SMALL AFRICAN TOWNS - BETWEEN RURAL NETWORKS AND URBAN HIERARCHIES

The Making of Modern Africa

Series Editors: Abebe Zegeye and John Higginson

Small African Towns - between Rural Networks and Urban Hierarchies

POUL OVE PEDERSEN
Centre for Development Research
Copenhagen

Avebury

Aldershot • Brookfield USA • Hong Kong • Singapore • Sydney

© Poul Ove Pedersen 1997

Published by
Avebury
Ashgate Publishing Ltd
Gower House
Croft Road
Aldershot
Hants GU11 3HR
England

Ashgate Publishing Company
Old Post Road
Brookfield
Vermont 05036
USA

British Library Cataloguing in Publication Data

Pedersen, Poul Ove
　　Small African towns : between rural networks and urban
　　hierarchies. - (The making of modern Africa)
　　1. Rural development - Africa
　　I. Title
　　307.7'2'096

Library of Congress Catalog Card Number: 97-70636

ISBN 1 85972 589 9

Printed in Great Britain by the Ipswich Book Company, Suffolk

Contents

Figures and tables

Preface

Since 1987 a group of researchers at the Centre for Development Research in Copenhagen has been studying small enterprises in development. In this research we have seen the small enterprise as performing specific tasks within the larger societal system of production and distribution, and as being shaped and adapted to the specific social and economic environment of which it is a part. This environment is locally specific, but comprises both local and non-local actors, small and large enterprises, public, private and cooperative organizations, households and social relations. Thus although we have studied the small enterprise, the focus has been not so much on the small enterprise itself as on the interaction between it and the environment in which it operates.

We have focused most of our research mostly on small enterprises in a specific type of environment, namely the small rural town serving a rural hinterland. Empirically, our research has been based on fieldwork in Kenya, Tanzania, Uganda, Zimbabwe and Bangladesh. The research has resulted in four Ph.D. dissertations, and a fifth is in preparation. Jesper Rasmussen (1992) has studied the building sector in Zimbabwean district service centres from a regional development perspective. Anders Ærøe (1992) has looked at the building sector in small Tanzanian towns from the perspective of rural industrialization. Jørgen Billetoft (1995) has studied small enterprises in Kenya and Bangladesh with a focus on small-enterprise support policies and the interaction between small enterprises and the public sector, donors and NGOs. On the basis of field work in Kenya, Steen Seierup (1995) has investigated the role of social structure on entrepreneurship and small-enterprise development; and Pernille Sørensen is presently studying the structure of small-scale grain-marketing in a small Ugandan town, and the restructuring taking place as a result of structural adjustment policies.

This book focuses more specifically on the small town itself and its role in the rural production and distribution system. It is primarily based on fieldwork carried out in Gutu and Gokwe, two district service centres in Zimbabwe's communal areas, during a number of visits in the period 1989 to 1995, but it also draws more broadly on the work in the research group. In particular, I have drawn heavily on Jesper Rasmussen's work, which has also been based partly on fieldwork in two Zimbabwean district service centres, namely Gutu and Murewa. Chapter 5 on industrial development in Zimbabwe and chapter 9 on the building sector in the district service centres are based to a large extent on his work.

I have drawn less directly on my other colleagues, but their empirical experiences and our theoretical discussions have in many ways influenced the work presented in this book. I therefore thank them all for their collaboration, and especially Jesper Rasmussen for permission to use his work.

During our fieldwork in Zimbabwe, Jesper Rasmussen and I were both based at the Department of Rural and Urban Planning at the University of Zimbabwe. I would like to thank our colleagues there for the kind reception and inspiration we have always received during our stays in Zimbabwe.

I would especially like to thank Philemon Jazi, who was research assistant to both Jesper Rasmussen and myself throughout our fieldwork in the district service centres, first as a student, and later as a colleague and Ph.D. student with a research project of his own on Zimbabwe's district service centres. His knowledge of people in the towns we researched, his never-failing energy in embarking on yet another interview, and his interest and understanding of our research project has been invaluable to the results.

Since 1992, Wilbert Gooneratne has invited me to a number of seminars organized by UNCRD in preparing and carrying out a project on small-town development in eastern and southern Africa. This has given me a valuable opportunity to meet a group of administrators and researchers from many African countries engaged in small-town development. Chapter 3 on the actual development of small African towns is to a large extent based on the work carried out by and the experience of that group. I would like to thank my colleagues in the group, both for their interest in my work and for the experiences they have shared with me, and especially Wilbert Gooneratne for inviting me to participate.

Theoretically, I have drawn much inspiration from the meetings of the EADI (European Association of Development Institutes) working group on industrialization strategies, and I would like to thank my colleagues there. Under the auspices of Meine Pieter van Dijk, this working group has organized a number of research seminars in recent years attempting to adjust and modify the theories of networking and flexible specialization to the realities of developing countries. Though the small rural towns I studied and their trading enterprises bear little physical resemblance to the production networks of Marshallian districts in northern Italy, which are usually associated with flexible specialization, the theory describes a diversified industrial structure and strategies of enterprises which on an abstract level differ little from what I found in Africa's small towns.

I would also like to thank the secretariat at CDR and, especially Gitte Munk Hindberg, Aase Møller Hansen and Marie Bille, who have carried out most of the labourious work required to transform my research papers into a book manuscript.

Finally, I would like to thank the businessmen and civil servants in Gutu and Gokwe who with great patience gave their time and answered our endless questions. My ultimate hope for this book is that it may prove useful to them in their efforts to develop their businesses and the small towns for the benefit of the rural population in their districts.

Although I owe these thanks to many people in Denmark, Zimbabwe and more generally in Europe and Africa, the responsibility for the contents of the book and for any errors and misunderstandings is of course mine alone.

Poul Ove Pedersen
Copenhagen, October 1996

Introduction

1.1   Why study small rural towns?

In the aspatial, dichotomous world of most development theories, there is no room for small rural towns. Here, the world is perceived as either rural or urban, and small towns are regarded either as an indiscriminate part of the urban sphere, as in Lipton's theory of urban bias (Lipton, 1976; Harris and Moore, 1984), or as an undifferentiated part of the rural sphere, as in Mellor's theory of rural industrialization and much of the rural development literature from the 1970s Mellor, 1986; Mellor *et al.*, 1987).

Just as the small towns have tended to be overlooked in the rural-urban dichotomy, so the intermediary functions and middlemen that inhabit the small town have tended to be overlooked in the agriculture-industry, large-small, formal-informal or capital-labour dichotomies; and even where their existence has been acknowledged, they have often been by-passed for theoretical or ideological reasons as unproductive or even superfluous.

In a spatial world, however, small towns and their intermediary functions become, for better or worse, important links between rural areas and the larger urban centres. Small towns become centres for the production and distribution of goods and services to the rural region, as well as for the exploitation and extraction of resources. In addition, they become centres for the growth and consolidation of rural non-agricultural activities and for the location of decentralized branches of government administration and services and of large private and parastatal enterprises. They also become centres of infrastructure and communication within and outside the rural region and for the articulation of regional politics. Finally, they become centres for the retention of some of the rural migrants who would otherwise migrate to the large urban centres, where social overhead costs are often considered to be larger.

1

In terms of population, employment and income, small towns may not seem very important to the national economy in developing countries. Their importance rests in the short term on the flows of agricultural produce, industrial products, services, money and people which pass through them between the rural areas and the larger towns in both directions, and on their ability to provide services which enhance rural productivity and incomes. In the long term, their importance rests on their ability to grow and increase their employment by diversifying their economic base, partly into a larger variety of local services and partly into manufacturing activities and exportable services.

Although some of the rapidly growing rural population in parts of Africa may still be absorbed by rural areas, most population growth in the future will have to migrate to the urban areas. Although most of these urban migrants move to the largest towns; in many parts of Africa today the small towns are growing relatively more rapidly, and small and medium-sized towns are likely to receive a growing proportion of urban migrants in the future. Their ability to provide improved living conditions to the migrants depends on their ability to transform and expand their economy, and that again depends on the structure of their links with both the rural areas and the larger towns and cities.

These relations are complicated by the coexistence of a highly concentrated, large-scale, mostly urban-based formal economy and a very decentralized, small-scale, both rural and urban informal economy. There is no clear-cut distinction between the two, and in many countries this has tended to change over time. The two parts of the economy are highly linked, and many households or even individuals are active in both the formal and the informal economy as customers, employees or entrepreneurs.

Rural-urban relations are also complicated, because in their attempts to draw resources from many different sources many households are divided, with members in both the rural and the urban areas and sometimes in both small towns and large cities.

Under these conditions, the ability of small towns to provide services to the rural areas and to transform their own economy is not at all evident. Historically, small towns in Africa have often played a doubtful role in rural development, and the major controversy in the literature about small towns has been waged over the question of whether they are exploitative or supportive of rural development.

Also, it is not at all obvious that 'small-town activities' should be located in rural centres. Both during the colonial period and after independence, potential small-town activities in eastern and southern Africa have often developed as part of uncoordinated sector plans and have therefore been dispersed over rural areas rather than being concentrated in rural centres. Other non-farm activities in rural areas developed as semi-subsistence activities by dispersed farm households and were not consolidated to a level where a small-town location was relevant. Yet other rural service facilities remained highly

2

centralized, and to the extent that rural areas were served at all, the small towns were by-passed.

The concentration of rural service functions in rural centres or small towns is desirable, because such a concentration can reduce the cost of the provision of services and improve access to an increased variety of services at reduced cost. However, there is no guarantee of this happening, because the concentration may enhance the creation of the economic and political monopolies used to exploit the rural areas. On the other hand, the concentration may also create a focal point for local economic and political power, which may be used as increased bargaining power in attracting resources from the state, the donors and the larger urban system.

The purpose of the present book is to investigate the role and economic *raison d'etre* of the small rural town, the structure and development of its economy, and its external relations to the rural hinterland, the larger urban centres and the national and international economy.

Why and how do small rural towns develop and grow (or why do they stagnate)? What role do they play in rural development, and under what conditions is that role beneficial to rural development? What are the external forces and policies which make them develop? Who are the local actors carrying the development?

1.2   The normative and the subjective

The study of small-town growth is the study of the potential for decentralizing and restructuring the economy, both because small towns tend to be geographically peripheral, and also because their economy tends to be dominated by small production and service units.

Such decentralization always comes up against structural resistance from the inertia of development and from groups with vested interests in the existing system. But contrary to the structuralist centre-periphery models which see this resistance as being impossible to overcome, I believe that it is possible and indeed that it sometimes happens. This book is an attempt to study both structural resistance and the strategies pursued by individuals, enterprises and organizations in order to overcome that resistance. This is carried out using an actor-structure framework, as is implicit in theories of enterprise networks and flexible specialization and not much different from that presented by Long and Long (1992).

Such a focus on the decentralization of the economy necessarily contains a considerable normative element. It implies that decentralization of the economy is generally seen as positive, and that a certain degree of decentralization is seen as a necessary (though not sufficient) condition for economic development. Not everyone may agree with that.

3

Although I hardly realized it when I started the research on which this book is based, it has become increasingly clear to me that I have at least two personal interests in the choice of research topic and approach. First, I come from a family of small retailers and for that reason have probably been fascinated by small-scale entrepreneurs and traders more than many other researchers. I have also had difficulty in understanding and accepting the almost automatically negative attitude towards small enterprises in general, especially traders, which permeates much of the development literature.

Secondly, although I was born and brought up in a capital city, I have spent many years of my research life in a small provincial town trying to develop a research environment there. This has taught me much about the actual and psychological differences between being at the centre and being on the periphery, about the skewed information and power relations between centre and periphery.

These personal experiences are part and parcel of the fascination with small enterprises, traders and small towns which I have vested in the present study of small towns in Africa.

1.3   The theoretical approach

The study focuses on economic activities located in small towns, and on the specific environment in which they operate. Small-town activities may involve production or services, but mostly they are engaged in retail or wholesale trade. They may be local enterprises or branches of larger regional, national or even international enterprises or organizations. They may be private, cooperative, government or parastatal enterprises.

These small-town activities operate in a complex environment comprising both local and non-local elements. This environment is far from the anonymous, homogeneous competitive market of neoclassical economics. It is also very different from the cut-throat competition of petty commodity markets, which completely dominated and controlled by large-scale corporate enterprises. Instead, the environment is seen as a competitive market where corporate enterprises play an important role, but where small enterprises may still be able to pursue strategies to overcome competition and dominance. Inspiration for such a theory is found in Scandinavian network theories, theories of flexible specialization and industrial clusters, and theories of institutional economics, all of which tend to focus on the interaction between the enterprise and its environment.

However, there are many ways of looking at small-town enterprises and their environment. First, small-town enterprises are an integral part of the sector to which they belong, and many studies of rural areas in Africa during the last twenty years have tended to see small-town enterprises in a purely sectoral perspective as part of the agricultural sector, the clothing sector etc., without considering the implications of their small-town location. Secondly, small-town activities are an integral part of rural areas, and many studies of small towns have focused on linkages between small towns and the surrounding rural areas. Thirdly, small-town activities are part of the larger urban system, on which they depend for supplies of the goods and services they distribute and as markets for the rural produce they collect. Finally, the small town can be seen to make up a small, open system of its own within which enterprises may compete or collaborate in order to improve their efficiency, either to service the rural areas or to exploit them.

In reality, of course, small-town enterprises are part of all these subsystems, and an understanding of small-town economies must rest on the integration of these different perspectives. I will focus especially on the link between the small town and the larger urban system, partly because relatively few studies of this link exist, and partly because the main controversy about small towns – namely whether they are exploitive or supportive of rural development – is centred on this link.

1.4   The empirical approach

As a consequence of the foregoing, the small-town enterprise must be seen as part of several interacting subsystems: it is part of a sector; it is part of a rural area serviced (or exploited) by the small town; it is part of the small town itself; and it is part of the larger urban system. In order to capture the relative importance of each of these subsystems to the enterprise, the empirical study is based on what has sometimes been called a subsector approach. Such an approach focuses on the horizontal and vertical differentiation into subsectors of a specific sector of the economy, and on the linkages among the subsectors and between the subsectors and the rest of the world. It is through these linkages that the economy of the sector operates, and it is also through them that structural changes in the sector take place. The subsector approach has most often been used to study sectors in the national economy. Here, I will apply it to the local, small-town economy instead, in order to investigate the role of the small town in the economy of the sector at the national level. Thus empirically we focus on the links of small-town enterprises in the sectors examined, both locally, in the rural areas, and up through the urban hierarchy.

Empirically, the book presents a case study of the development since independence of two rural district service centres in the communal areas of Zimbabwe. Zimbabwe has higher levels of both urbanization and industrialization than most other countries in eastern and southern Africa; therefore, these two small towns may not be considered very representative

5

of the region. However, both urban and economic development in Zimbabwe are highly concentrated, and the level of urbanization in the communal areas is lower, if anything, than in most other countries in the region, though labour emigration to the large cities may be higher. Therefore, the conditions under which small rural towns develop in Zimbabwe's communal areas may not be so very different from other parts of the region, and the external dominance, which is often seen as a hindrance to rural development, may even be stronger than elsewhere.

Both the forces which support small-town development and those which restrict it depend on organizational, economic and political structures which vary from country to country or even from region to region within the same country. Clearly, therefore a case study of two small towns in one country cannot in detail claim to be representative of small towns in eastern and southern Africa. However, through a detailed case study I do hope to be able to show that small-town development depends on a much more complex set of mechanisms than the black and white picture presented by traditional small-town theories.

Even within Zimbabwe, the two small towns examined cannot claim to be representative. They are both among the largest and most successful of the new district service centres developed after independence. The reason for choosing two relatively large and growing small towns is that it is not possible to study small-town growth processes in centres which do not grow, nor to study the mechanisms which restrict or support small-town economic activities in centres which are so small that few activities exist. In addition, the mechanisms of growth and stagnation are likely to be the same in smaller centres, though the balance between them will be different.

1.5   Content of the book

In addition to this introduction, the book contains three parts. Part I is theoretical and general and comprises chapters 2 to 4. Chapter 2 summarizes previous discussions about the role of small towns in rural development, especially in eastern and southern Africa. The role of small towns in rural development is not at all evident, and different development theories have perceived them very differently, from positive to negative, from supportive to exploitive of rural development. These changing perceptions of small towns in development theory are the theme of chapter 2.

Chapter 3 discusses the statistical problems involved in studying the development of small towns at a national level and presents some of the scant evidence on the development of small towns in eastern and southern Africa.

Chapter 4 presents the general model of small-town development on which the empirical case study presented in Part II will be based. The small town is the location of the more consolidated rural non-agricultural activities as well as of decentralized public administration and services, parastatal depots, and branches of large private enterprises, although the combination of these different activities will vary from country to country and from town to town. In the small town these diverse sets of activities interact and compete for markets and resources. Here, they develop under the impact of the small-town environment of which they are a part. Chapter 4 therefore discusses how these different small-town enterprises and their productive environment are perceived by different enterprise theories.

Part II is empirical and specific. It presents a case study of the development of two district service centres in the communal areas of Zimbabwe. It begins with chapter 5, which is a presentation of the historical background for the development of district service centres in communal areas since independence in 1980. Chapter 6 presents an analysis of the development of retail trade, services and wholesale trade in the two centres examined. Chapters 7, 8 and 9 analyse trade and production in three sectors which are important to the small towns, but also very differently structured, namely agro-processing and marketing, the clothing sector, and the building sector and building material trade and production. Chapters 10 and 11 focus on the development process up through the 1980s and early 1990s, summarizing the empirical material presented in chapters 6–9, but also including material from other sectors than those analysed in the earlier chapters. Chapter 10 focuses especially on the external forces of development: national government, parastatals and large private enterprises. Chapter 11 focuses on the internal, local forces of development: local entrepreneurs and managers, and local government policies.

Finally, Part III, consisting of chapter 12, presents the theoretical and general conclusions of the study.

Part I
THEORETICAL AND GENERAL

2 The changing perception of small towns in development theory

2.1 From a positive to a negative perception of small towns

During the early period of development theory, the 1950s and 1960s, small towns were generally seen as playing a positive role in rural development. Based on Christaller's service centre theory (Christaller, 1933; Berry, 1967), small towns were seen as centres for the distribution of urban services to the rural areas; and being based on innovation diffusion and growth-pole theory, they were seen as growth points or as the last link in the urban hierarchy through which innovations and modernization trickled down from the large urban centres to rural areas (for an overview of this early literature on East Africa, see Funnell, 1976). Through large public investments in infrastructure and services and publicly supported private investments in selected growth sectors, growth and development were supposed to spread to other sectors of the economy and down the urban hierarchy to the peripheral and rural regions. Unfortunately, this development vision seldom if ever materialized. The large-scale industries usually chosen as growth sectors did not develop the linkages to the local economy that were hoped for but became isolated enclaves generating few local incomes. Around 1970, therefore, under the impact of dependency theory and Marxist centre-periphery theory, small towns came increasingly to be seen as administrative and political centres of resource exploitation, taxation and control rather than as service centres for rural development.

In most developing countries, the urban system was dominated by one or a few large centres. These primate cities developed during colonial times as seats of colonial powers and export harbours for resources extracted from the colonies. The small towns became an important link in this process of resource exploitation. In most cases, independence did not change that. The primate city was still the seat of power and of the control of resources. In

11

order to be able to govern, the new states had to extract resources from rural areas just like the colonial powers. The centralist nature of the small towns was especially evident in Africa, where there was only a fragmentary urban system at the time of colonization. Here, the different administrative hierarchies (missionaries, police, civil administration) often located their branch networks independently of one another. Private sector trade and production activities in rural areas were not encouraged and often reserved for white or Indian traders. Where Africans were permitted to establish such activities, they were often obliged to locate outside the white administrative centres. As a result a dispersed pattern of functions emerged rather than a network of small multi-purpose rural centres.

Consequently, the small towns were no longer seen as a positive force in the development process but as centres for the control and exploitation of the rural areas. The growth and the decline of the small towns were seen as the result of restructuring processes decided upon in centralized ministries and the headquarters of large national or multinational corporations, and not as a result of rural development processes.

During the 1970s, the view of small towns as centres of resource extraction coincided with a very negative view of the rural bourgeoisie of traders and middlemen dominating the small towns. They were seen as agents of the exploitive, central economic powers, but also as superfluous profiteers in their own right. This negative view of small-town traders was in part based on Marxist theory; but in eastern and southern Africa, it merged on the one hand with the strong aversion to Asian and other foreign traders who had dominated rural trade during the colonial period and also after independence in many areas, and on the other hand with a traditional belief that success in business which led to a change in life-style and a separation from traditional rural consent might be caused by sorcery and witchcraft (see, e.g., Bourdillon, 1987; Aschwanda, 1987; also *The Herald*, Tuesday, January 24, 1995, on a case of the abduction and killing of children for body parts to be sold to businessmen and traditional healers).

Basing themselves on structuralist theories, many researchers saw the skewed rural-urban relations as resulting from the prevailing power relations, which could only be changed by radical changes in class relations and the political system. In his theory of the urban bias, Lipton (1976) sees rural poverty as a result of the dominance of the urban classes over the rural in much the same way as dependency theory sees underdeveloped countries as being held down by the dominance of industrialized countries (for discussions on urban bias, see also Harris and Moore, 1984; Varshney, 1993). Lipton includes the small rural towns within the urban sphere, but does not attribute any specific role to them (at least partly because his analysis is based on a spaceless rural-urban dichotomy), but other researchers who have reached conclusions similar to Lipton's have seen the urban bias as a narrower capital-city bias (e.g., Kongstad, 1985; 1986).

In a detailed study of a small town in Zaire, Schatzberg (1979; 1980) shows how the small-town bourgeoisie is infiltrated by the state bureaucracy and political elite and operates as an active agent for Lipton's urban classes.

In two volumes of papers focusing on specific small towns in fourteen African countries the editor, Southall (1979; 1988), similarly concludes that small towns play a predominantly negative role in African rural development. The negative forces are primarily caused by external forces which, according to the case, may be colonial powers, large multinational corporations, centralist national governments, local administrators or elites, or even major international donors. 'It is only where the stimulus to urban growth result in activity primarily by the people and for themselves that small-scale urbanization may be beneficial locally' (Southall, 1988, p.5). This, he concludes, has been the case especially where colonization took place through indirect rule, and he mentions Nigeria, Ghana and Uganda as examples.

2.2   Attempts to by-pass the small town: development from below

During the 1970s and early 1980s, many development researchers and planners responded to these negative conclusions with attempts to by-pass the small towns and focus directly on the rural areas and the peasant farmer. This is the case in most of the so-called integrated rural development programmes adopted by many donors during the 1970s. Here, the existence of rural centres and small towns is generally ignored, and rural development investigated in sectoral terms alone (Baker and Pedersen, 1992).

This is also reflected in the theories of development from below (Stöhr and Taylor, 1981) and of basic needs. Poor peasant farmers should be empowered, and the government and donor support needed for rural development should be provided directly to the farmers without the use of unnecessary intermediaries. This rural and agricultural focus was obviously important in understanding and supporting the rural development process. However, it has not led to the decentralization which was generally intended by donors and NGOs. Rather, it has on the one hand led to a strong concentration in the capital cities of decision-making powers and of processing and marketing activities related to agriculture and rural development (Hinkerdink and Titmus, 1988). On the other hand, it has led to the support of very small-scale rural processing and marketing activities at a subsistence or artisan level; but it has tended to block the development of that rural industrialization at an intermediate level which should have taken place in the small towns.

2.3 The small town in the national economy

Although the negative view of small towns as exploitive seems in most cases to be historically justified in eastern and southern Africa, this does not justify the conclusion that small towns should be by-passed. Obviously, this would not in itself reduce the central exploitive powers.

Whether the small town is dominantly exploitative or supportive of rural development does not depend primarily on the small town itself, but on the relationship between rural areas and the urban-based national economy. The development of small towns is not likely to change things if the relationship is exploitive of the rural areas: it may even make the exploitation more efficient. On the other hand, if the national urban economy is supportive of rural development, the development of small towns may make the support more efficient. Some researchers and especially regional development planners, have therefore continued to see small rural towns as playing a potentially important role in rural development. Here, small towns are often seen as an element in a larger national settlement plan intended both to decentralize the urban system away from the dominant capital cities and to supply rural areas with services and employment opportunities.

One such approach is Friedmann's model of 'agropolitan development' (Friedmann, 1988; Friedmann and Weaver, 1979; Friedmann and Douglas, 1978). Friedmann and his colleagues envision an integrated, locally controlled, rural development strategy for a rural region that forms a unit of local government and is centred around a small town of 10–25,000 inhabitants. The approach can be seen as an extended basic-needs strategy. Development will be based as far as possible on local resources and skills, and only goods and services which cannot be produced locally will be imported. It is conceived as a bottom-up strategy, but in order to retain locally produced surplus for local benefit and prevent the undermining of local activities by external competition, it requires a selective, territorial closure which can only be secured by a strong, central government. Such territorial closures, which have been difficult to achieve at a national level, are hardly realistic at a subnational level. It has also been argued that the approach presupposes a relatively equal social structure which seldom exists. Therefore, although the approach contains many interesting theoretical ideas and has been discussed and criticized extensively in the literature (see, e.g., Simon, 1992; Ærøe, 1992), it is hardly implementable.

Rondinelli and a group of predominantly American researchers have developed another much less ambitious and more empirically oriented approach known as 'the functional approach' (see, e.g., Rondinelli and Ruddle, 1978; Rondinelli, 1982; 1983a; 1983b; 1983c; 1984; 1985; 1986; 1987; 1988; 1990; Kammeier and Swan, 1984; Belsky and Karaska, 1990). They focus specifically on the small rural towns as service centres supplying a variety of services, agricultural inputs and consumer goods to the rural areas. Most of the theoretical work carried out and inspired by Rondinelli builds on and extends Christaller's central-place theory. Empirically, this tends to focus on the links between small towns and their rural hinterlands (e.g., Evans and Ngau, 1991) and often argues for the location of more rural service supply points (see, e.g., Wanmali, 1991; Wanmali and Zamchaya, 1992; Haggblade, Hazell and Brown, 1987; Funnell, 1988; Gaile, 1988).

The functional approach has been widely used by some of the larger donors such as the World Bank and USAID, but it has been highly criticized by researchers who argue that low rural consumption is caused by social inequality and low incomes rather than by difficult access to supply (see, e.g., Bromley, 1984). The approach also assumes implicitly that the linkages between the small town and the higher levels of the urban hierarchy are (as in Christaller's original work) served perfectly by the private sector or the state. In developing economies and especially in an African context, this is a doubtful assumption because supplies of commodities and services are often insufficient and irregular due to breakdowns in the production system, insufficient capacity in the distribution system, speculation and other market irregularities (e.g., Pedersen, 1992a; Smith, 1976).

Some of these non-market aspects of the development process are taken up by Hydén (1983; 1985; 1986) in his theory of the economy of affection, which refers to the various networks of support and interaction between different groups connected by blood, kin, community or other affinities. It links together in a systematic fashion different social and economic units which in other respects may be autonomous, thus giving rise to economic flows and exchanges based on criteria other than those that are expected to guide economic behaviour in either market or planned economies (Hydén, 1985).

The economy of affection provides the basis for survival strategies for the poor segments of the population, securing resources for education, informal credit, labour assistance, lodging etc. to members of the network, and creating the framework for social reproduction, with strong elements of patronage and clientalism. The economy of affection penetrates both local and central levels of the economy. Contrary to Friedmann, who to a large extent builds his development strategy on the local economy of affection, Hydén sees the economy of affection mainly as a hindrance to development because it diverts resources away from productive investments. Therefore the economy of affection must be broken down in order for development to occur. Also contrary to Friedmann, Hydén sees the urban centre rather than the rural areas as the dynamic force in development and the urban entrepreneur as the mediator of economic development (Ærøe, 1992).

2.4 A more diversified view of small towns: national resource allocation or local development processes

Up to the mid-1980s theories of small-town development were generally based on relatively few and mostly not very detailed case studies. This was changed in an important study by Hardoy and Satterthwaite (1986), in which they presented a series of detailed case studies of small towns from Latin America, Asia and Africa. In Baker's words, perhaps their most important conclusion is 'that the universal generalizations and prescriptions concerning small-town development are simply not valid' (Baker, 1990, p.18). They stress the uniqueness of individual small towns and 'point to the phenomenally rich and diverse set of circumstances particular to each' (Hardoy and Satterthwaite, 1986, p.399). They stress especially that a very unequal land distribution in the rural areas and income distribution in the small town itself is not conducive to small-town development because the many poor households consume few of the goods and services supplied by the town, while the small town often cannot supply the more specialized goods and services demanded by the wealthy few.

They also stress the negative impact of an unbalanced national urban system dominated by one or a few large cities which tend to attract resources and migrants from all over the country. At the same time, however, they emphasize the important role which government agricultural policies, investment in infrastructure, and urban services and decentralization of government and public administration may play in the development of small towns. Finally, they focus on the social dimensions of the small town, the complex networks of friendship, kinship and family ties which link the small towns to the larger towns and the rural areas, and which function as channels for the articulation of diverse socioeconomic and cultural demands in the rural areas.

In total, Hardoy and Satterthwaite's study presents a much more complex and differentiated picture of the small towns than most previous studies, which have tended to see them in either black or white. As a consequence, they suggest that centralized and standardized national models and prescriptions for small-town development may not be very efficient, because they cannot take into account the peculiarities of the individual small towns and their hinterlands. Instead, they argue that there is a need for a large decentralization of decision-making power and the establishment of effective representative local governments with investment and resource-raising capabilities at the local level. Through such local governments, local needs and priorities can be articulated and both rural and urban development stimulated on the basis of local resources, local actors and local capabilities. Many public-sector decisions are also more effectively taken at the local level because the level of information is higher and the pressure for accountability greater.

Although the increased focus on local development processes appears to be more promising than the very centralist national policies which have dominated until recently, local policies obviously cannot stand alone. There will continue to be a need for national resource allocation from rich regions (and donors) to poor regions, and national policies are also needed as a safeguard against upper-class dominance and minority-group repression in the local economy. It is on these grounds that Slater (1989) in his debate with Rondinelli (Rondinelli, McCullough and Johnson, 1989), argues that a locally based development process will not be possible because the powerful, dominant urban classes will drain resources from the periphery. The problem with this argument is that it is based on a dependency theory approach which implicitly assumes the development process to be a zero-sum game where one part has to win and the other has to lose. This, of course, may not be very wrong in a simple resource exploitation economy. However, it is more problematic in an economy which is undergoing commercialization and industrialization and in which rural and urban areas are increasingly integrated. Here, growth at the periphery may well be of greater advantage to the centre than stagnation, and dependencies are not likely to be one-sided but to a large extent mutual.

Another important reason for the change from centralist national policies toward more local-level policies is that national governments have had fewer and fewer resources to reallocate, while the large-scale formal economy has had increasing difficulties in supplying the periphery with commodities and services. This has led Mabogunje (1986), for example, to see the recent development of small towns in Africa as a retreat from the large-scale formal economy. He argues that the decline or even breakdown of the formal sector has left a void which has made it possible for small-scale, often informal activities to develop at the periphery. Similarly, Jamal and Weeks (1988; 1993) emphasize the decline in formal-sector employment in the larger urban areas and falling urban incomes, and see the growth of non-agricultural activities in the rural areas as a process of ruralization caused by falling urban incomes. Their argument can be seen as the opposite of Slater's, i.e. as a centre-periphery model where the centre has lost its dominance. There is, of course, some truth in the argument, but in its one-sided focus on incomes and consumption it completely overlooks the non-agricultural activities and development processes which are actually taking place in the rural areas and small towns[1] and which are slowly changing the balance between rural and urban areas.

Here, we argue instead that the shift from centralist national development policies towards a greater emphasis on local-level policies and development policies, which is presently taking place in many African countries, corresponds to the changing understanding of the concept of local and regional planning which has slowly taken place since the 1960s in both developed and developing countries.

In the 1960s, regional planning and growth centre policies were generally perceived as national plans and policies of resource allocation. The development of peripheral rural regions was seen as a result of relocating large-scale growth industries to the peripheral region. In the 1970s, the basic needs and development-from-below strategies stressed popular participation and the empowerment of the rural poor, but policies continued to be based primarily on national plans and national resource allocation, and the industrialization strategies associated with basic needs continued to build on the large-scale mass production of farm implements and consumer goods. During the 1980s, however, regional and local development policies were increasingly perceived not as national policies, but as regional or local policies based to a large extent on local resources and local small-scale and medium-scale enterprises. This change is partly a response to the findings of regional economics since the end of the 1970s, which show that small- and medium-sized enterprises are much more likely to develop local links in peripheral regions than large-scale, Fordist, mass-production enterprises.

In the economies based on small-scale commercialization and industrialization which are now developing for better or worse in most African countries, the small towns assume a role different from that perceived by the theories derived from either the dependency or the neo-classical paradigms. Here, small-town activities are often highly dependent on large-scale public, parastatal or private organizations and enterprises, but their dependence is not absolute, and small enterprises may have considerable room to manoeuvre, if for no other reason than that this is in the interest of the large enterprises themselves.

As we shall see in chapter 3, the small towns therefore play an increasingly important role in many African countries. However, their development also becomes less predictable, and there are considerable differences in the development trends of individual towns.

Note

1 Although Jamal and Weeks (1993) recognize and even emphasize the importance of multi-activities for both urban and rural households, they base their argument on a comparison between farm incomes (for subsistence farmers producing sufficient food to feed their families) and an urban minimum wage, thus, overlooking the contribution of the rural non-agricultural sector (and of the urban) both directly to rural household incomes, and indirectly to agricultural productivity and farm incomes.

3 The empirical trend of small-town growth in eastern and southern Africa

3.1 Deficiencies of the data

In this chapter, I shall attempt to provide a picture of the development of small towns in Africa. This is not easy, partly because the available statistics are scarce and deficient, but more importantly because a clear definition of what a small town is does not exist.

Ideally, small towns should be defined in terms of their function as urban centres which serve a rural hinterland and at the same time constitute a link between the rural area and higher levels of the urban hierarchy. Small towns are also places where larger rural non-agricultural activities meet decentralized urban functions. Such towns represent a broad range of centres, from large villages to often quite large provincial towns. In the smallest centres, public administration and private and public services often dominate, while in the larger centres manufacturing tends to play a larger role. Where in this broad range of centres development is taking place depends on the structure of the economy in the hinterland, the organization of intermediary trading and processing functions and public administration, and the strength of local forces versus national and international forces. Which levels of the urban hierarchy will be most important will therefore vary from country to country and from region to region, making it impossible to rely on standardized statistics.

In practice, a broad picture of small-town development in Africa can only be obtained through population statistics, and this creates a number of problems. First, the population of a centre may not give a fair picture of the centre's activity level, because many small centres in Africa are market centres, but only to a limited extent living centres. In other cases, small towns with a relatively large population might be large villages dominated by agricultural activities and with very few urban functions, such as the agro-towns of Botswana (Silitshena, 1990). In general, however, the type of small rural

19

towns we are concerned with here are in the range of between 5,000 and 50,000 inhabitants.

Secondly, population statistics even for small towns are both scarce and problematic, partly because there are few censuses and partly because the statistical definitions and delimitations of small towns vary from country to country and often also from census to census. Statistically, small towns are often defined by a fixed minimum size which typically varies from 2,000 to 20,000 inhabitants. This means that centres below that size are classified as part of the rural areas. In other cases, small towns are defined, independently of their size, as all centres at a specific low level of the administrative hierarchy, e.g. district centres. This means that often quite small centres in thinly populated poor regions are classified as urban, while much larger centres in other regions are considered rural.

A further problem is that small towns are often delimited so as to include large rural hinterlands, leading to an overestimation of their population (see, e.g., Hesselberg, 1986; Hardoy and Satterthwaite, 1986). In other cases, small-town population may be underestimated, because many small African towns are so dispersed that functions belonging to the town are located outside its boundaries. Also, the size of rapidly growing small towns may be underestimated if they grow over the town border and create suburbs which are not counted as part of the town. Such statistical problems often make it difficult to compare censuses from different years in order to obtain information on small-town growth. Finally, as a consequence of the infrequent censuses, it is difficult or impossible to relate the changing pattern of urban growth to changes in policies and economic trends. Most of our knowledge of small towns is therefore based on monographs on individual towns, which may not be comparable and do not permit broad comparative studies.

The following attempt to paint a picture of small-town growth in Africa south of the Sahara, especially in eastern and southern Africa, is therefore only indicative.

3.2   The causes of small-town growth

Where small towns grow, growth is caused by a combination of different factors. The most important are:

–   growing rural cash incomes, which increase the demand for urban goods and services;

–   the decentralization of public-sector administration and services to the small towns, which in themselves are an element of small-town growth, but which also increase the local demand for both public and private urban goods and services;

–   the development of a private (or public) sector to satisfy the local demand
    for goods and services either through the development of local activities
    or through the decentralization of branch activities from larger urban
    centres and centralized organizations.

Contrary to the stereotyped picture of African development presented in much
of the development literature, the realization of these three causes of small-
town development has varied widely from country to country and even from
region to region, as well as over time. The development of small towns must
have differed as well.

It is true that increases in agricultural productivity in general have been
small in African countries and that prices have often been low, either because
world market prices have been low or because agriculture has been taxed
through low producer prices. However, there have been large variations in
both productivity and prices from crop to crop, country to country and region
to region, depending on land and climate and on agricultural policies and
their administration: for example, peasant farmers in Tanzania during the
1970s and in Ethiopia during the 1980s were heavily exploited through low
producer prices, while following independence in 1980, African farmers in
Zimbabwe experienced both increasing prices and increased market access.
In addition, rural households in most African countries rely not only on farm
incomes, but also on incomes from rural non-farm activities and on remittances
from family members working in urban areas. Thus rural incomes to a large
extent depend indirectly on development in urban areas. This has also meant,
however, that where the urban economy has collapsed, as in Zambia and
Uganda, this has had serious negative repercussions on rural incomes.

In most African countries, public administration and services have to a
greater or lesser extent been decentralized after independence. Most countries
have had policies to decentralize primary schools and health clinics to the
rural areas and village level, although the extent to which this has actually
happened varies. However, there are big differences in the extent to which
secondary schools and formal vocational training have been diffused.
Zimbabwe, which already had a relatively widespread system of primary
schools before independence, has attempted to create a universal system of
secondary schools with considerable success since independence. Tanzania,
on the other hand, limited the secondary school system to a minimum until
around 1980, when it was partly privatized and started to expand rapidly,
especially in the more wealthy areas.

Administration has also been decentralized in many African countries,
although decentralization has mostly been administrative and only to a limited
extent political. In Zimbabwe, administration has partly been decentralized
to the district level and has made an important contribution to the growth
which has taken place in the 55 new district service centres established in the

communal areas after independence. In Tanzania decentralization appears to have been more thorough, but it has mostly favoured the eighteen regional capitals which as a result have grown rapidly during the 1970s. The effect of public and parastatal decentralization appears to have been much smaller at the lower levels of the urban hierarchy. In Kenya, administrative decentralization, especially after the introduction of the District Focus for Rural Development in 1983, has focused on the 35 district centres, but decentralization has probably been less extensive than in Tanzania and Zimbabwe.

Finally, the experience has been very different in different countries with respect to private-sector development too. In Kenya there have been relatively few restrictions on the development of the private sector, and although there has been a certain bias in favour of large formal enterprises, there have been few obstacles to the development of the small-scale formal or informal sectors

In Zimbabwe since independence, the small-scale sector has been able to develop relatively freely, but the bias in favour of the large-scale sector has been much greater. During the 1980s, the large (mostly white-owned) retail chains were urged to set up branches in the new district service centres, which to a considerable extent they did. Manufacturing, however, has remained highly centralized.

In Tanzania (as in other countries with a socialist government, such as Ethiopia), the development of the private sector has been much more restricted. The Indian and Arab traders which dominated rural trade before independence were restricted in their activities, especially in the rural areas, or even thrown out. During the 1970s, attempts were made to monopolize rural trade especially in a parastatal wholesale organization and in local cooperative stores, while private retail trade was closed down or relegated to black-market status. This parastatal distribution system never came to function very efficiently. As a result, the distribution of consumer goods almost broke down during the early 1980s, and since 1984 the development of a private sector has increasingly been accepted, although it has only become fully legalized during the 1990s.

In Uganda the Indian businessmen who owned most of the private enterprises at independence were thrown out in 1972 and their activities taken over by parastatals and African businessmen. However, because of civil war and unrest these activities never functioned properly, and a large parallel, informal, small-scale sector developed, which since the end of the 1980s has become increasingly formalized.

3.3   The pattern of small-town growth

As a consequence of these very different growth trends, small towns can be expected to have grown very differently in different African countries. Here,

I will try here to present a picture of how small towns have developed in different countries in eastern and southern Africa.

Ethiopia

The 1984 population census for Ethiopia (see also Gebre, 1991) found that slightly over 10 per cent of the Ethiopian population lived in 325 urban localities with 2,000 or more inhabitants. Of the urban population, 32.4 per cent lived in Addis Ababa, 30.8 per cent lived in 25 other towns with more than 20,000 inhabitants, and 36.9 per cent lived in smaller towns with from 2,000 to 20,000 inhabitants. Since the 1967 census, the urban population had grown by 4.75 per cent a year. Urban growth was most rapid in Addis Ababa (6.5 per cent) and decreased in size to 3.47 per cent for the 186 towns with a population of 2,000–5,000. Thus the small towns were not growing much more than the total population. Gebre (1991) explains that this is a result of very low agricultural prices and a strong urban bias. The growth which has taken place in the small towns is mainly due to the very limited growth in public administration and agricultural services.

According to Baker (1990) the growth of Addis Ababa fell during the 1980s to about 3.5 per cent, and although there is no precise data, he suggests that the small towns are now growing more rapidly than the large ones. This seems to be supported by Tirfie (1993), who attributes the change in growth pattern to the land reform, which has stopped urban migration, and to increased agricultural prices, which have increased the demand for goods and services in rural areas.

Kenya

Kenya has experienced high urban growth since independence, especially during the 1970s, when the urban population grew by 7.8 per cent per annum. During the 1980s the growth rate decreased to 5.3 per cent, with small towns especially growing. The number of small towns with a population between 2,000 and 20,000 inhabitants grew from 30 in 1962 to 215 in 1989, while the number of towns with more than 20,000 inhabitants grew from 4 to 27 (Obudho, 1993; Ng'ethe and Ngunyi, 1991). At the same time, the dominance of Nairobi and Mombasa decreased from 67 per cent in 1962 to 46 per cent in 1989. Mombasa's share loss was especially great from 31 per cent to 12 per cent. The next nine towns kept their share of the urban population at about 20 per cent, while the smaller towns increased their share from 13 per cent to 34 per cent. This rapid growth is, of course, partly caused by many new towns growing to 2,000 inhabitants; however, individual small towns (2,000–20,000) also appear to have grown more rapidly than the larger towns since 1969. This was especially the case during the 1980s, when the falling urban growth rate mainly hit the larger towns (see, e.g., Billetoft, 1989).

In spite of its rather centralized government, Kenya since independence has formulated policies for the development of small centres. The focus of these policies has changed over time from regional centres via district centres to small rural trade and production centres. These policies may have been instrumental in enhancing the growth of the small towns.

Malawi

Malawi is one of the least urbanized countries in Africa. According to a study by Rasmussen and Ærøe (1987), the level of urbanization increased from only 6.4 per cent of the total population in 1966 to 8.4 per cent in 1977. They found that between 1966 and 1977 the two largest cities, Blantyre and Lilongwe, grew by 6.9 per cent a year, while all the smaller centres only grew by 3.2 per cent a year. As a result, the two large cities increased their share of the total urban population from 60 per cent in 1966 to 69 per cent in 1977.

Rasmussen and Ærøe estimate that the growth rate of both large and small towns increased from 1977 to the mid-1980s, but that the large centres continued to grow more rapidly (more than 7 per cent a year) than the small ones (4.2 per cent a year). As a result, the level of urbanization in the mid-1980s had increased to 12 per cent of the total population, and the dominance of the large centres had increased still further.

Tanzania

At independence, Tanzania, even by African standards, had a very low level of urbanization; but since then, it has experienced rapid urban growth both in Dar es Salaam and in the eighteen regional capitals. In 1967, the regional capitals were still relatively small towns with populations ranging from 5,000 to 34,000 inhabitants (except Tanga, which had 60,000). Since then, they have grown dramatically to populations ranging from 18,000 to 156,000 in 1988. In the same period, Dar es Salaam grew from 272,000 to 1,117,000 inhabitants. This growth took place especially in the intercensal period of 1967–78, when the town grew by almost 10 per cent a year, while it grew by less than 5 per cent a year in the period 1978–88. Therkildsen (1991) explains the rapid urban growth in the 1967–78 period with reference to the rapid growth and decentralization in public and parastatal employment which took place from 1972–84, when expansion in the public sector stopped. He sees the falling urban growth of the period 1978–88 as a result of the reduced urban growth after 1984. There is no reason to doubt that growth in the public sector was an important stimulus for urban growth in that period; however, although the public sector makes up the major part of the formal sector, to a large extent urban growth must be accounted for by the unregistered and unknown growth in the informal sector. And it must also be the informal sector which led Dar es Salaam to grow more rapidly than the regional capitals, in spite of the dramatic decentralization in the public sector documented by Therkildsen.

Forced villagization during the 1970s led to a rapid, rural-urban migration of people wanting to escape the lack of resources and strong social control in the rural areas. The rapid migration is documented by frequent attempts by urban authorities to return the swelling number of street vendors and small informal entrepreneurs to the rural areas.

During the period 1978–88, the growth of both Dar es Salaam and the regional capitals fell to about half the earlier period, and for the first time the regional capitals grew on average more rapidly than Dar es Salaam, and as documented by Holm (1994) for 5 regions, the small towns below the regional capitals grew even more rapidly (see Table 1). Mbonile's (1994) survey of migrants to three trading centres in Makete district in southern Tanzania shows similar rapid growth of the small towns.

Table 1
Growth of Dar es Salaam, regional capitals and smaller towns in five selected regions, 1978–88

	No. of towns	Average town size		Growth rate p.a.
		1978	1988	
Dar es Salaam	1	769,445	1,217,590	4.7%
Regional capitals	5	61,068	105,456	5.6%
Small towns >10,000 inhabitants	12	8,120	15,994	7.0%
Small towns <10,000 inhabitants	21	2,965	5,53	6.4%

Note: Based on comparable recalculations of data taken from the censuses of 1978 and 1988 for towns in the Iringa, Arusha, Kilimanjaro, Morogoro and Mbeya regions.

Source: Holm (1994)

Although we do not have data for the growth of the small towns during the 1970s, there is no reason to believe that they have grown more rapidly than the larger towns. Public-sector decentralization did not proceed much below the regional capitals, and apparently the private sector in the small towns and villages was to a large extent forced to close or go underground (Lerise, 1991).

Thus in spite of the very different development histories of Tanzania and Kenya, the development trends of the small towns during the 1970s and 1980s appear to have been surprisingly similar, with a lower general urban growth during the 1980s, but with a relatively more rapid growth of the small towns and a rapid slow-down in the growth of the large towns.

Uganda

At independence, Uganda inherited an urban system completely dominated by the two largest towns, Kampala and Jinla. Since then, however, Kampala and Jinla have stagnated. According to Mugabi (1993), Kampala only grew by 3.2 per cent a year during the 1970s, while Jinla even declined by 0.7 per cent a year. In contrast, some of the smaller centres grew rapidly, e.g. Bombo by 23.3 per cent a year, Kigoba by 15.6 per cent a year, Bugiri by 14 per cent a year and Kisoro by 13.8 per cent a year. However, growth rates vary widely from town to town and between different parts of the country.

Zambia

When Zambia became independent in 1963, 20.5 per cent of its population lived in urban areas. This was one of the highest levels of urbanization found in Africa south of Sahara, and since then it has continued to grow rapidly so that it was 39.9 per cent at the census of 1980 and today probably above 50 per cent. Most of the urban population is spread over a number of large cities around Lusaka and in the copper belt, and unlike in many other African countries, the capital city is not a primate city. In 1963 it housed only 17 per cent of the total urban population, and although it has grown rapidly since independence, it still had only 24 per cent of the urban population in 1980. In the latter year, ten cities had more than 50,000 inhabitants and in total 75 per cent of the urban population, but although they had grown rapidly, their share of the urban population had dropped from 95 per cent in 1963.

The ten large towns grew especially rapidly during the 1960s (9.4 per cent a year), but when the copper industries were hit by crises in the early 1970s, the growth of the large towns was reduced to half (4.6 per cent p.a.). The towns in the copper belt were hit especially. During the 1980s, many of them experienced growth below the national population growth rate, which means that they must have experienced net out-migration. However, the smaller towns continued to grow rapidly, both because of the growth of individual towns and the increase in the number of small towns. The next nine towns in the urban hierarchy (with populations between 9,000 and 34,000 inhabitants in 1980) grew by 9.6 per cent a year in the period 1963–69 and by 10.6 per cent a year in the period 1969–80. The total number of small towns (those below the top ten) grew in the same periods by 14.8 per cent a year and 18.9 per cent a year, respectively. As a consequence, their share grew from 5 per cent to 25 per cent of the total urban population.

The large rate of urbanization in combination with rapid urban growth has meant that contrary to most African countries, rural population growth has been very limited (0.6 per cent a year in 1963–69 and 1.6 per cent in 1969–80), and many of the thinly populated rural areas have even lost population. During the 1980s the urbanization process apparently slowed down further in both the large and small towns. According to Melange (1993) the small towns did not grow by more than 2.5 per cent a year in the census period 1980–90.

Zimbabwe

The level of urbanization in Zimbabwe increased from 16.6 per cent in 1962 to 27.3 per cent in 1992 (towns with more than 2,500 inhabitants). The urban system is greatly dominated by Harare (including Chitungwiza) and Bulawayo, which in 1992 accounted for 73 per cent of the total urban population, a figure which has not changed much since 1962. (However, Bulawayo has been growing much slower than Harare and has reduced its share of the urban population from 40 per cent to 22 per cent.)

In addition to Harare and Bulawayo, a number of smaller towns developed before independence that were located in and serviced the white commercial farm areas. In the African farm areas, on the other hand, urban development was generally held back until the 1970s. During both the 1970s and the 1980s, the fourteen largest of these towns (with populations from 16,000 to 124,000 in 1992) grew at almost the same rate (4.7 per cent a year in 1969–82 and 5.0 per cent a year in 1982–92) as Harare (including Chitungwiza) and Bulawayo together (5.2 per cent a year in 1969–82 and 5.3 per cent a year in 1982–92). However, below these major towns, a number of smaller towns have developed, both in the white commercial farm areas and, especially after independence, also in the communal areas. The number of these small settlements with more than 2,500 inhabitants has increased from 12 in 1962 to 23 in 1969, 46 in 1982 and about 60 in 1992. Although most of them are still small, some grew very rapidly during the 1980s (Mlalazi, 1993).

3.4   Conclusions on the pattern of small-town growth in eastern and southern Africa

To draw any general conclusions on the development of small towns in eastern and southern Africa on the basis of the data presented above may well be unwise. The data are mostly revised and adjusted data taken from infrequent population censuses, which especially for urban areas are often highly questionable because definitions of what is urban have tended to change from town to town as well as over time. However, in spite of these difficulties, which make more detailed conclusions impossible, the country studies above point to a number of different processes which together and in different combinations have been important in determining the pattern of urban growth:

– in the British colonies especially the urban migration of Africans was generally highly restricted. The growth of European urban centres was therefore often limited before independence. Also, the possibilities for Africans to open their own businesses in trade and production outside the European towns were often restricted, so that rural towns tended not to develop in African rural areas either. At independence this changed, and the result was often a rapid migration to urban areas, at first to obtain wage labour in the large towns, but increasingly also to create new small businesses both there and in the often new smaller towns. This influx especially to the capital cities was further supported by the development of the new state's administration and flows from donor activities. This rapid migration to the large cities just after independence is seen especially in Zambia, probably in Tanzania and also in Malawi, but apparently not in Kenya;

– guerilla warfare in rural areas both before and after independence often forced people to migrate to urban areas. This led to rapid urban growth in Mozambique during the 1980s and to a lesser extent Zimbabwe during the 1970s, but apparently not in Uganda, which also suffered rural warfare during the 1970s and 1980s;

– at low levels of economic development and urbanization, urban growth tends to be concentrated in the large cities, while development of the smaller towns tends to take place at higher levels of urbanization, when rural money incomes and the level of rural commercialization increase. This may be the explanation for the pattern of urban development found in Malawi and Tanzania;

– government policies on urban centre development may favour the development of different levels in the urban hierarchy, from the capital city via regional capitals or district centres to small rural centres. Most countries have had such policies. However, whether or not they have had the desired effect is often doubtful, because they are often counteracted by other policies. Thus a strong urban bias in agricultural policies has often counteracted small town development policies. There are indications, however, that such policies have been important in, for example, the gradual decentralization of urban growth in Kenya, in the development of regional capitals in Tanzania, and in the development of district service centres in Zimbabwe;

–   externally generated economic crises and the negative effects of structural
    adjustment policies have generally tended to hit urban areas relatively
    harder than rural areas. This seems to have been the case in a number of
    countries, e.g. Kenya, Tanzania, Zambia, Uganda, and possibly Ethiopia,
    during the 1970s and/or 1980s, when urban growth in general decreased,
    especially in the large cities, while smaller towns continued to grow at a
    more rapid rate. This partly corresponds to Jamal and Week's (1993)
    thesis of the vanishing rural-urban gap, except that they postulate a return
    to the rural areas rather than a growth in small rural centres. This
    difference is significant in that if the 'return to the rural areas' is not a
    return to the rural household but a growth in the small towns, the
    development is likely to take place at a considerably higher level of
    accumulation, as small town activities tend to be larger than rural non-
    town activities.

In Zimbabwe, small and large towns appear to have grown almost equally
rapidly both in the 1970s, before independence, and in the 1980s since. The
explanation may be that restrictions on urban migration were gradually being
lifted already during the 1970s, and urban migration was in addition furthered
by the civil war in the rural areas. On the other hand, after 1980 independent
Zimbabwe introduced relatively efficient rural development policies, which
may have been successful in dampening migration to the large cities.

4 A small-enterprise theory of small-town development

4.1 The structure of the small-town economy

The small African town is the location of small and sometimes not so small local hawkers, artisans, traders, businessmen and even small-scale industrialists. Some of these run businesses which on the surface may not be so different from the retailers described in traditional central place theory. But the small town may also house branches of large national or multi-national corporations of a type implied by dependency theories, which attempt to exploit local resources or markets. And it is the seat of branches of mostly agricultural parastatals which are governed at least partly by bureaucratic regulations, and which are often conceived to be part of the rural area rather than of the small town in which they are located. In the small town, these different forms of business organizations meet, compete and sometimes collaborate, but in any case influencing one another so that in the end they may not be what they seem on the surface.

Economic activities in small towns may be concerned with:

- the local distribution of local produce;

- the collection and processing of local agricultural products for export out of the local region;

- the distribution of products produced outside the region, both consumer goods and production inputs and investment goods for local production; and

- the local processing of non-local inputs for a non-local market (often called enclave or footloose industries).

The collection and processing of local agricultural produce for export out of the region is typically carried out by parastatal organizations or large enterprises and their branches, partly because these activities often require large amounts of capital and are often based on technologies with considerable scale economies, and partly because trade in such commodities is often government controlled. Small local enterprises dominate the supply of products which are both produced and distributed locally, while goods imported into the region may be distributed by both small and large enterprises. Finally, enclave production may be carried out by both small local enterprises and branch plants, but in any case they are often closely linked to larger external enterprises.

There is often a certain segmentation, which is sometimes legally enforced, between the branches and the small and larger local enterprises. However, the line of demarcation between them is usually not fixed absolutely, and small and large enterprises and branches develop in response to one another and under the influence of the available technologies, national and regional policies, and the general level of development. In the end they all compete for the same resources and the same rural market, but they do not, as assumed by the Christallian central-place theory, have a locational monopoly on the local rural market. They often compete with both rural non-farm activities and direct deliveries from suppliers in the larger towns in a market which is often highly unstable and insecure. It is unstable because agricultural production in many parts of Africa is a risky business, with frequent years of drought, flood or pests which destroy the harvest. It is also unstable because the supply of industrial goods, whether consumer goods, production inputs or machinery, is often unreliable; infrastructure is insufficient and dilapidated, cash-flow problems recurrent, speculation endemic, and political and administrative decisions often arbitrary. In this risky environment, small entrepreneurs often depend on family relations and on the patronage of wealthier businessmen or administrators with political influence for credit, government permits and allocations, supply of scarce commodities and food in time of crisis. On the other hand, branch offices and shops are guaranteed such supplies from their head offices.

4.2   Enterprise networks

This complex web of interdependencies between enterprises is not well described by the enterprise concept implicit in traditional development theories and informal sector literature (e.g., ILO, 1972, 1985; Little, 1987; Liedholm and Mead, 1987; Moyo, 1984; Peattie, 1987; Portes, 1983; Mkandawire, 1986; Castells and Portes, 1989). Neo-classical-inspired modernization theories assume that enterprises operate on equal terms in anonymous, homogeneous and stable markets, thus precluding interaction and adaptation between enterprises. On the other hand, Marxist-inspired dominance or dependency theories reduce enterprise relations to simple dominance and subordination, and therefore a priori preclude meaningful actions and strategies on the part of the small enterprises.

In order to describe the complex web of interdependencies in which the small-town enterprise operates, we need an enterprise concept which places the enterprise in a much more differentiated and dynamic environment, taking into account specific relations between the small enterprise and other small and large enterprises, organizations and households.

Such approaches to understanding the small enterprise and its interaction with the environment have been developed since the end of the 1970s for example in theories of economic restructuring (Massey, 1984) and flexible specialization (Scott, 1988; Scott and Storper 1988; Storper, 1991; Sabel, 1982; Piore and Sabel, 1984), the Scandinavian network theory (Hägg and Johanson, 1982; Johanson and Mattson, 1986; NordReFo, 1987), the regulation school (Lipietz, 1985), institutional economics (Williamson, 1981) and theories of global-local relationships (Dicken, 1994). Some of these approaches are developed from Marxist tradition, others from neo-classical tradition, but the arguments are increasingly being mixed. The different approaches emphasize different arguments and different aspects of the production system; but they share a new understanding of the enterprise on which I am also basing my theory of small-town development.

This new understanding places the enterprise in a network of enterprises, organizations and households through which commodities, labour, services, money, information and innovations flow, and through which learning processes and power relations are transmitted and enterprises adapt to each other. Although the existence of both market and command relations is recognized, personal relations based on reciprocity and trust are seen to be important in determining flows.

The enterprise is no longer seen as a black box with fixed borders, but rather as an open dynamic organization performing many different functions which may be carried out in-house or be external to branch plants or offices, subcontractors or other suppliers as a matter of strategy. The composition of enterprises in a sector may therefore vary from place to place and over time as a result of differences in the physical, social and political production environment.

Small enterprises are looked upon neither as completely independent enterprises operating on free markets, nor as completely dependent on large-scale formal enterprises and state policy. Interdependence between enterprises is seen as determined not only by ownership and size, but also by many other often qualitative factors such as technology, market and financial relations. The small enterprise will often be dependent on one or more large enterprises.

32

But at the same time, the productivity of the large enterprise will often depend on the existence, not of a specific small enterprise, but of a network of small service and production enterprises. The small/informal enterprise is seen as operating in interaction with other small and large enterprises and public authorities in an interplay which in some situations may lead to dependence, but which in others may lead to considerable autonomy (NordReFo, 1987; Johanson and Mattson, 1986). This has also led to a more differentiated view of branches and independent enterprises, where differences in dependence are relative rather than absolute and where branches may have considerable degrees of freedom, while formally independent enterprises may not be independent at all.

Last but not least, scale economies are seen to be much less important than is assumed in the traditional development theories. Thus small enterprises are not necessarily seen as being less efficient or less important than large ones; rather, they are seen to perform at least partly different functions which sometimes may be of strategic importance in the integrated and dynamic production and social system.

Scale economies are important, but large-scale production requires large markets which often, especially in developing countries, are not there, or are very expensive for large enterprises to reach because of poor infrastructure. Therefore, small enterprises typically produce specialized or different quality products for different markets, either specialized, high-quality products for specialized markets or low-quality cheap products for low-income, peripheral markets. Such small enterprises will, of course, often be less efficient than large enterprises supplying the core market, in the sense that the unit cost of the specialized product produced by the small enterprise will be higher than that of the standardized product produced by the large enterprise. However, if the large enterprise were forced to supply the small market actually supplied by the small enterprise, the costs would often be even higher; thus one cannot say a priori that the small enterprise is less efficient than the large, because they do not carry out the same functions.

In developing countries, small producers are typically also retailers of their own products, and often earn a larger share of value added as retailers than as producers. Large producers, on the other hand, typically sell their products through wholesalers. Comparisons of the efficiency of small and large enterprises should therefore include the cost of wholesaling, retailing, transport and possibly marketing.

To be able to exploit large-scale scale economies not only requires a sufficiently large market, but also resources, capital and labour available in sufficiently large quantities of the right quality and at the right time. On the other hand, by using different technologies small and medium-sized formal or informal enterprises may be able to exploit small amounts of resources, e.g. waste products which would not be attractive to the large enterprise, small individual savings which would not be available to the large enterprise, and labourers who are not able or willing to sell their labour on the conditions offered by the large enterprise or who have the wrong qualifications. Small enterprises, therefore, may also be able to survive by exploiting such small input markets, which would otherwise lay idle.

The argument sometimes advanced, that the development of a small enterprise sector is a waste of development resources, therefore seldom holds true. Investments in small enterprises are almost completely based on people's own savings, and they use labour and other resources which would most often not be available for the large-scale sector, if the small-scale sector were suppressed. Small and large enterprises should therefore be seen as complementary rather than as alternatives. Small and large enterprises should co-exist, because although they compete, they do different things, use different resources and serve different markets.

A theory of small enterprises (and therefore also a theory of small towns) must specifically take into account these specializations and market segmentations – both between small and large enterprises and within the small-scale sector – because they are the *raison d'etre* of the small enterprise.

4.3   The hierarchy of enterprises and flexible specialization

Large-scale production requires large investments and therefore it has large fixed costs and requires large and stable markets to be profitable. In order to understand the role of small and medium-sized enterprises in the economy, we must understand the process of specialization and market creation. Large stable markets are created by:

– policies of spatial integration through improved transport and communication networks, which permit increasingly larger markets and stabilize supplies through the standardization of products and markets, and through the creation of efficient market and financial institutions;

– policies of market stabilization, which increase predictability and reduce risks, e.g. agricultural policies to increase food production and security, the setting-up of insurance and social institutions, the creation of political, administrative and legal systems based on rules rather than arbitrary decisions, and macro-economic policies.

In the industrialized countries such a process of market integration and stabilization has gradually taken place during the last 100–200 years, culminating in the Fordist and Keynesian polices in the period after the second world war. During this period African countries were increasingly being drawn into the economy of the industrialized countries, but their own economies are still little integrated. In the industrialized countries, increased market integration and stabilization has meant that an increasing proportion of total production is produced by large-scale industries; but contrary to the expectations of both neo-classical and Marxist theories, this has not meant that there is no room for small enterprises (see, e.g., Pedersen, 1991b). The reason for this is that while transportation improvements, product standardization and stabilization policies have promoted large-scale production, they have also tended to create new room for small enterprises, because the large producers often choose to opt out of the smallest, less profitable and most unstable markets and leave them to niche producers and subcontractors or else unserved.

In the process of industrialization, spatial market niches have therefore increasingly been replaced by technical and product niches. Small enterprises venturing into these small and unstable market niches have three strategic options in surviving this instability:

–   they can invest in multi-purpose machinery and employ skilled labour in order to shift production between different markets and thus create stable production for themselves, even though their individual markets fluctuate. This strategy corresponds to what is sometimes known as 'flexible specialization',[1] or what Sengenberger and Pyke (1992) call the 'high road' to industrial restructuring;

–   they can minimize their investments in machinery (and preferably treat the investments as sunken costs) and rely on unskilled labour, which can be hired and fired on short notice. In this way, the enterprise can reduce its fixed costs and be able to survive even though its market fluctuates wildly. This strategy leads to what could be called 'sweatshops', often operated as simple subcontractors. It corresponds to what Sengenberger and Pyke call the 'low road' to industrial restructuring;

–   finally, it can be possible for very small, often household-based enterprises to survive in a semi-subsistence economy in the smallest and most unstable markets by doing out-work for larger enterprises. They can do this by investing very little capital and only part of the household labour force, if at the same time they draw on other sources of income from agriculture or from formal or informal wage labour.

These strategies form a hierarchy with respect to size, capital intensity, productivity and market. The competitiveness of each of these strategies depends on the structure of the commodity and labour markets and on the general social context in which the enterprise operates. The actual specification of the three strategies therefore depends not only on the enterprise itself, but also on the sector and environment in which it operates. Two enterprises following the same strategy but operating in different environments may therefore look very different, and the three strategies cannot be used directly as a basis for the classification of enterprises (see, e.g., McCormick, 1994).

For the large capital-intensive enterprise, the stability of its labour force is important in securing stable production and high capacity utilization. The necessary qualifications are often highly specialized and enterprise-specific, and in order to reduce training costs and labour turnover, the enterprise often tries to train people so narrowly that their qualifications cannot be utilized in other enterprises. On the other hand, the enterprise is also willing to pay above-average wages in order to keep its trained personnel. Thus it will attempt to create an internal labour market where the enterprise and at least its core personnel have a common interest in reducing labour turnover, but also a situation where the labour force has few attractive alternative job opportunities, and therefore relatively little bargaining power in cases of conflict. Labour unions are often organized on an enterprise basis.

Enterprises choosing the flexible specialization strategy require a core labour force with broader and more general qualifications, so that they can switch from one production to another. However, with such a qualified labour force the enterprise is in a poor bargaining position, because it should be relatively easy for qualified workers to switch from one enterprise to another. As a result, such enterprises are unwilling to finance training, which instead has to be paid for by the trainees themselves or by the government. On the other hand, the high mobility of labour is important for a rapid diffusion of innovation among enterprises. Unions will often have a relatively strong bargaining power, emphasizing the importance of training, but also trying to control access to the sector by new trainees in order to maintain this bargaining power. On the other hand, broad qualifications and in many cases limited capital requirements also mean that workers can start their own enterprises with relative ease.

Enterprises choosing a sweatshop strategy typically offer relatively poor working conditions, low wages and unstable employment. They employ unskilled or low-skilled workers, who have little bargaining power even where unions exist , since they are easy to replace in areas with surplus labour. However, even in the sweatshop, on-the-job training is often important, and even though the enterprise hires and fires workers according to seasonal and cyclical swings, the same workers may often be attached to the enterprise for long periods. Patron-client relations often develop between workers and owners. Especially in rural areas, there may be a mutual interest in such permanent seasonal employment if it complements the agricultural work seasons.

Finally, the very small semi-subsistence enterprise typically offers employment only to the owner and possibly to some of his or her family members. It is often a part-time activity supplementing agricultural work or some type of wage labour. The income earned at such activities varies widely depending on the activity, the qualifications of the owner, his investments and the priority he is able and willing to give to the enterprise. Often this is small.

Thus the burden of market instability is transmitted first from large-scale production down the enterprise hierarchy, and secondly from the enterprises to their workers. In order to absorb the instability, workers attempt to use partly their social and family networks and partly the state, organizations (e.g. unions, unemployment insurance, NGOs) or patron-client relations.

Enterprise collaboration tends to be more frequent among flexibly specialized enterprises than among sweatshops. Flexibly specialized enterprises tend to compete on quality and product specialization rather than on price and therefore often complement each other in terms of both technological capability and markets. Areas dominated by flexibly specialized enterprises may therefore develop into partially integrated production areas or what has become knows as Marshallian districts, after the British economist who described such districts at the start of the twentieth century (Becattini, 1990).

Sweatshops, on the other hand, tend to operate with simpler technologies and compete mostly on price. In order to reduce costs, they often minimize management functions and develop into simple subcontractors strongly dependent on large customers who provide the management services that are lacking.

Government and inter-firm organizations also tend to play a more active role in the flexible specialization environment than in large-scale and sweatshop environments. Government and inter-firm organizations are important, especially in vocational training, development and the transfer of new technology, and organization for collective efficiency. It is no coincidence that the role of local governments in enterprise-support in the industrialized countries has been increasing since the 1970s concurrently with the growth of flexible specialization.

In the industrialized countries, flexible specialization is often said to have become increasingly important partly because the market for high-income consumer goods has increased, and partly because the market for intermediate goods and the informalization of the labour market have become more important. However, the increasing demand for small flexible production is also a more direct result of the development of large-scale production. This is first, because larger production units require a greater product standardization, and this increases the need for niche products to serve markets which are not satisfied by standardized products; secondly, because large-scale production with increased mechanization and automatization has an increasing demand for highly specialized machinery and equipment to maintain and renew the production system.

Over time, many areas in the industrialized world have developed into specialized Fordist production centres, Marshallian districts characterized by flexible specialization, or sweatshop peripheries through processes of mutual adaptation between industry, labour, social groups and government. Such social production structures take a long time to develop and are difficult to replicate. The experience of the last twenty years in Europe also indicates that they may be difficult to change when there is no longer an economic basis for them. However, experience also shows that this is possible, although it often takes a long time.

4.4 The hierarchy of enterprises and the flexibility of production in African countries

In African countries, the situation is very different. Market instability is typically much larger and the total market much smaller. Consequently, there is much less room for large-scale production than in industrialized countries. Still the goal of industrialization policies in most African countries has been to develop large-scale industry. Supported by government and donor funds, the large-scale production capacity has often been expanded much beyond what is feasible given the existing market and distribution system. This has often resulted in a very low capacity utilization which governments have attempted to increase by granting enterprises monopoly status and preferential treatment in the allocation of scarce resources and foreign currency. This has effectively blocked the development of other alternatives than very small semi-subsistence producers and traders, and the official attitude toward them has in general been negative and they have often been harassed by the authorities.

Large excess capacity in combination with a lack of small service and input suppliers in the local environment has often led large enterprises to develop side productions and workshops within the enterprise to produce inputs and services which in the industrialized countries would usually be bought on the market. Such non-marketed side production is often carried out on a less than optimal scale, which therefore reduces further the efficiency of the large enterprise while undercutting the chances of developing such activities on a market basis.

As a result, the intermediate enterprises which do develop tend to grow out of the demands of semi-subsistence producers and consumers, rather than as a response to the large-scale sector. Their development is therefore limited by the low purchasing power of their main customers and by the closed, monolithic and monopolistic nature of the large-scale producers. Intermediate enterprises which have developed out of the large-scale sector are more likely to be sweatshops than flexible producers.

The monopolistic nature of the industry also means that the large industries tend to organize their own distribution, and as a result the wholesale sector is under-developed. It is therefore difficult for small enterprises to reach non-local markets except as subcontractors to large producers or distributors.

At the same time, public education and training are geared to produce the general academic qualifications demanded by the large enterprises – which often provide their own enterprise-specific training – rather than to a sector-specific vocational training which is the basis for developing a flexible production environment. Such sector-specific vocational training has mainly taken place through private initiative and expense as informal apprenticeship schemes in the small-scale informal sector, often low in quality.

Finally, the low income levels and considerable instability in the economy often forces people to rely for their survival not on one activity, but on a mixture of wage labour and entrepreneurial activities in small or large enterprises. Their association with labour market organizations and unions, where they exist, therefore tends to be rather weak, while social and family networks become more important. As a result, the small entrepreneurs are often only able to focus part of their energy and resources on their enterprises, and are therefore less likely to succeed.

Another consequence is that a clear difference between sweatshops and flexible producers has seldom developed. Where flexible production and Marshallian districts can be said to exist in Africa (e.g. in Kenya and Ghana), they do not supply the large enterprises but rather the low-income households and the small farms. And they are often at the same or even a lower social level than the sweatshops.

Flexible specialization and enterprise networks of the type described in Europe and some of the NIC countries are seldom found in Africa (see, e.g., Masinde, 1996; Mead and Kunjeku, 1993; Ndlela, 1993). This does not mean, however, that flexibility and networking are less important in Africa than in Europe. Flexibility and networking in the production system are a response to the instability and insecurity of markets (Salais and Storper, 1992). In the industrialized countries, this instability is to a large extent created by rapid innovation, product specialization and market segmentation in the production system itself. In developing countries, the instability is due rather to large income differences, unstable and seasonal incomes, a lack of infrastructure and unstable commodity supplies. However, just as in the industrial countries, enterprises respond to instability with networking and flexible specialization, albeit of a different kind. To counteract the effect of the high degree of instability, small enterprises rely on family networks and hierarchical patron-client relations, which may often be exploitative but which do give some guarantee of survival in crisis situations; and specialization and market segmentation are often based on distribution services (transport, credit and commodity availability) rather than product specialization.

Due to the high degree of instability and the importance of local networks, successful businessmen tend to expand by diversifying into different sectors within the local area, rather than by expanding into the regional or national market. To expand into such larger markets requires the establishment of new social, economic and political networks, which may be both difficult and costly to develop. As a result, where such market expansion takes place, it is often based on extended and geographically dispersed family or clan relations.

4.5   The small enterprise as a reproductive activity of the household

The small enterprise and the household of the entrepreneur are often highly integrated and difficult or impossible to distinguish empirically (Redclift and Mingione, 1985). However, in order to understand the interaction between the enterprise and the household, we shall here make this distinction, which is important because the enterprise must be competitive in the market in order to survive, while the household need not survive on the market but must command sufficient resources to reproduce itself.

However, the competitiveness of the enterprise need not be based on technical efficiency; it may be due to resource transfers from the household or from external sources, e.g. donor or government institutions. Also, the rules of the market need not be purely economic, though in general neither the small enterprise nor the household will be able to change them. Usually, the entrepreneur and his or her household will provide the enterprise with capital, working time and management, receiving a profit in return, but sometimes the household may have to subsidize the enterprise.

The purpose of the enterprise will usually be to contribute to the reproduction of the household and to the accumulation of capital. The reproduction of the household may be secured by a combination of agricultural activities, wage labour in either the formal or the informal sector, government transfers (or taxation) or the family enterprise. The decision of a person or household to try to develop some private or cooperative enterprise depends partly on its prospects and partly on the possible alternatives.

Where reproduction of the entrepreneurial household is based on agriculture, the small informal activities will often be designed to supplement seasonal farm incomes by utilizing seasonal surpluses of farm labour and exploiting seasonal variations in local resources and markets. Unfortunately, periods with labour surplus often coincide with periods when the market for small businesses is low and the competition fierce. Therefore, although farm incomes may be subject to large seasonal and climatic swings, in the long run land represents a more stable source of income than most non-farm activities. Partly for this reason, land ownership and farming have first priority in most rural societies, even if incomes are lower. Consequently, both formal low-wage jobs and especially informal non-agricultural activities will in many cases be considered supplementary, often part-time activities which people try to enter and leave again, depending on the amount of surplus time from agriculture.

Entrance requirements to the small-scale sector

Such a strategy is obviously only possible for small-scale/informal activities with few entrance requirements. In a large part of the small-scale/informal sector, such rapid mobility in and out is prevented by entrance requirements in the form of necessary production capital, qualifications, contact network and government permits and allocations. However, investigations into entrance requirements often appear to conflict. Some studies show that formal educational qualifications are not a prerequisite and may even be a hindrance, partly because they are often geared toward very specialized jobs in capital-intensive industries, and partly because they create expectations for employment in a secure, stable wage job (e.g., Aboagye, 1986). However, one should not conclude from this that no qualifications are necessary. Former work experience (e.g. with rural crafts), on-the-job training and family (or other) networks may often be more appropriate qualifications than formal education.

The prospects of the new enterprise depend on the resources that the entrepreneur commands in the form of qualifications, experience, networks, and access to capital. Consequently, the types of enterprise set up by educated and non-educated, by rich and poor, and by men and women tend to have different prospects. These are not only different because of the difference in resources, but also because people with many resources will also usually have better alternatives and more time to wait for them (Gugler, 1988). They are therefore less likely to engage in enterprises with few prospects. Consequently, many of the least lucrative small businesses are run by old people, single women, the handicapped or children, who are marginalized on the wage-labour market (Nattras, 1987).

The small entrepreneur is seldom able to borrow money from the formal banking system because he does not have the necessary security. Therefore his own savings or access to family money are very important. Even if he were able to borrow money, however, this could be very risky because he will often operate on very unstable markets where he may not be able to pay interest and amortization on the loan. Most small entrepreneurs therefore treat their investments as sunken costs in order to reduce their fixed costs. This is especially important for small enterprises adapted to the seasonal and climatic cycles of agriculture. By treating investments as sunken costs, small enterprises may be able to reduce their fixed costs to almost nothing and thus survive for long periods, even though their turnover fluctuates wildly and

41

they are actually closed for long periods. This also means that small enterprises often have a larger demand for borrowing working capital than for borrowing investment capital. This is especially the case in rural economies which fluctuate with agricultural cycles and therefore suffer permanent cash-flow problems.

In the literature on small enterprises in the Third World today, it is often assumed that entrance requirements in terms of both training and capital are much lower in trade and commerce than in crafts and production, because no tools or machinery are required. This hardly holds true, however. Except for the very lowest level of commercial activity, the capital invested by traders in stocks is likely to be larger than that invested by craftsmen in tools. And although the necessary qualifications in trade and commerce are different from those in crafts, there is no reason to believe that they are lower. Training in trade and commerce can to a large extent be seen as training in network building, and the lack of emphasis on such training may well be one of the most serious bottlenecks in the development process (see, e.g., King, 1987).

The role of household structure in the small-scale sector

The resources that a person (or household) commands depend not only on own resources, but also on access to other resources, such as private loans, supplier credit and public resource allocations and contracts. Such access to resources other than one's own often depends either on family and other social networks or on wage labour and the contacts which accompany it. The structure of the small-enterprise sector therefore depends both on family structure and social organization and on the experience and incomes earned in the formal sector.

This access to family resources may be especially important for women because it is more difficult for them than for men to find well-paid jobs which permit them to save starting capital and to borrow from the formal financial system. For divorced women especially, it may also be more difficult to obtain family loans, because they have often broken family ties.

The family structure also influences the ability to accumulate. Where the successful entrepreneur has a customary obligation to support members of a large family, it may be very difficult to save enough to invest, even though in periods of crises the entrepreneur could expect to receive help from his family (Hydén, 1983). Many entrepreneurs, especially the more successful, therefore attempt to avoid or reduce such family obligations. In a fluctuating economic environment, however, it can be very risky to dissociate oneself from the security of the family network. In other parts of the world, the family organization operates rather as a mutual investment circle and thus tends to support the ability to accumulate. To a large extent, this seems to be the case among Indians in East Africa.

The growth of enterprises from small to large often takes several generations. The way enterprises are carried over from one generation to the next is therefore important for the process of accumulation. It is often claimed that the businesses of successful African businessmen tend to dissolve at their deaths, when assets are distributed among children and brothers (see, e.g., Rasmussen, 1992).

These interactions between small enterprises and the different family relations surrounding them depend not only on how traditional gender relations and family institutions have adapted to the modern legal regulation of marriage, family responsibility and inheritance, but also on the economic consolidation of both households and businesses and their ability to withstand fluctuations in the economy. However, our knowledge about these relationships is still very limited.

The household-based enterprise: a response to crisis or to development?

African governments have generally had a very ambivalent attitude toward small/informal enterprises, and many have periodically attempted to halt their development. They have been able to draw support for such a policy from both neo-classical and Marxist theories, which both prophesy the contraction of the small-enterprise sector in the course of development through its being outstripped by the more efficient and modern large-scale sector. Contrary to these theoretical expectations, the number of small formal and informal enterprises has been growing rapidly in most African countries, in which they make up an increasing part of the economy and employment.

There is no general agreement, however, about why the small-enterprise sector is growing. Marxist-inspired, petty commodity theories tend to see the growth as a response to economic crisis and growing unemployment which forces people with no other options into the small-enterprise sector. Consequently, the present growth in small enterprises is seen as a response to the social crisis and contraction of the large-scale, formal sector resulting from structural adjustment policies. The small enterprises are therefore expected to disappear again when and if the economy takes off.

The perception of the small-enterprise sector as a response to crises and a last resort for surplus labour rests on the assumption that there is free and easy access to it. This is generally not supported by empirical studies. During major crises especially, the poorer sections of the population are unlikely to have the resources necessary to start and run an enterprise (Scoones, 1994).

A second problem with the crisis theory is that the large-scale formal sector in most African countries, even in good years, has only been able to absorb a relatively small part of the annual growth in the labour force. Therefore, even quite dramatic swings in formal-sector employment will have limited impact on the total national employment situation, although, of course, it may be important locally, especially in the large urban areas. The close links between urban and rural households that exist in Africa make it more likely that the swings in the formal and informal urban economy are absorbed into peasant agriculture.

Neo-classical modernization theory would also see the present growth in small enterprises as a result of structural adjustment, but it would focus on the economic liberalization which permits small enterprises to compete on more equal terms with the rather inefficient large enterprises. But also, that will only last until the efficiency of the large enterprises improves.

However, on the basis of theories of networks and economic interdependencies in the production system two other arguments may be advanced. First, it has become evident from many empirical studies that large and small, formal and informal enterprises are very interdependent and complement rather than conflict with one another. This indicates that the informal sector should grow in response to growth in the total economy, not in response to crisis, and thus be pro-cyclical rather than counter-cyclical. Secondly, there are strong reasons to believe that especially in rural areas, the informal sector grows concurrently with the commercialization and monetization of the rural economy, a process which, while it may be influenced by the swings in the economy, is basically long term (Pedersen, 1994a).

Thus there are many alternative explanations for the growth of small enterprises. In reality, the small-enterprise sector is very heterogeneous, and different small enterprises are likely to respond differently to both crisis and development. However, the long-term growth trend is probably much more important for growth in the small-enterprise sector than cyclical swings in the economy.

4.6   The branch

One of the recurrent issues in regional studies has been the debate on the role of branches versus independent enterprises in regional development. Regional development theories have mostly argued against branches and in favour of development based on local independent enterprises (Thwaits, 1978; Watts, 1981; Sweeney, 1987; Maleckie, 1990). In practice, however, regional policies have often attempted to induce branches of large national or international corporations or government organizations to locate in peripheral regions. In Africa, branches of private corporations as well as of parastatal, governmental and non-governmental organizations play an important role in small-town development, and it is often through branches that the national and international economy makes itself felt at the local level.

In favour of the branches is, the fact that whenever a large corporation or organization decides to locate a branch, large investments and many jobs may be created in a short time. Against this, it is argued that the effect of the branch on local development is often limited, because it employs mainly unskilled low-wage labour, withdraws its profits from the region, and is usually not integrated into the local economy, thus resulting in few external economies. In addition, it is risky to base the local economy on branches, since a branch may be closed down not only because it becomes unprofitable in itself, but also as a result of technological restructuring in the large corporation to which it belongs (see, e.g., Massey and Meegan, 1979; Massey, 1984; Watts and Stafford, 1986).

On the other hand, it is argued that development based on local independent enterprises tends to be more stable. The independent enterprises tend to be better integrated into the local economy and thus to have larger derived effects. More of both profit and technological capacity developed in the production tends to stay in the region. However, especially in developing regions with little tradition for entrepreneurship and little local capital accumulation, development based on local enterprises alone may be very slow.

The debate has therefore never been satisfactorily resolved. In fact, both empirical and theoretical developments during the last ten years indicate that the issue is more complicated than it appears from the traditional debate (see, e.g., Dicken, 1994). Dependence is increasingly seen as a relative rather than an absolute concept. Formally independent enterprises are often not independent at all, but highly dependent on both their main customers and suppliers. On the other hand, dependent branches may be run with little interference from the head office, but with the advantage of having access to services, credit and marketing facilities which are not accessible to the local enterprise. And although it is true that even if the branch is profitable, it may be closed as a result of long-term structural considerations, in the short term it will often be more stable than the local enterprise because it has greater financial backing to weather out cyclical or seasonal swings (see, e.g., Pedersen, 1978).

In most of the regional literature from the 1960s and 1970s, the branch was usually conceived as a simple production unit with only limited investments and limited management of its own, and set up in a peripheral region in order to exploit the cheap labour force available there. During the 1980s, this picture of the branch has gradually changed and become more diversified. At least four different types of branch may be identified:

1   a commercial retail or wholesale outlet set up by a large commercial or production enterprise in order to exploit a larger spatial market;

2   a simple production branch, mostly set up to exploit cheap unskilled or semi-skilled labour. It will usually be based on limited fixed capital and costs, and have a limited management capacity of its own. However, it

45

may also be established to exploit localized resources, e.g. in agricultural processing. It will often produce for a very cyclical or seasonal market and be operated on a hire-and-fire basis. It may produce either simple finished products for a commercial enterprise, e.g. a retail chain, or simple inputs for a production enterprise. This is the classical conception of a branch. Technologically, it corresponds to the independent enterprise on the low road to development;

3   a vertically integrated production plant producing intermediate goods for the mother firm. It will typically be more capital intensive and use more highly skilled labour on a permanent basis. It often operates with a limited management capacity of its own. But it may also function as an almost independent enterprise or profit centre which in addition to its deliveries to the mother firm also attempts to develop its own market. However, the innovative capacity in product or process development will usually be concentrated in the mother firm;

4   an innovative branch with full managerial capacity basically run as an independent enterprise. It is typically orga nized as a limited company where the mother firm owns the majority of the shares, but is not technologically closely integrated into the mother firm. The latter is typically a finance corporation, but it might also be a production corporation attempting to innovate by buying and integrating small successful innovative enterprises into the corporation. It has a greater chance of becoming integrated into the local economy and tends to have a structure similar to the independent enterprise on the high road to development.

The different types of branch are the result of different corporate strategies which have developed in response to the growth of large corporations from national to multinational to global, and from product-specific production corporations to broad financial conglomerates with interests in many sectors (see, e.g., Giaoutzi, 1990). Corporate strategies also depend on the ownership of the corporation and may vary from private via cooperative to parastatal ownership.

The peripheral branches of large enterprises usually operate in a local economy where there are also smaller independent enterprises with which they have to compete or cooperate. However, in a world dominated by large corporations, it is the latter that determine the rules of the game to a large extent. The result is that small enterprises tend to be structured in response to the strategies of the large enterprises and their branches.

Branches of types 1 and 2 often compete intensively with local enterprises for local markets, cheap labour or other resources. Branches of type 3 and especially type 4, on the other hand, may play a potentially important role in the development of a local productive environment, where branches and local enterprises share a joint interest in collaboration because their resources tend to complement each other.

The local enterprise may have access to local financial and labour resources which are not accessible to the hierarchical system, whether private or public, and it may also have better access to the local market. The branch, on the other hand, has access through its mother firm both to the national market and to public and private services, to which the local independent enterprise often has difficult access or none at all.

In choosing a strategy for the development of his enterprise, the local small-town entrepreneur has to strike a balance between expansion and diversification on the local market, and specialization and expansion on non-local markets. Under the right conditions, the branch and branch manager may well be key elements in such a strategy because the branch is a part of both the hierarchy and the local agglomeration.

There are a number of difficulties in the development of such collaboration, however. The local entrepreneur will often regard the branch as an unwelcome competitor on the local market, which of course is often true. The branch manager is often a non-local person with few or no local contacts, and he is often moved around within the large corporation so frequently that he may have little chance to develop such contacts. He is also often more oriented towards the hierarchy, where his career opportunities are, than towards the local environment. Finally, the rules for his actions laid down by his head office may not really permit him to integrate locally, because the corporation to which he belongs is more concerned with its sectoral objectives than with exploiting local opportunities (Pedersen, 1992b). Realization of entrepreneurial potential therefore depends on the management strategies of the large organizations as well as on the qualifications, experience and attitude of both entrepreneurs and branch managers. However, a development strategy based on the greater integration of branches, whether private or governmental, into the local economy in order for it to gain increased access to non-local resources and markets may well be more efficient than attempts at territorial closure.

4.7 Agglomeration economies and collective efficiency

The small town can be seen as a way of organizing economic activities or enterprises in space. Thus the theoretical views of the small town depend to a large extent on the view of the enterprise and the way it interacts with its environment.

To explain the spatial concentration of enterprises in towns, classical location theories (e.g., Weber, 1929; Christaller, 1933; Lösch, 1954) invented the concept of agglomeration economies (Mulligan, 1984). In Weber's industrial-location theory, agglomeration economies are production-oriented, based on economic interaction among specialized and vertically integrated enterprises. Agglomeration economies consist of the advantages of reduced costs and increased intensity of interaction that enterprises may obtain by joint location. Subsequently, the idea of industrial-agglomeration economies in combination with input-output models has been developed into industrial complex analysis (see, e.g., Isard *et al.*, 1960) and, by a further combination with innovation theory, into Perroux's (1955) growth-centre theory. In the socialist economies, similar considerations led to the development of the concept of territorial industrial complexes.

The basic problem with this line of reasoning is that technical innovations, both in transport and communication and in production (Pedersen, 1987a), have led to reduced interaction costs, especially over long distances, so that in many cases it has been possible to exploit production-oriented agglomeration economies over long distances. At the same time, vertical specialization has been carried out to such an extent that the local market of a small town will seldom be sufficient to support specialized enterprises. The Weberian agglomeration economies among vertically integrated enterprises will thus seldom be relevant in small towns and will be found only in large metropolitan areas or city regions.

Another type of agglomeration economy, which may be either production oriented (backward linkages) or market-oriented (forward linkages), may occur where many similar enterprises agglomerate to exploit and develop a common resource base, a common labour market with specific qualifications or a common local market. They are sometimes termed location economies. They may be found in, for example, market towns where all enterprises in a specific trade are located in the same street, quarter or market place to attract as many customers as possible. There are many examples of this in African towns. Local economies may also be found in traditional textile regions or in certain mining areas, where many small enterprises agglomerate to exploit a common qualified labour market or a common mineral resource. Such industrial districts or agglomerations of similar activities are also known as Marshallian districts after Marshall, who described them at the start of this century in England.

Christaller's and Lösch's service-centre theories, however, are the most specific attempts to explain the existence of small towns. Here, agglomeration (or urban) economies are market-oriented (though they might also be oriented towards a dispersed resource base or labour market). They are based both on horizontal specialization among local enterprises interacting with the same local market (rather than with each other), and on vertical specialization and interaction with enterprises at higher levels of the urban hierarchy. Here, the small town becomes a service centre which serves the surrounding rural area and smaller towns with products and services, but which on the other hand receives inputs from the larger higher-order centres through a perfect market mechanism.

Christaller's and Lösch's theories of the development of small towns were originally developed for a market economy, but a modified version has also been used for the design of centres in planned economies where provisions are assumed to be supplied by a perfect administrative distribution system. If this assumption about perfect market or administrative distribution systems is not fulfilled, which is often the case in the Third World, the small towns may not develop as expected. Very low and unstable rural incomes, and efficient transportation also tend to reduce the role of small towns.

In the newer Marxist-inspired location theories, the role of the local environment has been largely discarded. Especially in underdeveloped regions, industries are often regarded as enclave industries with little or no local interaction except with the labour market. Instead, these theories explain location in terms of internal enterprise and concern structure. Production takes place in footloose production plants which can be moved around the world at will and located in those regions which offer the lowest labour costs and the highest locational subsidies (see, e.g., Massey, 1984; Maskell, 1984). The small towns are not seen as service centres, but rather as locations for agents or branches of multinationals and other large organizations attempting to exploit rural resources and labour markets. Attempts to engage the local rural population in the development of local market trade and production are doomed to failure, because this would only be possible for activities with very low entry requirements; and here the competition would be so fierce that no accumulation would be possible.

The new theories of networks and flexible specialization recognize the importance of the large multi-locational concerns and their footloose branch plants, but see small enterprises agglomerated in Marshallian districts as a potentially competitive alternative. At the same time, the very aggregate concept of location economies has been replaced by the more precise concept of collective efficiency (Schmitz, 1990). Groups of small enterprises may achieve increased collective efficiency through collaboration in more or less formalized enterprise networks. Where the concepts of agglomeration and locational economies were based on a neoclassical understanding of the enterprise as a black box operating in an anonymous and homogeneous market, the concept of collective efficiency is based on the new understanding of the enterprise as an open system operating in a network of other enterprises, organizations and individual actors. Interaction in such networks will be based at least partly on reciprocity and trust, although market or command relations may be involved as well (see also Section 4.2; also Pedersen, 1994c).

Such networks may take many different forms. Different authors have tended to focus on different types of networks, depending on their theoretical standpoint and the empirical cases:

49

- non-hierarchical production networks of small and medium-sized enterprises which through collaboration and flexible specialization can achieve a greater collective efficiency than they would individually (Schmitz, 1990; Rasmussen, Schmitz and van Dijk, 1992);

- primarily hierarchical networks, generated and controlled from the top by large enterprises which, in order to reduce costs and/or exploit cheap labour and illegal practices, externalize (Williamson, 1981; Johanson and Mattson, 1986) or informalize (Castells and Portes, 1989) functions which would otherwise have been performed within the large organization itself;

- formal membership organizations or cooperatives of small entrepreneurs fighting for political recognition and benefits for the small enterprises (Burrows, 1992; Moore and Hamalai, 1993);

- unions of informal labour fighting for higher wages, better working conditions and greater job security, but in many developing countries also promoting self-employment for the unemployed (Sanyal, 1991);

- non-hierarchical social-support networks (often family-, clan-, class- or neighbourhood-based) through which resources may be generated in times of crisis, but which can also lead to the distribution rather than re-investment of profits (Hydén, 1983, 1985);

- hierarchical patron-client relations which may guarantee the survival of the client and his enterprise in time of crisis, but may also exploit him in good years (Smith, 1976; Pedersen, 1992a; Bryceson, 1990).

Much of the literature on collective efficiency and Marshallian districts focuses on the local and non-hierarchical nature of small-enterprise networks. There is, therefore, reason to stress that such networks often comprise both non-local and hierarchical elements. And even where they are local and non-hierarchical, they often compete with large non-local enterprises or are linked to larger national or international enterprise networks which are hierarchical.

A second problem with most discussions of collective efficiency is that they focus on the efficiency that small individual enterprises may achieve through active collaboration with other enterprises. However, much of the collective efficiency in a Marshallian district or a small town is achieved through specialization and market segmentation *vis-à-vis* the non-local market. Such a process of specialization and market segmentation entails mutual adaptation among local enterprises, but not necessarily active collaboration or commodity flows between them. However, it may still increase the ranges of goods and services delivered by the centre, improving the delivery conditions and thus increasing collective efficiency. As is documented in the empirical study below, such processes of mutual adaptation play an important role in small-town development.

The increasing focus on small-enterprise networks and flexible specialization since the end of the 1970s is often seen to be the result of the introduction of a more flexible technology based on microelectronics. However, flexible technology may also be used by the large enterprises and there is no reason to believe that flexible technology in itself should support small enterprises. It could just as well lead to the development of larger enterprises because it makes it possible for them to capture small market niches which are not profitable for mass production. Still, it is probably true that new flexible technology has led to flexible specialization and small-enterprise development, not because flexible technology is flexible, but because it has made it possible to produce standardized components and intermediate products on a smaller scale and with greater precision, and therefore to a large extent made it possible to trade with them. The flexibility which leads to flexible specialization and collective efficiency among enterprises is built into the trade and distribution system rather than into the technology. It is therefore important that the system of agents, wholesalers, retailers and other middlemen is seen as an integrated part of the production system.

4.8 Conclusion: the small town as a spatial organization of enterprises

The small town in a developing rural region can be seen as a way of organizing activities in space. Small-town activities develop in competition or collaboration with rural households and their agricultural and non-agricultural activities on the one hand, and with direct deliveries from the large urban-based formal organizations and enterprises on the other. The development of small rural towns may play an important role in improving the level of rural services and infrastructure (see, e.g., Moser, 1984; Hardoy and Satterthwaite, 1986; Rondinelli, 1986).

A necessary condition for the creation of urban places in a non-metropolitan region is the existence of a sufficient economic surplus in the region. Such a surplus may come from local (agricultural) production, or from external sources, e.g. wages to the administrative hierarchy, pensions to local citizens, visits to the region by pilgrims and tourists, development aid, government services, construction projects and military establishments. The structure of the urban system depends, of course, on the structure and size of its economic base. The urban system may be seen as a way of organizing economic activity inspace. Seen from the local area, local economic activities may be concerned with:

- the local distribution of local production;

- the collection and processing of local (agricultural) products for export out of the region;

- the distribution of products produced outside the region, both consumer goods and inputs and investment goods for local production;

- the local processing of non-local inputs for a non-local market (often called enclave industries).

These functions may be carried out by branches of formal, large-scale, multi-location organizations or by small formal or informal single-location enterprises. Collecting and processing local exports is usually carried out by large enterprises and organizations, because these activities often require large capital and are often based on technologies with large-scale economies. The small enterprises will mainly supply products and services which are both produced and distributed locally, while goods imported into the region may be distributed by both small and large enterprises. Finally, enclave industries may also be carried out by both small and large enterprises, but they will usually be closely linked to larger external enterprises.

The line of demarcation, however, between small and large enterprises is not fixed. Small and large enterprises develop in response to one another under the influence of available technologies, national and regional policies and the general level of development. The development and structure of the urban system depends to a large extent on the resulting balance between small and large enterprises. At the same time, the development of enterprises, especially small enterprises, also depends on the structure of the urban system.

The large organizations and the urban system

Large, formal, multi-location organizations may be governmental, parastatal, cooperative or private, they may be national or multi-national, but they will usually be hierarchical in structure and have a more or less centralized management located in a metropolitan area or some other large town. The large enterprises may be able to attract important resources in the form of capital and qualified labour to a peripheral region. On the other hand, they are often run in such a way that the production surplus is extracted from the peripheral region, as profits, if they are private, as taxation, if they are governmental.

The advantage of the large enterprise is its ability to exploit scale economies. To be able to do this effectively, it tends to standardize its activities and production. Product standardization is often also necessary to sell products on export markets. However, such standardization tends to be determined by the situation in the centre region or by some average conditions and therefore may be less favourable to some of the peripheral regions. Thus at the same time as the large enterprises are increasing their competitiveness by exploiting scale economies, they often also open up new local markets which may be exploited by small local enterprises.

Especially where transport and communication infrastructure is little developed and management personnel scarce, the large organizations tend to concentrate as many functions as possible near their headquarters, where control functions are most easily carried out. Also, structural rationalization within large, multi-location organizations (e.g. parastatals) often results in centralization and the closing of local services and activities in small towns, even in situations where the local demand would be sufficient to justify the activity if all the large organizations operating in the town pooled their demand. Consequently, such concentrations often go much further than can be defended by scale economies, with the result that the lower levels of the urban hierarchy are little developed.

A possible solution to this problem would be to allow one of the large organizations open their local service activities (e.g. transport, telecommunications, administration or repair services) for other users on a market basis. In this way, a better utilization of scarce resources and an increase in the availability of local services for both small and large enterprises could be obtained.

Small enterprises and the urban system

Small formal or informal single-location enterprises are usually private, but they may be public or collective. They usually cater mainly to the local market in the town and its hinterland, and are better able to adapt to local market conditions. They are often more dependent on the local supply of inputs and services than large enterprises and their local branches, which often obtain such services from their own hierarchy.

The fact that small enterprises cater primarily to the local market does not mean, however, that they only operate with local contacts. Rather, they often function as mediators between the local market and outside sources of consumer goods, production inputs and information. These outside connections may be provided by a series of middlemen or wholesalers up through the urban hierarchy, or they may be provided by one of the large organizations (Freeman and Norcliffe, 1985; Kongstad and Mønsted, 1980; Schmith, 1979). Ideally, the large organizations may provide a limited range of standardized services cheaply, while the small middlemen are often more expensive; many, on the other hand, offer a wider range of services. But of course this may not hold true in situations where the large organizations are subsidized, where the supply of resources is deficient, or where small enterprises are restricted or illegal, as is often the case in the Third World today.

Small enterprises typically operate in market niches where it does not pay for the large-scale sector to operate. This may be in markets where the standardization of large enterprises and organizations is not appropriate, or it may be on markets where buying power is so low or diffuse that it becomes too costly for the large organizations to exploit them. This means that the small-scale and large-scale sectors often do not compete directly; however, if the market for small enterprises expands, it may become attractive for large organizations to enter into direct competition and attempt to take over the market, e.g. by establishing local branches. The large-scale sector may also attempt to monopolize the market through legislation, especially where it is governmental or parastatal. In other cases, small enterprises may be directly linked to large enterprises or organizations, whether as subcontractors, by processing inputs or by distributing their products.

Contact between the peripheral rural region and the outside world, and the resulting development or exploitation, thus follows either the 'open' urban network and the infrastructure and agglomeration economies it offers, or the internal and often closed networks of the large organizations. In many cases, of course, these organizational networks follow the structure of the urban system; but in other cases, the large formal organizations may be powerful enough to create their own networks, often short-cutting the lower levels of the urban hierarchy. Thus although the urban network and the large organizational networks are linked, they are not identical, and both are decisive for the development of the peripheral region.

Small-town development: local development processes versus national resource allocation

If the local market for the small-scale sector is very small, the sector will develop only as the part-time, informal activities of agricultural households. With larger market density, periodic markets or seasonal travel to markets (e.g. with livestock) may develop. However, only with a relatively large market density will the permanent full-time jobs which are the basis for the development of small towns be created in the non-agricultural small-scale sector.

When the local market expands and the small town grows, some small-scale artisan producers may get a chance to increase their scale of production. For Kenya, Hosier (1987) shows that while small enterprises in the regional centres mainly produce to order, the small enterprises in Nairobi tend to produce longer series for the market. This tendency is, of course, limited by the competition from large enterprises within or outside the town. On the other hand, the growing local market means that the market for specialized goods and services is likely to increase and thus open the way for an increased diversification in the local economy.

This growing diversification of the local economy will especially benefit, on the one hand, the middle-income households which have sufficient money to use the new services and still have a demand which is sufficiently simple to be satisfied locally, and on the other hand, the small local enterprises which are more dependent on local supplies than the large enterprises, which to a great extent obtain their inputs through their internal hierarchies. This is one of the reasons why the growth-centre policies of the 1960s did not succeed. In most cases, these policies attempted to generate local growth in peripheral regions by implanting one or a few large mass-producing enterprises in the region. However, these are exactly the type of enclave enterprises which have proved to generate very few local contacts other than the employment of cheap labour (Pedersen, 1986b).

Also the theories of the 1970s about restructuring the world economy and its negative impact on many peripheral regions hit by plant closures during recessions were primarily based on studies of regions dominated by a few large, mass-producing enterprises and lacking a diversified economy.

Though the trend toward centralization and product standardization in the large organizations and enterprises tends to hit the peripheral regions and their towns especially , it also creates new local niches in the production system which may be exploited by small enterprises. Seen from a small-town perspective, therefore, potential strategies for small-scale improvement of the local production system always exist in response to external changes.

In the short run, such strategies will seldom be sufficient to offset losses from closures of large plants in small towns. However, in the long run, there seem to be much better prospects for success with local development policies based on small-enterprise networks and a mixture of small and medium-sized enterprises.

Although the small towns may not seem very important when seen from a national perspective, this is hardly the case. Experience with regional development policies during the 1960s and 1970s clearly showed that long-term regional development cannot be achieved through a reallocation of national resources alone. Growth and development are basically local processes in which local actors attempt to develop the local area in response to and in competition with other regions and the large organizations. The reallocation of national and international resources may, of course, have a positive impact on the regions that benefit, just as structural rationalization may have strong negative impact on the regions that are hit. However, no amount of external subsidy is likely to have any lasting effect on local development if there are no actors in the area who are able and willing to exploit the subsidy for the benefit of the region. On the other hand, the positive development of activities in small towns is likely to have a positive effect not only on the towns themselves, but also on the efficiency of both the rural areas and large-scale activities in the larger cities. Small towns and their activities may therefore play a crucial role in the development process, even though their relative importance does not grow.

Note

1   The term *flexible specialization* is sometimes only used for enterprises following the first strategy. However, the term is also used more broadly for the whole process of de-concentration which comprises all the different strategies enterprises can pursue in order to survive in an unstable environment.

Part II
EMPIRICAL AND SPECIFIC

5 The development of small towns in Zimbabwe's communal areas: background

5.1 Introduction to the empirical study

This second part of the study focuses on the economic structure of the small towns that have grown up in Zimbabwe's communal areas since independence. Although at independence Zimbabwe was relatively highly urbanized and industrialized compared to other African countries, the level of urban and industrial development in the communal areas was very low. This was a result first, of the skewed development of agriculture in Zimbabwe during the colonial period and, secondly, of the development in the largest towns of commercial and industrial sectors which were almost completely white-owned, highly monopolistic, and to a large extent based on migrant labour from the communal areas.

One of the goals of the post-independence government in Zimbabwe has been to change the skewed structure it inherited. In order to improve living conditions, the communal areas should be provided with urban services and industries. Policies to develop rural centres have therefore been high on the agenda, although not consistently so. As we shall see, there has also been considerable growth in many of the centres in the communal areas, although in general growth has hardly lived up to the expectations of policy-makers.

In order to be able to evaluate the future potential of small towns in the following chapters, we shall look in more detail at the development since independence of economic activities in two large district service centres, Gutu and Gokwe. These two centres are among the largest and most successful district service centres. Larger centres have been chosen for the study because in order to investigate sectoral links and obstacles in enterprise development, we have to be sure that there is a differentiated commercial sector and at least some production activities in the centres already. The danger, of course, is that we may overlook some of the problems specific to the smaller centres. Other criteria for choosing the two centres were that they should have different types of agricultural hinterland and thus represent different patterns of agricultural development.

Gutu and Gokwe are presented in chapter 6, which also examines the structure of the retail and wholesale trade in the two centres with specific reference to farm input supplies. Chapter 6 also examines activities in some of the smaller rural business centres in their hinterland.

In chapters 7 to 9, three sectors which are important in most small towns, namely agro-processing and marketing, the building sector and the clothing sector, are investigated. These three sectors are not only structured very differently but also represent different ways in which small towns are linked to the national economy. While agro-processing is highly centralized and monopolistic, the building sector is relatively decentralized. The clothing sector represents a more mixed position, with both an important large-scale industry and a large number of very small enterprises. Within each of the three sectors, both trade and production will be examined, focusing especially on their interaction and the way they create possibilities of or obstacles to the development of production in small towns.

Finally, in chapters 10 and 11, we examine the changing structure of small-town development since 1980. In chapter 10, we focus on the external national forces of development, and in chapter 11 on the internal, local forces.

However, as background for the more detailed investigation of small-town development, this first chapter of part two presents a short account of Zimbabwean development and development policies before and especially after independence. The chapter focuses successively on agriculture and the rural areas, on the manufacturing industry and the urban system, and on the small rural towns.

5.2   The structure of agriculture and rural development

Zimbabwe is a country with wide variations in rainfall and therefore also in the quality of agricultural land. During the colonial period, white farmers gradually took over most of the good-quality land, where they established a small number of large commercial farms (at present about 4,500) covering 40 per cent of the land. These are still mostly white-owned, although some have been taken over by black politicians and businessmen since independence.

As the white farmers took over the good agricultural land, the African population was pushed out to what are now called the communal areas, where most of the African rural population was concentrated on a large number (about 800,000) of very small farms with an average size of four to five acres, but in some areas less. The communal areas cover 42 per cent of the agricultural land; of this, 75 per cent is located in areas with low rainfall. In the communal areas, land is government-owned and allocated to individual users; private ownership of land is not possible. The colonial government designated areas where African farmers could buy small-scale commercial farms. Here, 8–9000 farmers, mostly African, own farms of 20–100 acres, covering in total only 4 per cent of the land.

Since independence, a number of 'resettlement areas' have been designated, mostly on former white commercial farms and therefore on relatively good farm land. The original plan was to resettle 162,000 households before 1990. However, by this date only about 52,000 households had been resettled (Cousins, 1993). These four different types of agricultural land still play an important role in rural administration and development policies in Zimbabwe.

Until 1990, the Lancaster House agreement, which required the government to buy agricultural land at market prices and in hard currency, hindered the realization of large-scale land reform (see, e.g., Cousins, 1993). Since 1990, there has been a hectic debate on the nature of future land reform, and in 1992, a land reform bill was carried through parliament. However, more active steps towards land reform have still not been taken.

During the colonial period, the development of towns, infrastructure and services primarily took place in the large-scale commercial farming areas which produced most of the marketed surplus of agricultural products. Access to most communal areas remained very poor and most agricultural products produced there went for subsistence.

However, during the last years of the colonial period and especially since independence, a successful effort has been made to increase cash-crop production in the communal areas. Road access, agricultural services and marketing facilities have been improved, and the focus of agricultural research and development policies has shifted from only serving the large-scale commercial farms to the needs of the communal and small-scale commercial farmers. Especially in years with good rainfall, this has led to considerable increases in both yields (although they are still low) and marketed output. Thus by the end of the 1980s, the communal areas produced more than half the maize and cotton marketed in Zimbabwe. This has led to a considerable increase in rural cash incomes.

However, cash-crop production in the communal areas is very unevenly distributed. Although the communal areas as a whole have a considerable maize surplus, just 18 out of 170 communal areas account for most of this surplus (Amin, 1989). While only 10 per cent of communal farmers control about half of the marketed surplus, 40 per cent have a deficit, even in an average year (Jackson and Collier, 1988). Thus although agricultural cash incomes have increased, they are still very limited for most rural households (see also Cousins, Weiner and Amin, 1992; Jayne and Chisvo, 1991).

Income from cash-crop production is also very unevenly distributed over time because rainfall in many communal areas is very erratic: since 1980,

1984, 1987, 1992 and 1995 have been especially dry. Most rural households therefore depend on wage incomes, incomes from non-agricultural activities, or remittances from family members working in urban areas.

Several investigations (Bonnevie, 1987; Göttlisher, 1986; World Bank, 1982) indicate that about half the income in the communal areas in the early 1980s came from remittances. This is not a new phenomenon. Arrighi (1973a) found that the percentage of all male adult Africans engaged in wage labour in the 1950s had already increased to 50–60 per cent.

Immediately after independence, when constraints on the migration of Africans to large cities were liberalized and many new jobs for Africans were created, labour migration may well have increased. However, during the 1980s, remittances seem to have become relatively less important. Jackson and Collier (1988) thus found that only 19 per cent of total rural household incomes were due to remittances, and that 37 per cent of all households received such remittances. The reasons for this reduction in the role of remittances in the rural economy are partly that the new freedom to migrate after independence not only opened new possibilities for labour migrants but also made it possible for them to bring their families with them to the town, and partly that both agricultural and rural non-agricultural activities during the 1980s became relatively more important. At the same time, during the late 1980s and early 1990s the stagnating urban economy made it increasingly difficult for rural youth to find urban jobs (Cousins, Weiner and Amin, 1992). However, in spite of their reduced significance, remittances still play a very important role.

The proportion of non-agricultural activity in the rural areas before independence appears to have been lower than in many other African countries. Helmsing (1987) quotes a World Bank (1982) estimate that only 3–4 per cent of rural households are engaged in non-agricultural activities. This estimate is probably too low (see, e.g., Scott, 1995), but a low level of non-agricultural activities in Zimbabwe's communal areas at independence can be explained by the well-developed (by African standards), but also very centralized manufacturing industry and service sector. This, combined with the considerable labour migration to the large towns, meant that many of the commodities consumed in the rural areas were purchased in the large towns.

Since independence, however, rural non-agricultural activity has grown rapidly. In a survey from 1983–84 Helmsing (1987) found that 15 per cent of rural households were engaged in non-agricultural activities, while the Gemini Study (McPherson, 1991) found that more than a third of all rural households carried out at least one non-agricultural activity in 1991. This corresponds to a growth of at least 10 per cent per year between the two surveys. Finally, the Gemini II Study of 1993 found that the number of non-agricultural enterprises had grown by 12 per cent between 1991–93 (Daniels, 1994).

A more detailed comparison between Helmsing's data and the results of the Gemini studies shows that in 1986 small-scale manufacturers made up more than 80 per cent of rural non-agricultural activities, though this figure fell to about 67 per cent in 1993. At the same time, commerce, which is second in importance, increased from only 8 per cent of all non-agricultural activities in 1986 to 25 per cent in 1993. Construction was reduced from 7.6 per cent in 1986 to 3.8 per cent in 1993, while services increased from only 2.1 per cent to 3.3 per cent (for a more detailed analysis of these data, see Pedersen 1994a).

The rapid increase in commerce and decrease in manufacturing is the combined result of increased commercialization of the rural areas and increased competition from industrial goods. The drop in the construction sector is probably caused by industrialization of that sector, resulting in a shift of building material production and trade from the building sector to manufacturing and commerce.

The great majority of these rural non-agricultural activities consists of small farm- or homestead-based enterprises and only 20 per cent are either mobile or located in rural centres according to the Gemini survey. Even in the small towns themselves more than half the enterprises are home-based (see Table 2). However, most of the larger rural non-agricultural activities are likely to be located in the small towns and rural centres.

Table 2
Distribution of rural non-agricultural activities by location,
Zimbabwe 1991

Location	Rural areas			Small towns and growth points		
	%			%		
Homestead	79.7			56.7		
Traditional market	2.3	}		9.2	}	
Commercial district	5.5	}	20.3	25.2	}	43.3
Roadside	1.6	}		2.2	}	
Mobile	10.9	}		6.7	}	
Total	**100.0**			**100.0**		
Total no. of enterprises	488,224			86,828		
Estimated population	6,590,000			893,000		

Source: The Gemini Study (McPherson, 1991)

5.3   The structure and development of manufacturing industry[1]

At independence, Zimbabwe inherited from Rhodesia one of the most industrialized economies in Africa south of Sahara, in which about 25 per cent of GDP came from manufacturing industry. However, Zimbabwe also inherited a highly centralized industry dominated by monopolies or near-monopolies with very hierarchical organizational structures, owned and managed to a very large extent by white or foreign capital, an industry in deep crisis after years of international economic sanctions and civil war.

The foundations for the development of a manufacturing industry in Zimbabwe, then Southern Rhodesia, were laid during the second world war, but the manufacturing sector only started to grow rapidly during the first post-war decade. Southern Rhodesia experienced a boom involving mainly British and South African white immigrants and foreign investors. The value of foreign investment in Southern Rhodesia almost quadrupled from 1947–51 (Arrighi, 1973b), and manufacturing employment doubled from 35,000 in 1946 to 70,000 in 1953 (Riddell, 1988). The predominantly foreign origin of manufacturing investments generated a highly centralized industrial structure which still prevails, dominated by large-scale mechanized factories owned by multinational corporations.

The establishment in 1953 of the Federation of Nyasaland, Northern and Southern Rhodesia and its common market gave a further impetus to growth in the manufacturing sector in Southern Rhodesia, and during the 1960s it became the leading sector in the economy, more important than agriculture. In 1965, the manufacturing industry employed 79,000 and contributed almost 20 per cent to GDP.

A precondition for this rapid urbanization was a literate labour force with higher qualifications than those needed on the farms and in the mines. The foundation for the qualitative upgrading of the labour force was established around 1940, when blacks increasingly began to divert resources to education. Enrolment in mission primary education quadrupled from 1936–47 (Arrighi, 1973a).

In order to secure a more stable work force, African workers (who had earlier only been permitted in the urban areas on a temporary basis) were from 1941 allowed permanent residence in urban townships if they were employed, and from 1960 they could obtain freehold titles and thus stay in town regardless of employment.

As an incentive to maintain a permanent work force, industrial wages were raised during the 1950s in real terms, while agricultural wages remained constant (Arrighi, 1973a). Wage increases together with a persistent labour shortage stimulated the mechanization of production as well as the large-scale immigration of African labourers from the other federal territories, especially Nyasaland. The proportion of African males in wage employment

64

rose to 55–60 per cent in 1951, and in 1956, the foreign share of the total labour force of 602,000 was 43 per cent. Most of the foreign workers were employed in agriculture, while blacks from Southern Rhodesia dominated in unskilled non-farm employment (Bonnevie, 1987).

Skilled workers, however, were recruited predominantly among the white population and from South Africa and Britain. They established a 'skill aristocracy' which was maintained to a large extent by regulating the entry to apprenticeships and maintaining very high standards of training (Arrighi, 1973b; King, 1989). Their interest was in preventing Africans from being educated and trained for skilled jobs and from residing permanently in the urban areas. Monopolization of skills in the white labour force resulted in the creation of a very rigid work structure with strong hierarchical controls in management and standardized work processes on the factory floor (Blunt, 1983).

When the Federation broke down in 1963 and the Smith government declared Southern Rhodesia independent from Britain in 1965 (the Unilateral Declaration of Independence or UDI), the scene was set for a more open economy; however, this only lasted until 1966, when new protection was involuntarily reinstalled in the form of sanctions imposed by the international community.

As a result of sanctions, the market was now reduced to Southern Rhodesia itself. The costs of imported inputs increased, and the nationalist government was forced to initiate an import substitution policy. A comprehensive system of foreign exchange controls favouring domestic manufacturers was introduced and capital outflow from non-South African companies was frozen. The government actively encouraged and influenced investments in priority sectors such as steel and metal products, chemicals and textiles (Wield, 1981). The freezing of foreign investments left most market growth to small Rhodesian industrialists, who gradually grew into larger conglomerates producing a wide range of products needed in the sanction-hit economy.

Consequently, manufacturing rose from 20 per cent of GDP in 1965 to 25 per cent in 1974. Manufacturing value added more than doubled and employment grew to 152,000 in 1975. The number of different products produced in Rhodesia increased from 1,059 to 3,837 between 1966–70. Of these about 2500 were produced by monopolies or near-monopolies.

The indigenization and domestic orientation of the economy engendered closer links between the different sectors. In 1965, manufacturing only absorbed 13 per cent of the total marketed agricultural output, but by 1981/82 this increased to 44 per cent, corresponding to a tripling of the manufacturing input derived from agriculture from 10 to 29 per cent (Riddell, 1988).

A large share of the growing manufacturing output was directed towards the white minority, but the blacks' share of the market was also growing and became increasingly crucial. In 1978, demand from blacks accounted for 51 per cent of furniture, 73 per cent of tea and 68 per cent of clothing and footwear (Wield, 1981). The booming growth in manufacturing led to the increased employment of African workers, but few acquired skills. In the factories, 100,000 whites still constituted more than 80 per cent of the skilled manpower in 1969 (Stoneman, 1978). In 1975, blacks only occupied 8 per cent of the skilled or technical jobs (review article in *Financial Gazette*, 18/8/1989).

From 1974, the rapid growth in manufacturing was halted by a combination of intensive guerilla war in the rural areas and the adverse effect of the international recession and oil crisis. The value of oil imports tripled to 22 per cent of total imports (Riddell, 1988) and excess on the world market of steel, sugar etc. had a severe impact on Rhodesian manufacturing industry (Wield, 1981). Due to the civil war, a large proportion of those skilled whites who had been operating the industry left the country or were about to do so, and few blacks had been trained to take over. Thus on the eve of independence the manufacturing sector was in a state of crisis. White and foreign dominance in manufacturing was almost absolute. Out of 1300 manufacturing units, scarcely a dozen black manufacturers were registered (Riddell, 1988).

In spite of the sanctions, foreign companies still owned 48 per cent of the total assets in the manufacturing sector in 1982 and accounted for 80 per cent of the total private capital of private manufacturing companies (Riddell, 1988). As the only country open to Rhodesia during the UDI period, South African enterprises had increased their control over the Rhodesian economy and owned about half of the foreign controlled assets (Stoneman, 1981).

After independence, one of the main aims of the new majority government was state control over the foreign and white-dominated productive sectors, particularly as South Africa had now become an enemy. Driven by a Marxist and statist ideology – and in the absence of a qualified class of black industrialists – this was done by buying up existing industries rather than creating new ones. In 1982, the state and the inherited parastatals accounted for 14 per cent of manufacturing industry, but later both the state and the party directly or indirectly acquired majority or part-ownership in an increasing number of key manufacturing corporations (Riddell, 1988). This happened mostly through the Industrial Development Corporation (IDC), which had already been set up in 1963 to take over minority shares in private ventures. Similarly, the existing manufacturing parastatals (e.g. the Cold Storage Commission, Dairy Marketing Board and Cotton Marketing Board) were expanded.

After the slump years of the late 1970s, the manufacturing sector resumed its growth and in 1985 accounted for 29 per cent of GDP. This impressive post-independence growth was based on boundless demand after the long period of constraint during the UDI period. At the beginning of the 1980s, employment also grew rapidly from a low of 138,000 in 1978 to 176,000 in

1982. Then in 1983–84, a slump due at least partly to two years of drought caused manufacturing employment to drop to 164,000 in 1984. Thanks to increases in productivity employment only recovered slowly after the slump and did not reach the 1982 level until 1987–88. However, during the last years of the 1980s, employment again grew fairly rapidly (at about 3 per cent a year from 1985 to 1990) to 197,000 in 1990 (see Figure 1).

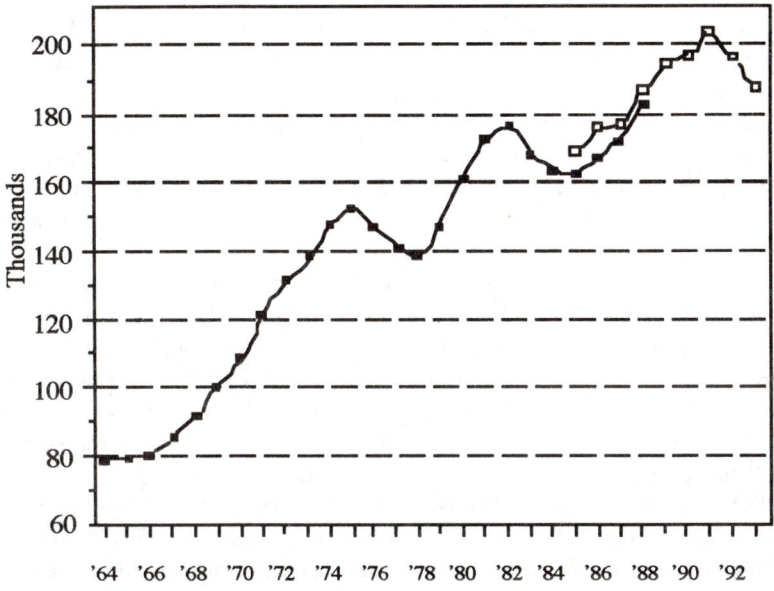

Figure 1   Manufacturing employment, Zimbabwe 1964–93
Sources based on: Census of production 1988/89, Statistical Yearbook 1989
        and *Quarterly Digest of Statistics*, October, 1994, Central
        Statistical Office, Harare

After the significant white exodus (it was estimated that between one-third and one-half of the white population left), it was feared that lack of adequate skills would cause a dramatic drop in manufacturing efficiency and production. This has not been the case. Blacks have succeeded remarkably in overtaking many office tasks (Riddell, 1988). Thus in 1989, blacks held 78 per cent of minor management and 65 per cent of middle management positions in industry. However, whites still remained in control of senior management, although blacks occupy 38 per cent of the executive chairs (*Financial Gazette*, 18/8/89). Similarly, employment in technical fields, where in 1981 whites occupied 44 per cent of all professional and technical posts, had already in 1985 plunged to 11 per cent. This relatively smooth and rapid succession from whites to blacks contributed to the preservation of the hierarchical organizational structure and enclave nature of the manufacturing sector and did not call for any substantial policy changes.

The manufacturing sector also remained monopolistic or oligopolistic during the 1980s. In fact, concentration accelerated. Approximately 50 per cent of the more than 6,000 items on the market in 1982 were produced by a single firm, and 80 per cent by up to three firms. From 1977–86/87, the number of registered manufacturing firms dropped from 1355 to 1094 at the same time as employment rose from 141,000 to 168,000, and enterprises with more then 750 employees increased their share from 26 per cent to 46 per cent of the total employment in manufacturing.

Small enterprises with less than 50 employees decreased in number by 18 per cent. The white exodus is likely to have caused this diminution of the already tiny small-scale to medium-scale enterprise group. Although the new government established a Small Enterprise Development Corporation in 1983–84 (SEDCO, based on the already existing Small Industry Advisory Board dating from 1972), government support for the development of new black entrepreneurs was at best half-hearted. SEDCO was given only limited funds and has not been very efficient in reaching its potential clientele. During the 1980s, 80 per cent of the funds went into retail businesses rather than production, and mostly to towns larger than district service centres. In addition, loan conditions were not very attractive compared to bank loans (for a more detailed discussion of SEDCO, see Sverrisson, 1990; 1993).

The most striking feature of the post-independence period has been the continuity in policies toward the manufacturing sector since the UDI period (Riddell, 1988) in spite of the radical change in formal policies from capitalist to socialist and from pro-white to pro-African. Prices and foreign-exchange allocations have remained under firm government control, and most of the pre-independence institutions and organizations have continued almost unchanged except for some shift in orientation. The existing industries owned by white Zimbabweans have still been favoured with forex allocations and protection.

Black businessmen who wanted to invest in small industries were in general not favoured. On the contrary, zoning, building and local planning regulations and by-laws often made it difficult and unreasonably expensive for small entrepreneurs to establish themselves. Instead, forex allocations and import permits were given to emerging African businessmen who established import-export businesses. The hope was that they would eventually earn enough to invest in larger production enterprises; a hope that seems to have been fulfilled in only a few cases. Instead, they have become expensive middlemen who have thrived on their scarce forex allocations rather than on their services to industry.

On the urban industrial labour market, minimum wages, job security and worker-protection legislation were introduced during the first half of the 1980s

(Fallon and Lucas, 1991; Østergaard, 1994). It became very difficult for employers to dismiss permanent employees; piece-rate systems were made illegal; provisions were made for maternity leave; a 45-hour work week and high overtime pay were introduced; and protective clothes were made compulsory. The introduction of minimum wages just after independence increased the urban industrial wage level rapidly during the early 1980s. However, state regulation of the labour market continued much as under UDI. Attempts to strike were impeded, and during most of the 1980s wages increased at a lower rate than inflation. In addition, minimum wages were only valid in the urban industries. In rural areas, minimum wages continued at a much lower level than in urban areas.

At the same time, the introduction of job-security regulations created a division between the permanently employed and temporary workers. This division has been further strengthened by the education and training policies which followed independence. Before independence, black youth had very much less access to education than white youth, and one of the most important goals of the new government was to change this. Before independence the majority of Africans received some primary education, but few continued into secondary school. The goal of the new government was to introduce universal secondary education. Although it has not quite succeeded, especially in the rural areas, it has come a long way, and the general level of education increased rapidly during the 1980s. Vocational training opportunities and job openings in the public and large private sector did not, however, grow nearly as rapidly as the number of school leavers (dropouts and graduates). Apprenticeship training in industry and trade before independence was largely reserved for white youth. In order to change this, the government insisted on controlling the intake of new apprentices after independence. However, this only led the intake of formal apprentices in private industry to drop to a clearly unsatisfactory level (for a more detailed account of vocational training policies in Zimbabwe, see King, 1989). Instead, the government has built a number of vocational schools in the larger towns, but compared to the rapid expansion of the secondary schools, the capacity of the vocations schools is still very limited, and they have only been able to cater to a small proportion of those seeking admittance. As a result, entrance requirements have risen steadily. Today, young people without a very good secondary school exam have few chances to be admitted to any vocational training or employment in the formal sector.

An increasing part of the rapidly growing number of school leavers has therefore found employment in the small enterprise sector, although they aspire to permanent formal-sector employment (understandable enough, considering the often very large income differences). Informal apprenticeship schemes operate in the small-enterprise sector. They are undoubtedly of a much lower training quality than the formal apprenticeship schemes, but are possibly better suited to the small-enterprise sector. Little is known about their number and quality, however, and until recently the government has shown very little positive interest in them.

Although industrial policies have fostered a more competitive industry and increasing manufacturing exports, industry has mostly been inward-looking and export earnings have not been large enough to cover the sector's increasing need for foreign currency. Similarly, although the industry has become increasingly efficient on its own terms, it employs a constantly falling share of the growing population and has increasingly been unable to serve low-income groups satisfactorily. As a result, a sector of small-scale activities has rapidly developed outside the so-called formal sector in production, trade and services and in both urban and rural areas. It is not recognized by the formal economy, but it plays an increasing role in the economy. A country-wide survey from 1991 (Daniels, 1994) estimated the number of small (formal and informal) enterprises with less than 50 employees at 868,000 with a total employment of 1,351,000. About 30 per cent of these enterprises were located in the larger urban areas, the rest in rural areas and small towns. In total, 72 per cent were manufacturing activities, about half in clothing and textiles.

Against this background, in 1990 Zimbabwe introduced a structural-adjustment programme similar to those advocated by the IMF in many other developing countries (see, e.g., Gibbon, 1995a and b; van Dijk, 1995). Over a number of years, these new policies have opened up the economy to foreign trade, started a process of privatizing state-controlled industries, and are increasingly focusing on the development of small enterprises and preferential support for indigenous businessmen. But the programme has also led to increased prices, especially for food and imported goods, and to increased competition, which has especially hit the smaller enterprises and led to a massive retrenchment of workers. These negative effects of the reforms have coincided with and been magnified by the serious drought in 1992, which decimated incomes in the rural areas and in agriculturally related sectors. According to sources at the time about 45–50,000 workers may have lost their jobs during the drought (Gibbon, 1995a; Kanji, 1995), especially in the clothing and food-processing industries, where about one-third of employees seem to have lost their jobs. However, according to the statistics, manufacturing employment only dropped from 205,400 in 1991 to 187,700 in 1993, and in March 1994 it increased again to 199,300, which is bad enough in a country with a rapidly growing workforce.

A large and throughout the 1980s increasing proportion of industrial production depended on agriculture, both agro-processing industries dependent on agricultural inputs, and the production of consumer goods and farm inputs for the rural population. Thus the agro-processing and textile sectors now make up about half of all manufacturing industry (see Table 3). The increasing instability of agricultural production caused by the expansion

Table 3
Manufacturing employment by sector, Zimbabwe, 1980–88

Sector	1980	%	1983	%	1986	%	1988	%
Agroprocessing	36,375	22.6	40,393	24.0	40,767	24.3	40,059	21.9
food	23,971	14.9	26,961	16.0	28,131	16.7	28,337	15.5
drink and tobacco	12,404	7.7	13,432	7.9	12,636	7.5	11,722	6.4
Textile and apparel	36,543	22.7	40,471	24.0	40,906	24.3	48,316	26.5
textiles	17,373	10.8	20,607	12.2	20,576	12.2	24,322	13.3
apparel and foot ware	19,170	11.9	19,864	11.8	20,330	12.1	23,994	13.1
Wood and furniture	13,772	8.6	10,719	6.4	9,413	5.6	10,036	5.5
Paper and printing	7,612	4.7	9,191	5.5	8,706	5.2	8,935	4.9
Chemicals	11,580	7.2	13,774	8.2	14,769	8.8	17,113	9.4
Clay, cement and glass	7,110	4.4	7,090	4.2	7,896	4.7	8,605	4.7
Metal industries	44,561	27.7	43,799	26.0	42,933	25.6	46,588	25.5
Other manufacturing	3,194	2.0	2,881	1.7	2,609	1.6	2,997	1.6
Total manufacturing	**160,748**	**100.0**	**168,318**	**100.0**	**168,005**	**100.0**	**182,649**	**100.0**

Source: Census of Production 1986/87, Central Statistical Office, Harare

of commercial agriculture into the dryer parts of the country therefore appears to have had an increasing impact on manufacturing production.

5.4   Processes of urban development and rural urbanization

Industrial development in Zimbabwe has been centralized not only organizationally, but also geographically. Since the 1960s, Harare and Bulawayo accounted rather constantly for about 75 per cent of industrial production. Some of the medium-sized towns along the railroad, like Mutara (tea, food products, wood and pulp), Gweru (textiles) and Kwekwe (steel), also have important industries. In total, Harare, Bulawayo and five medium-sized towns accounted for 92 per cent of industrial production in 1977, and this pattern has remained constant since.

During the colonial period, public services and infrastructural investments were also concentrated in the same towns and in other smaller towns in the commercial farm areas, and although some decentralization of public services and infrastructure investments has taken place since independence, total formal non-agricultural employment is still highly concentrated. Before independence, 69 per cent (in 1977) of all formal non-agricultural employment was found in the seven largest towns. Since then, the employment level has increased from 664,000 in 1977 to 940,000 in 1991,[2] but two-thirds are still located in the same seven towns (see Figure 2 and Table 4).

In spite of this strong concentration of both manufacturing industry and urban services during the colonial period, the process of the urbanization of the African population was slowed down by very strict migration controls. Until 1941, African workers were not allowed to settle permanently in the urban townships. From 1941, this became possible for individuals with jobs, but only since 1960 have Africans been able to stay in town regardless of employment. However, in spite of this relative liberalization and the rapid industrial growth of the 1960s, the share of Africans in the urban areas remained rather constant at around 14 per cent during the decade. The rate of urbanization only began to climb at the end of the 1960s, and in the period 1969–77, urban areas grew by 4.5 per cent a year or 1 per cent more than the general rate of population growth. In the later part of the 1970s, this increase in the rate of urbanization was increasingly caused by the civil war in the rural areas.

In the communal areas, little urban development took place. Very few public services and almost no infrastructural investments were located there before the 1970s, and few private non-farm activities developed.[3] Due to extensive labour migration, the industrial goods consumed by the rural population were to a large extent bought in the large towns, and until the 1950s licenses for rural shops were given primarily to whites. However, from the early 1950s,

Table 4

Non-agricultural formal employment by sector, Zimbabwe 1977–93 (in thousands + percentile)

	1977 '000	1977 %	1980 '000	1980 %	1983 '000	1983 %	1986 '000	1986 %	1989 '000	1989 %	1990 '000	1990 %	1993 '000	1993 %
Mining	61,6	9.3	66,2	9.7	60,4	7.8	54,9	6.8	55,7	6.3	51,4	5.7	47.7	5.2
Manufacturing	145,1	21.9	159,4	23.3	173,4	22.5	176,9	22.0	195,3	22.1	197,1	21.9	187.7	20.5
Electricity, water etc.	6,6	1.0	6,7	1.0	6,9	0.9	8,2	1.0	8,8	1.0	8,7	1.0	7.9	0.9
Construction	46,5	7.0	42,2	6.2	49,4	6.4	47,4	5.9	66,6	7.6	75,8	8.4	90.5	9.9
Finance	12,2	1.8	12,5	1.8	15,8	2.1	15,4	1.9	17,1	1.9	17,6	2.0	20.2	2.2
Distribution, hotels etc.	72,5	10.9	70,8	10.3	80,6	10.5	81,2	10.1	91,9	10.4	96,0	10.7	95.9	10.5
Transport + communication	45,5	6.9	45,6	6.7	49,4	6.4	50,7	6.3	51,8	5.9	53,3	5.9	49.8	5.4
Public administration	60,6	9.1	71,1	10.4	82,5	10.7	90,8	11.3	93,5	10.6	93,4	10.4	89.0	9.7
Education	36,6	5.5	41,9	6.1	78,0	10.1	95,7	11.9	104,2	11.8	108,1	12.0	111.3	12.1
Health	14,5	2.2	15,2	2.2	19,0	2.5	21,8	2.7	23,6	2.7	25,0	2.8	25.7	2.8
Private/domestic services	120,0	18.1	108,0	15.8	99,8	13.0	100,1	12.4	102,4	11.6	102,1	11.3	102.1	11.1
Other services	42,3	6.4	43,8	6.4	54,7	7.1	62,5	7.8	71,2	8.1	73,7	8.2	88.4	9.6
Total	**6640**	**100.0**	**682,9**	**100.0**	**769,9**	**100.0**	**805,6**	**100.0**	**882,1**	**100.0**	**900,2**	**100.0**	**916.2**	**100.0**
Of these in the 7 largest towns	68.6		68.9		64.6		64.6		65.8		65.6		67.4	

Sources: Statistical Yearbook 1989 and Quarterly Digest of Statistics, Central Statistical Office, Harare

73

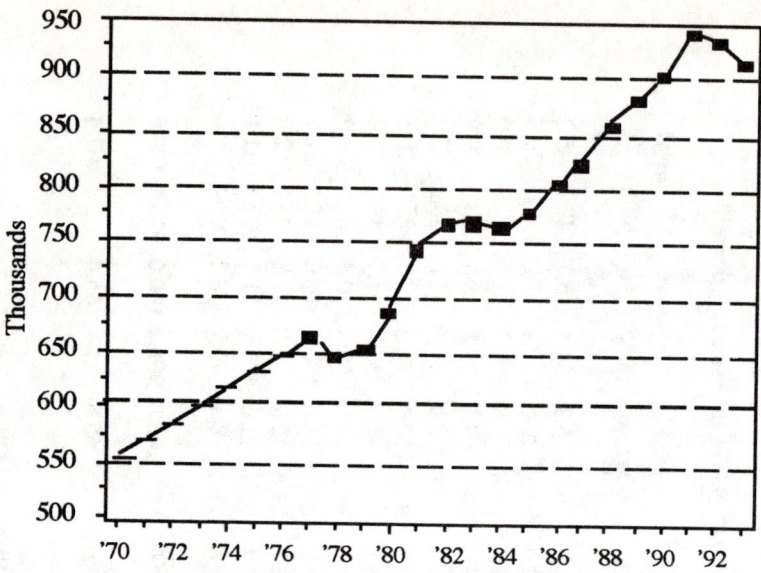

Figure 2   Total non-agricultural formal employment, Zimbabwe 1970–93

Sources: *Statistical Yearbook 1989*; *Quarterly Digest of Statistics*, October 1994, Central Statistical Office, Harare

Africans established themselves in larger numbers as shopkeepers, building contractors and bus operators in the rural areas, gradually taking over from the white traders until by 1977, 95 per cent of all licenses in the communal areas were held by Africans (Gasper, 1988).

Although African businessmen were not allowed to run businesses from urban premises, some (e.g. building contractors and bus operators) were able to extend their more mobile activities to the urban areas. Already in the 1950s, it appears to have been a general administrative practice to limit new licenses to the already existing centres (Gasper, 1988; Bessant and Muringai, 1993). This led to the development of small rival business centres, many of which continued to grow throughout the 1960s and 1970s, and formed the foundations of the small towns on which this study focuses. However, these new emerging centres were generally located at a distance from both the missions and the white administrative centres, thus developing into purely business centres.

In the late 1960s and especially during the 1970s, these rural centres became the object of a planning exercise initiated by the white government, which was increasingly worried by the growth in the migration of Africans to the urban areas. By developing new urban centres within the communal areas, it was hoped that migration to the larger white towns could be reduced.

In 1972, TILCOR (the Tribal Land Development Corporation, established in 1968) initiated a strategy of 'growth points' based on large agricultural estates in areas remote from existing centres. The growth points should be commercially viable and cover the costs of their own infrastructure. They were intended to grow into small towns serving the workers of the core estate, plus outgrowers and the population in a wider area (Gasper, 1988). Three such growth points were started during the 1970s (Sanyati, Tshotshoto and Maphisa).

Parallel to TILCOR's experiments, broader settlement planning for the communal areas was developed during the later part of the 1970s, resting partly on research based on central-place theory carried out at the University of Rhodesia (Heath, 1978). In 1978, this resulted in an 'Integrated Plan for Rural Development' which proposed the designation of 300 rural service centres and 20–25 new small towns to serve the communal areas. Of these, ten were proposed for immediate growth-point development. Public investment funds were to be allocated to the designated centres, and new finance organizations were formed to encourage job creation in the new centres through support to small industries and emerging businessmen.

After independence, one of the new government's central policies was to develop the communal areas and change the skewed pattern of urbanization which had developed during the white regime. As an important element in this rural development policy, the idea of a settlement hierarchy which had emerged before independence was taken over and even expanded. For each of the 55 communal districts, a district service centre was identified as the seat of the new district administration and local government, and for the government's rural development activities (see Figure 3, chapter 6). In addition, the 300 rural service centres proposed by TILCOR were increased to about 450.

On the basis of the existence of either a mineral resource or a larger agricultural government estate the district service centres, together with about ten growth points (some of which are also district service centres), were considered potentially new small towns.[4] The purposes of the new centres were:

– to support agricultural development in the surrounding district;

– to be the seat of the district administration and local government;

– to create new non-agricultural employment in the rural areas which could retain population in the rural areas and reduce migration to the large urban areas.

Policies to develop the district service centres have especially focused on:

75

- infrastructure investments, which have linked most of the district service centres to the national hard-surface road and electricity networks. Investments have also been made in local water and sewage systems, market places and bus terminals;

- investments in public services, especially primary and secondary education and health services;

- housing schemes, especially for the increasing number of public and parastatal employees who have moved to the district centres, but also to some extent to lower income households (Wekwete, 1987; Gasper, 1988).

Several industrial development policies could be used in support of the small town, for example:

- foreign-currency allocations and tax deductions for enterprises which establish themselves in the new centre;

- support to small-enterprise development through the Small Enterprise Development Corporation (SEDCO);

- support to housing and industrial development through the Urban Development Corporation (UDCORP).

Most of these measures, however, have not been geared specifically towards the small towns, and their impact on small-town development has probably been limited. In addition, much of the support has been allocated to the retail trade rather than production.

Last but not least, many of the agricultural services which were primarily geared towards the large commercial farmers before independence, were extended to the district service centres, e.g. the Grain and Cotton Marketing Board's depots, agricultural and veterinary extension services, and branches of the Agricultural Finance Corporation. This, together with agricultural pricing policies, led to increased cash incomes and commercialization in the rural areas, and therefore to a growing market for these activities in the district service centres.

The rapid growth in the public sector has been important not only for the services it provides, but also for the non-farm jobs and money incomes it creates. Thus public employees make up an important market for local retail trade.

Though these different policies have probably been of varying effect, together they have led to remarkable growth in many of the district service centres since independence. Both public services and trade have increased rapidly in many centres (more than doubling between 1976–86; see Table 5), and the largest of the centres have grown from very small centres to towns of 10–20,000 inhabitants. However, the development of productive activities has been much slower, and therefore in terms of job creation, the centres have in general not lived up to original expectations. This has led some writers to draw a rather pessimistic picture of the future of small towns (i.e., Wekwete, 1990), in spite of the rapid growth which has actually taken place in many of them in both public and private services, especially commerce.

Table 5

Growth in the number of private licenses and public services in selected district and smaller service centres, 1976–86

	No. of different types of activities		No. of establishments							
			Total		General dealers		Other public + private services		Production and repair activities	
	1976	1986	1976	1986	1976	1986	1976	1986	1976	1986
Murewa	33	68	101	198	29	55	58	119	14	24
Gutu	30	54	79	148	23	31	40	90	16	27
Jereza	11	20	27	67	12	30	11	30	4	7
Mataga	8	21	20	42	6	13	6	20	8	9
Basera	12	17	28	40	10	11	8	18	10	11
Total	**94**	**180**	**255**	**495**	**80**	**140**	**123**	**277**	**52**	**78**
Growth (% p.a.)	6.7		6.9		5.8		8.4		4.1	

Note: Precise data on the growth of the district service centres are not available. The data presented above originates from a number of bachelor theses from the Dept. of Geography, University of Zimbabwe. For five small centres, they give data for the number of activities in 1976 and 1986. The data covers both the private and public sector, though the public sector appears to be included to a varying degree in the different studies. The data for the private sector are based on licenses rather than actual operating activities and are likely to be somewhat overestimated, though one might hope that the overestimation is the same for both years.

This pessimistic view of the future of the district service centres is reinforced by their unsatisfactory development in many of the smaller districts and in the poorest parts of the country. Here, many of them still have less than 2,000 inhabitants and a limited supply of services. In some cases, this is because the designated centres have been out-stripped by larger towns nearby. In other cases, government services and infrastructure have not been developed as planned, due to a lack of resources or excessive costs. Compared with other African countries, the number of designated district service centres also appears to be very high (Gasper, 1988). Many of the smaller communal areas are too small to support a district service centre of their own. Other communal areas are located close to former white towns, which have taken over most commercial services.

However, the slow development of production in the district service centres is also caused by the very centralistic industrial policies followed both before and after independence. Therefore, in spite of the positive action taken to support small towns, in general the policies have not been conducive to industrial development there, and the attitude towards small entrepreneurs has often been rather negative. The structural adjustment policies initiated around 1990 may change this. This is discussed in chapter 10.

Notes

1 This section is to a large extent based on chapter 5 in Rasmussen 1992.
2 Due to drought and structural-adjustment, employment dropped to 916,200 in 1993, but in March 1994 it increased again to 944,600 (*Quarterly Digest of Statistics*, October, 1994).
3 Bessant and Muringai (1993) describe African businesses going back to the late 1920s.
4 Although the district service centres were originally not thought of as growth points, the terminology soon became blurred even in government papers, and today the term 'growth point' often comprises both the original growth points and the district service centres.

6 Two districts and their service centres: retail and wholesale trade in Gutu and Gokwe

6.1 Introduction

The most important function of the district service centres is the distribution of consumer goods and farm inputs to the rural areas, a function they share with a network of small rural business centres and rural stores spread throughout the rural districts. The purpose of this chapter is to investigate the structure of this distribution system in Gutu and Gokwe districts. Section 6.2 presents the two district service centres and their districts. Sections 6.3 and 6.4 analyse the structure and development of retail and wholesale trade in the two district service centres. Sections 6.5 and 6.6 examine two subsectors of special importance for rural development in greater detail, namely the distribution of farm implements, especially scotch carts, and farm inputs, especially fertilizer. Section 6.7 focuses on the development and structure of some of the small rural service centres in Gutu district, which – partly in competition with the district service centres – play an important role in the rural distribution system. Finally, Section 6.8 discusses the theoretical consequences of the findings for understanding competition and markets in the distribution systems of developing rural regions.

6.2 The two district service centres and their districts

Gutu and Gokwe are among the largest district service centres in rural Zimbabwe. Supported by public investments and increased cash-crop production in their rural hinterlands, they have grown into small towns since independence. They owe their size in part to the large districts of which they are centres and to their location at a considerable distance from larger towns. Gutu centre is located 225 km south of Harare and 90 km north of the nearest provincial town, Masvingo, which has about 50,000 inhabitants. Gokwe centre is located 300 km west of Harare and about 140 km northwest of the nearest provincial towns, Kwekwe (75,000 inhabitants) and Kadoma (67,000 inhabitants) (see Figure 3).

Gutu district is located in a relatively dry area. Most of it consists of communal land, but the western part is covered by large-scale commercial farms and resettlement areas; there are also some small-scale commercial farms in the district. Maize is the dominant crop, although large parts of the district are unsuitable for it. Sunflower seems to be developing as an alternative.

The district has a total population of 195,000 (1992), of which more than 80 per cent live in the communal areas. The communal areas have long been settled and are very densely populated, with an average farm size of only three to five acres of arable but rather dry land. Consequently, most agricultural production is for subsistence. Cash-crop production is limited, and most households depend on non-agricultural activities and remittances from mostly male family members working in the urban areas.

There has also been considerable out-migration and the population grew by only about 10 per cent between the two censuses of 1982 (177,000 inhabitants) and 1992. The large male labour migration is documented by a sex ratio for the working age group (20–55 years) in 1982 of only 60.8 men per 100 women; this low sex ratio has not changed much during the 1980s. From 1982 to 1992, the sex ratio for the whole population in the district only increased from 85.2 to 85.8.

Gokwe centre is located in an area with better rainfall and lower population pressure. It consists primarily of communal land, though there are some areas with small-scale commercial farms. In the areas around Gokwe centre, maize is the dominant crop, while the rest of the district is an important cotton-growing area. A large proportion of the cotton grown by communal farmers in Zimbabwe comes from Gokwe. The district has therefore much greater cash-crop production than Gutu district.

Until the 1950s, Gokwe district was very sparsely populated, because it was infected by tsetse flies and malaria. However, since the 1950s, and concurrently with the retreat of the tsetse fly (malaria is still a serious problem), there has been rapid immigration from other overpopulated rural areas; there are, for example, many immigrants from Gutu district. Gokwe continues to have a large net immigration, and in the period 1982–92, the population grew by 76 per cent from 229,000 to 403,000. The scale of immigration is also reflected in the sex ratio, which is much higher than in Gutu district and has been growing during the 1980s from 90.8 in 1982 to 93.1 in 1992.

Gutu centre

Gutu centre is located on the western rim of Gutu communal area and thus serves both the communal area and some commercial farming and resettlement

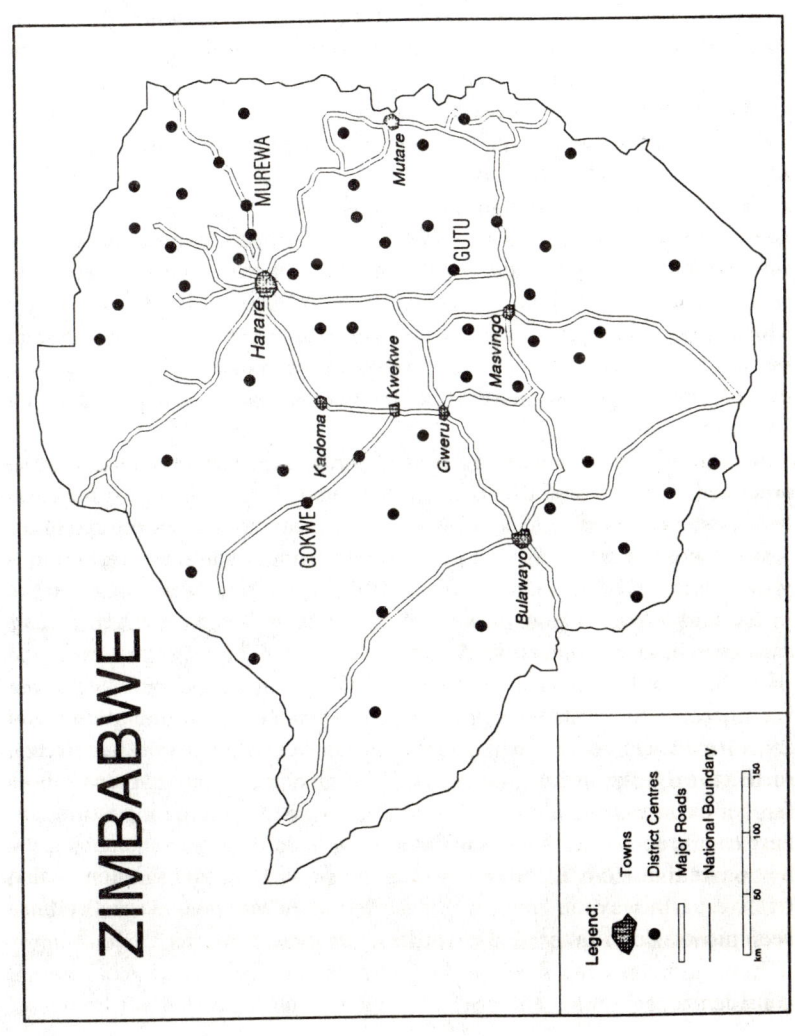

Figure 3   District service centres in Zimbabwe

81

areas. The old Mupandawana business centre, which makes up the core of the present Gutu district service centre was started in the 1950s as an African business centre, and some of the present businesses date back to that early period. The centre is located in the communal area 2–3 km east of the existing small white Gutu centre located at the road junction between what is today the administrative and industrial areas. Gutu Mission, which dates back to the early colonial period around the turn of the century, is located 5 km further to the east. It comprises a hospital and schools, among the latter being the only secondary school with A-levels in the district (see Figure 4). Early in the 1980s, Göttlicher (1986) estimated the population of Gutu/ Mupandawana centre to be 2,400, and the total population within a radius of 10–15 km around the centre to be about 14,000.

Since independence, the government has invested in infrastructure and in public and parastatal services. A new, more direct, hard-surface road was built to Harare and Masvingo, but the roads into communal areas have not been improved. Electricity, water and sewage infrastructure were built or improved in the centre, and schools and agricultural services provided both in the centre and beyond. As a result, the administrative areas and the Mupandawana business centre have been expanding especially. Housing areas have also been expanding, though generally not rapidly enough to satisfy the demand. Finally, a large industrial area has been established, but few industries have moved in.

In the war years before independence, many of the businesses in the white Gutu centre closed, and during the 1980s most of the commercial activities became concentrated in Mupandawana centre. However, since the end of the 1980s there has been renewed growth in the former white centre, which is well located near the new hard-surface road to Harare and Masvingo (finished in the mid-1980s). The expansion of activities in Gutu centre has led to a rapidly increasing population. According to the 1992 census, the town ward had 15,600 inhabitants in that year of which, however, only 6,200 are considered urban. This is considerably lower than the guesstimates of about 20,000 made before the census and may be due to a rather narrow delimitation of the town. Like many rural centres in Zimbabwe, Gutu is spread over a large area, stretching along ten kilometres of road from the mission to the east (with more than 2,000 inhabitants) past the business centre and the administrative and housing areas to the industrial area and the military camp furthest to the west. In between and around it are a number of small village settlements which have tended to grow in response to the insufficient supply of housing in the town itself, although the council has tried to avoid what it considers illegal settlements with raids and the burning of illegally built huts.

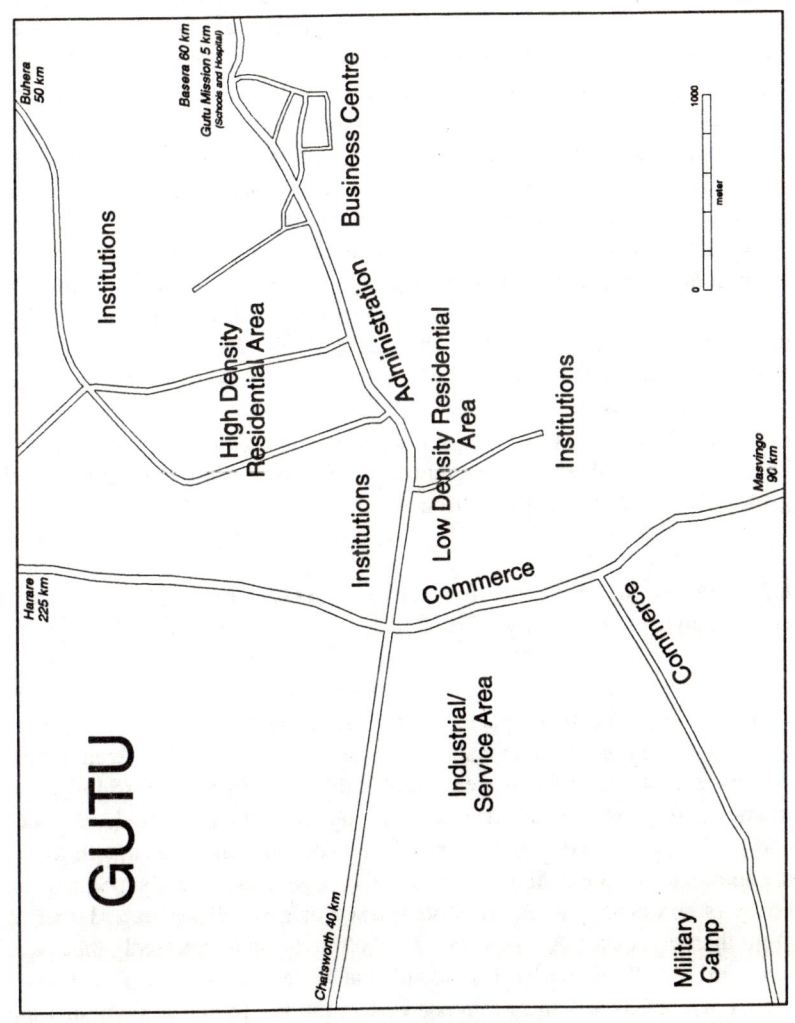

Figure 4   Gutu district service centre

83

Gokwe centre is both smaller and newer than Gutu/Mupandawana centre (see map in Figure 5). The first African businesses hardly go back further than 1970. As in Gutu, African businesses were not allowed to locate near the white administrative centre. A small business centre therefore developed 3–4 km southeast of the centre, but did not become very large. After independence, it was decided to develop a new business centre close to the administrative centre. Retail activities at the old centre have therefore stagnated, although other new activities have been developing around it (e.g. a military camp, the Grain Marketing Board's depot and a hotel). Close to the new business centre a large industrial area was developed with both large and small plots. Some housing areas were also developed, but far too few, and the lack of housing has been even more acute than in Gutu. A new hard-surface road linking Gokwe to Kwekwe and the urban system was built, and urban infrastructures were provided in the centre, although not rapidly enough to match the rapidly growing demand. From a very small centre at independence, Gokwe has grown to a small town. According to the 1992 census, Gokwe centre had 7,200 inhabitants in 1972. However, as with Gutu, this is likely to be a low figure because of the lack of housing and the dispersed structure of the town.

In terms of new activities, Gokwe has grown more rapidly than Gutu, and in time it may well grow larger than Gutu due to the high immigration and greater cash incomes in the district.

6.3 The structure of business activities in Gutu and Gokwe service centres

The two towns, Gutu and Gokwe, are primarily service centres, their most important functions being the retail and wholesale trade in consumer goods and agricultural inputs and small service and repair shops of different kinds. To give a more detailed impression of the business activities in the small towns Table 6 presents an overview of retail and wholesale trade, services and production activities in the two towns. The table shows that both towns are dominated by the traditional types of shops, general dealers, supermarkets, butchers and bottle stores. This dominance of general dealers is larger in Gutu than in Gokwe. An important reason for this is undoubtedly that there are more old shops run by traditional rural traders in Gutu than in Gokwe, which has developed since independence. Another reason may be that the lower incomes in Gutu make it more difficult for traders to specialize. However, in spite of the dominance of general dealers, more specialized shops have increasingly been established, especially clothing, hardware, book and

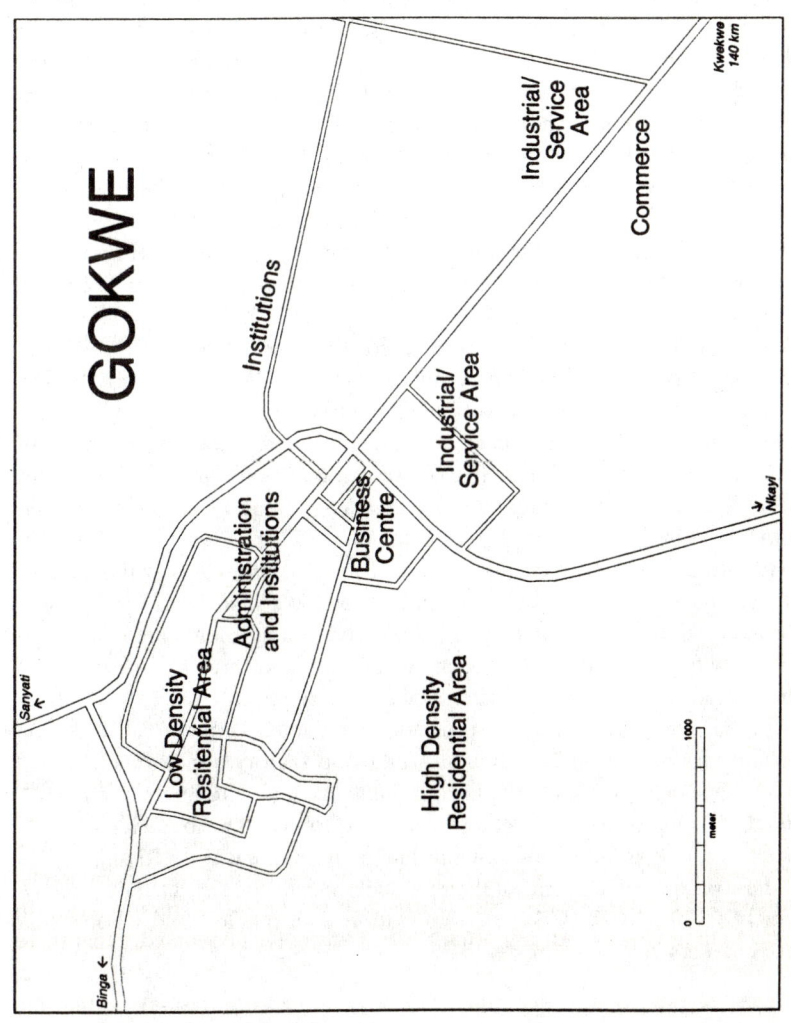

Figure 5   Gokwe district service centre

85

furniture stores, though in recent years also more specialized stores and workshops such as shoe and record shops, confectionary and take-away stores, photographic studios, hairdressers, gift shops and agents for dry cleaners in the larger neighbouring towns. Many of these new types of outlet combine activities in order to achieve a sufficient turnover. Furniture is also often sold together with either clothing or hardware. This makes it difficult to classify the shops into specific commodity groups. In order to overcome this difficulty, Table 6 shows figures for both the number of shops classified according to the most important activity and for the number of outlets for specific commodity groups. Here, each shop may appear more than once if it distributes more than one commodity group. General dealers and supermarkets, however, are only counted once. The data are based on a simple survey of shop premises in May 1990 and not on ownership or licenses. Thus the number of shops in Table 6 will be smaller than the number of licenses, partly because some shops are likely to have more than one license and partly because not all licenses are utilized. On the other hand, the number of shops will be larger than the number of businessmen because many businessmen run more than one shop.

Only small enterprises run from fixed premises, owned or rented, are included in the survey, while enterprises run from a dwelling are not. Except for the fruit and vegetable market (see chapter 7), such activities play a limited role in the retail sector. However, such small enterprises play a larger role in artisan production and repair. The figures for this sector presented in Tables 6 and 7 are clearly too small (see also chapter 9, Table 14, for more detailed data on the building sector; also Rasmussen, 1992).

Besides the small service, repair and artisan workshops, a growing number of medium-sized manufacturing industries have also been established. Typically, they have from 10 to 40 employees, though some are smaller. In 1990, there were four such enterprises in Gutu and three in Gokwe. 1994 showed an increase to nine enterprises in operation in Gutu (two clothing factories, one bakery, one oil-processor, one small commercial mill, one bookbinder/printer/chalk producer, one soup factory/pop-corn/soft-drink producer, one scotch-cart producer and one brick moulding enterprise with about 250 employees all together) and six in Gokwe (three bakeries, one oil-processor, one mill and one sawmill and more on the way). Although some of these producers sell some of their products outside the district, they produce mostly for the local market in competition with retailers and wholesalers (see chapters 7–9 for more details).

Table 6
Shops and activities in Gutu and Gokwe centres, May 1990

	No. of shops		No. of activities	
	Gutu	Gokwe	Gutu	Gokwe
Retail				
General dealer	31	16 }	42	20
Supermarket	4	3		
Butchery	7	4	9	4
Bottle store	3	3	3	4
Fish	1	–	1	–
Clothing	7	10	10	14
Clothing and furniture	3	1	–	–
Furniture	2	1	7	2
Hardware and furniture	2	–	–	–
Hardware	3	6	5	6
Shoes	2	1	2	1
Books and stationary	4	2	6	2
Spare parts	6	–	6	–
Petrol station	4	4	4	4
Automobile dealer	–	1	–	1
Diverse mixed shops	4	2	–	–
Records			3	3
Photography			1	2
Gifts			2	–
Magazines			1	–
Dry cleaning			2	–
Wholesale				
Farm input/coop/chemicals	3	3	4	4
Wholesale	4	3	4	3
Vegetable wholesale	2	1	2	1
Banking	–	3	4	4
Hotels and restaurants				
Restaurant/eating house	4	2	4	2
Beerhall/bar/nightclub	4	3	4	3
Hotel, restaurant and bar	1	1	1	1
Resthouse	–	1	–	1
Take-away food/confectionary	1	1	1	1

Table 6 (cont'd)
Shops and activities in Gutu and Gokwe centres, May 1990

	No. of shops		No. of activities	
	Gutu	Gokwe	Gutu	Gokwe
Artisan production, repair and service				
Automobile repair	6	–	6	2
Electric repair	1	–	1	–
Watch repair	–	–	1	–
Radio repair	3	–	4	1
Tyre service	–	1	–	1
Scotchcart seller/producer	1	3	2	3
Welder	3	2	4	4
Carpentry	2	1	3	1
Fencing	1	1	1	1
Hairdresser	–	–	5	1
Tailor/knitting	5	1	7	2
Tailor/knitting school	2	–	2	–
Grinding mill	4	3	4	3
Agricultural and other processing and marketing				
Large mill	1	–	1	–
Bakery	1	2	1	2
Soap factory	1	1	1	1
Candle factory	1	–	1	–
Beer depot	2	1	2	1
Dairy Marketing Board's depot	1	–	1	–
Grain Marketing Board's depot	1	1	1	1
Bus depot/office	1	2	1	2
Saw mill	1	2	1	2

Note: For detailed comments on the table, see text

Table 7
Shops and activities in Gutu and Gokwe centres, May 1990
Summary of Table 6

	No. of shops Gutu 1982[a]	No. of shops Gutu	No. of shops Gokwe	No. of activities Gutu	No. of activities Gokwe
General dealer/supermarkets	26	35	19	42	20
Other retail	20	48	35	62	43
Wholesale	3	9	7	10	9
Banks		3	4	4	4
Restaurant/hotel etc.	9	10	8	10	8
Production, repair and service	10	32	15	42	22
Total	**68**	**137**	**88**	**170**	**106**

Note: For detailed comments on the table, see text
a *Source:* Göttlicher 1986

6.4 The development of district service centre activities since independence

A comparison between the data in Table 6 and Göttlicher's (1986) data from Gutu in 1982 (see Table 7) indicate that the number of businesses doubled between 1982 and 1990, but that the number of specialized shops, wholesalers and producers grew even more rapidly and almost tripled, while the number of general dealers only grew by a third. This trend is also supported by Basera (1994), who presents a distribution of activities in Gutu at five points in time from 1978–94 (see Table 8). Precisely how these data have been obtained is not clear from the source. However, they appear to be based on activities rather than on shops, and in particular the production enterprises have been split into more activities than in the data in Table 6. On the other hand, a number of different specialized retail and service activities existing in 1992 seem to have been left out (e.g. furniture shops), while others are clearly under-represented (e.g. some clothing shops, a security company, training schools). However, in crude terms, the data correspond well to both Göttlicher's data from 1982 and our own from 1990. The data indicate that the number of activities quadrupled between 1978–94, but that the most rapid increase was in the period 1982–86. In this period, retail trade and services in particular grew rapidly, while production activities grew more rapidly after 1986, a growth which seems to have continued after 1992.

Many of the specialized retailers are branches of large retail chains, trading mostly in clothing but also in hardware and furniture. Such chains have played an important role in Zimbabwe since long before independence, but they

Table 8
Number of activities in Gutu centre, 1978–94

	1978	1982	1986	1992	1994
General dealers/supermarkets	15	24	40	45	52
Other retail	11	24	50	55	58
Wholesale	1	4	5	8	8
Banks	1	2	3	5	5
Restaurants/hotels etc.	8	10	11	15	18
Services and repair shops	5	8	17	23	24
Production	6	10	13	28	34
Total	**47**	**82**	**139**	**179**	**199**

Source: Basera 1994

were not then active in the communal areas. Since independence, the government has encouraged them to set up stores in the new district service centres, and since 1986 a number of large retail firms have opened branch stores in the large centres (Zinyama, 1990). Gutu and Gokwe now have between ten and fifteen such branch stores, which now dominate the market for clothing, hardware and furniture. Most of these chain stores are branches of large national or even South African owned corporations with headquarters in Harare, but others are branches of more regional chains, those in Gutu with headquarters in Masvingo or Marondera, those in Gokwe with headquarters in Kwekwe, Kadoma or Bulawayo. The branch stores tend to be relatively more important in Gokwe than in Gutu, probably because the local traders were much less developed in Gokwe than in Gutu when the branches were opened in the mid-1980s. On the other hand, more branch stores in Gokwe belong to smaller regional companies from Kwekwe or Kadoma, and they often seem to be better integrated into the local economy than the national chain stores.

Understandably enough, local traders tend to see the invasion of branch stores as unfair competition and a hindrance to local development because they tend to cream off the most profitable part of the market and invest little if any of the profit locally (most of them have not even invested in their own stores, but operate from rented premises). However, although the branch stores have taken over a large share of the market for clothing and hardware, growth in local businesses does not appear to have ceased.

Before independence and during the early 1980s, the prices of many consumer goods were considerably higher in the district service centres than in the large cities. Labour migrants and others travelling to the large cities therefore often bought goods there, so that much trade by-passed local traders.

In contrast, many retail chains have operated with fixed national prices and thus forced local traders to reduce their prices. As a result, district service centres have probably regained a large part of that market share which earlier went to the large towns. At the same time, lower prices have increased the already growing rural markets still further. There is thus reason to believe that branch stores have been one of the reasons behind the growth of the district service centres in the late 1980s and not an obstacle. However, as explained in a later chapter, retail chains may have created problems for the development of local manufacturing.

Branch stores have also forced local traders into a changed business strategy and a larger degree of specialization. For the general dealer in the more stable pre-independence society, his stock of commodities was his capital. As one old trader said: 'What I do not sell this year I shall sell next year'. Depreciation of goods was limited; he did not pay interest because he usually could not borrow money; and if anything prices went up. If he had the necessary capital, it was immaterial that part of his stock was held over to the next season. Commodities with a slow turnover might not be so profitable, but it would be important for him to have them in order to satisfy his customers, and they might be cross-subsidized by goods with a more rapid turnover. The branch stores, on the other hand, only sell goods with a rapid turnover. Goods which are not sold this season cost money to store and are often worth little next season because fashions have changed. This has also forced old traders to change their ways of doing business, because they have lost some of the more profitable wares to the branch stores. Many general dealers have been reduced to selling groceries; others have been forced to specialize in market segments not served by the branch stores (although they often keep some groceries as well). In clothing, which is mostly dominated by the branch stores, such locally owned, specialized shops have tended to specialize either in high-quality goods for the small but growing middle class of civil servants and successful traders, or in lower quality goods that are often produced in small workshops run by themselves or family members in Harare or other large towns. But retail shops and services have also developed in other narrow specializations such as shoes, books and paper, dispensaries, dried fish (which has become a popular substitute for meat after the large increase in meat prices in 1992), radios and other industrial goods imported on a small scale from South Africa or Botswana,[1] different spare parts often combined with repair services, hairdressing, photographic studios, dry cleaning, business and secretarial services, legal services, debt collectors and private training institutions. In Gutu, a local security firm has developed into the largest enterprise in Gutu since 1992, employing 140 young men and women as security guards and to a large extent taking over business from non-local security firms and creating at the same time a partial solution to the mounting youth unemployment problem.

This growing specialization has become possible because of the growth in the rural market up through the 1980s, but has also become a necessity because of the influx of new groups of young entrepreneurs, often with very little capital at their disposal. The result of this development has been the creation of a competitive environment in the small towns where many different types of actors compete in an increasingly segmented market. In many commodity markets, locally owned specialized stores compete with general dealers, branch stores and local small-scale producers, while they all compete with rural shops and suppliers in the larger towns. In the following two sections, we shall take a closer look at the structure of this competition by examining the distribution of two specific commodity groups, first farm implements with special focus on scotch carts, and then farm inputs with special focus on fertilizer.

6.5   The distribution of hardware goods, especially scotchcarts

Tools, equipment and machinery are increasingly important inputs into agriculture. Table 9 shows the availability of various types of equipment among communal farmers in Zimbabwe, based on a ZIDS survey of 759 communal farm households throughout the country (Sunga *et al.*, 1990). The table shows that the hoe is by far the most important tool, but most farm households also have their own plough and about one-third have cultivators, scotchcarts, wheelbarrows and bikes; many also have harrows. In general, farm households in the high rainfall areas are better equipped than households in the low rainfall areas because they grow more cash crops and have larger cash incomes. Consequently, demand for agricultural hardware is likely to be larger in Gokwe than in Gutu.

Tools and equipment are distributed locally by the larger general dealers and supermarkets, by specialized hardware stores, and in Gutu also by the Masvingo Cooperative Union (MCU). In addition, hardware stores in the larger towns also distribute directly to farmers, and the farmers themselves fetch goods in the large towns and bring it in by bus. Welders, and to some extent also car repair workshops, carry out some repair work on farm implements, but few of them produce farm implements. For both hardware stores and welders, the building sector is a more important customer than the agricultural sector

There are some indications that the cooperative and the growing number of hardware stores are taking over an increasing part of the market from both the general stores and direct sales from out-of-district enterprises. However, the number of hardware stores and welders is probably determined by building activity rather than agricultural activity and is thus not a good indicator of sales of farm implements.

Table 9
Agricultural equipment per 100 communal farm households

	Rainfall area				Total
	I+II	III	IV	V	
Hoes	531	545	437	489	470
Chains	129	173	213	110	161
Yorks	167	200	163	54	146
Ploughs	96	96	87	54	82
Granaries	101	81	83	82	83
Drums	58	86	88	37	69
Wheelbarrows	28	56	45	38	41
Bicycles	26	42	48	35	38
Scotchcarts	36	40	35	24	33
Cultivators	49	33	26	10	28
Harrows	15	21	31	12	21
Can sprays	26	21	5	13	13
Planters	2	18	5	13	8
Water pumps	1	2	11	12	7
Sledges	8	2	3	4	4
Water carts	3	5	3	5	3
Trailers	1	1	1	0	1
Shellers	3	0	1	0	1
Grinding mills	3	3	1	0	1
Tractors	1	1	2	0	1
Tractor implements	1	0	2	0	1
Total no. of households in sample	156	154	313	136	759

Source: Sunga *et al.*, 1990, Table 3.11

Many of the new hardware stores are branches of larger out-of-district enterprises, and thus even if the local stores take over an increasing part of the market, out-of-district enterprises may in fact keep their share or even increase it.

In the following we examine in more detail one specific farm implement, the scotch-cart, which undoubtedly represents a growing market with increasing competition. In Gutu, a local entrepreneur runs a relatively large welding and car repair workshop which also produces scotch carts. He supplies a considerable part of the local market, but also receives increasing competition, especially from branch hardware dealers. He competes by producing a scotch-cart which is more durable but probably has less finish than the non-local products.

In Gokwe, the distribution of scotchcarts is dominated by three local sales outlets of producers in Bulawayo and other large towns. In addition, hardware stores sell some scotchcarts. One of them, which also runs a welding shop, claims to produce scotchcarts, but on a much smaller scale than in Gutu. Since the total market for scotchcarts is probably larger in Gokwe than in Gutu, it should be possible to establish a local production in Gokwe; and in fact by the end of 1993, after the first good harvest following the drought, a number of welders in Gokwe had started scotch-cart production.

Local production in Gutu was also increasing. The local producer in Gutu in 1993 almost doubled his production relative to the pre-drought level in 1991 (in the drought year of 1992 he did not produce any at all). In 1994 his production increased by 25 per cent. However, sales of farm implements may well have increased more rapidly than local production. One trader in Gutu claimed his sales of farm implements in 1993 increased tenfold over the 1991 level, in spite of considerable price increases (e.g. plough prices increased from 250 Z$ to 400 Z$ and scotch-cart prices from approximately 2,300 Z$ to approximately 3,000 Z$). The reason for this is apparently that the price of maize rose even more rapidly, so that prices in terms of maize equivalent dropped to almost one-third.

6.6   The distribution of farm inputs, especially fertilizer

The most important farm inputs are fertilizers, seeds, chemicals and stockfeed. It is characteristic of these products that they are produced for the national market by only a few producers and that the market has been partly regulated. In the communal areas, farm inputs are distributed directly from the producer or via wholesalers, large general stores, specialized farm input traders or cooperatives; however, competition between the different distribution channels varies from product to product and from area to area. To give an impression of the distribution system and its dynamics, we focus especially on fertilizer, which is probably the most important of the farm inputs in both value and amount.

Fertilizer in Zimbabwe is produced by only two large industrial enterprises: ZFC (Zimbabwe Fertilizer Corporation) and Windmill, both with headquarters in Harare. In the early 1990s, ZFC was the largest of the two, with 58 per cent of the market. This share is about the same for both the communal and the commercial farmers' markets, but the communal farmers only buy one quarter of all fertilizer used.

Fertilizer is sold at a price at producer's gate, and the buyers pay for the transport. The producers have no transport capacity of their own, but they do help farmers and traders organize transport. Windmill distributes three-quarters of its sales directly to communal farmers and only one quarter through traders and cooperatives. ZFC sells a much larger share through traders and cooperatives.

Fertilizer distribution appears to be very different in the two districts. In Gutu centre, there is a large and apparently growing trade in fertilizer. Partly with support from the CARD programme[2] and GTZ, Masvingo Cooperative Union (MCU) has managed to increase its sales several times; two new specialized dealers in farm inputs have recently been established, and a third opened just after fieldwork was carried out (April 1990). The large general dealers, which have traditionally distributed the fertilizer, claim that their sales have not decreased (this may not be true). In Gokwe centre, on the other hand, fertilizer sales appear to be very limited. The cooperative is apparently almost bankrupt, and neither wholesalers, large general dealers, hardware stores or any others appear to sell much fertilizer. Several outlets sell chemicals especially for cotton farmers, but they sell hardly any fertilizer.

This very clearcut difference between the two centres is all the more peculiar given that Agritex claims that the use of fertilizer ought to be larger in Gokwe than in Gutu, because there is more rainfall. This prognosis is supported by Sunga *et al.* (1990), who show that while only 10 per cent of farmers in dry areas (natural regions IV and V) use fertilizer, 25 per cent or more of the farmers in areas with more rain use it. With more detailed data from Gutu and Sanyati (which in many ways is similar to Gokwe) districts in 1982, Göttlicher (1986), similarly shows that Sanyati farmers use much more fertilizer than Gutu farmers, partly because they use more fertilizer on their maize and partly because even more fertilizer is used on cotton, which is not grown in Gutu at all

On the other hand, neither Sunga's national survey nor Göttlicher's data from Sanyati can be representative for Gokwe, because a large part of Gokwe has only recently been settled and thus has not yet reached a level of exploitation where the use of fertilizer is necessary. In some areas not even cotton growers use any fertilizer.[3]

However, no matter how large a proportion of farmers in Gokwe use fertilizer, the actual users are likely to use more fertilizer than the users in Gutu, not only because rainfall is higher, but also because farm size is larger and cotton requires more fertilizer than maize. This makes direct sales to farmers much easier in Gokwe than in Gutu, because a small number of farmers will often be able to fill a truck. In Gutu, where both fertilizer use and farm size is smaller, more farmers will need to collaborate in order to fill a truck and organize direct delivery of fertilizer from the producer. Consequently, it is easier for traders and the cooperative to compete in Gutu.

The recent growth in fertilizer sales in Gutu also seems to have been spurred by GTZ and CARD programme support to the Gutu branch of the MCU. GTZ has provided MCU with working capital in the form of a revolving fund of 100,000 Z$, though at the same time it required it to reduce its markup to 15 per cent. This has made it possible for MCU to improve its distribution of farm inputs in Gutu district and at the same time reduce its prices. The result is that MCU was able to increase its fertilizer sales rapidly during the early 1990s. Some of this increase is likely to be a genuine increase in fertilizer use, but some of it is likely to be due to reduced direct sales from the producers and reduced local sales, especially from the small general dealers.

MCU gets its fertilizer from ZFC and has become the sole distributor for ZFC in Gutu. Windmill delivers to the private traders, either directly or through a major businessman in Masvingo who operates as a sort of agent or intermediary for Windmill. The success of MCU has forced Windmill and the local traders to become more competitive in order to maintain market share. The price for a bag of AN fertilizer at producer's gate is 20.30 Z$ (1990). The price of transportation to Gokwe or Gutu would typically be around 5 Z$, but earlier, private traders took up to 32 Z$ a bag. MCU in Gutu now charges about 27 Z$, and private traders have therefore been forced to reduce their price considerably.

Part of MCU's strategy has been to open five depots and ten sub-depots in the district to improve delivery. This has also forced private traders to improve their distribution service. However, only the larger traders have been able to do this, and this has probably led to a concentration of private fertilizer sale with specialized farm input dealers and the largest of the general dealers. It has also led to market segmentation, where private traders concentrate on segments of the market which are not supplied by MCU.

Membership of MCU is not open but largely limited to full-time communal farmers, many of whom are master farmers with relatively large fertilizer use and relatively easy access to credit from the Agricultural Finance Corporation (AFC). On the other hand, very few part-time farmers and farmers with non-farm jobs are members of MCU, and it is among these groups that the large general dealers with rural branches have their customers. They buy relatively little fertilizer, but often need the credit which general dealers may give; they also need the close access to rural stores. They are therefore willing (or forced) to pay excessively for fertilizer in order to receive these services.

Finally, most of the market for specialized farm input is among small commercial and resettlement farmers who order relatively large amounts of fertilizer and are therefore relatively easy to supply. They are therefore able to keep both costs and prices relatively low. Consequently, there is considerable market segmentation based on relative advantages, not in product or production but in credit and delivery services.

After the introduction of structural-adjustment policies in the early 1990s, the price of fertilizer rose. To counteract these price increases and the negative effects of the serious drought in the 1991–92 season, the government distributed large amounts of fertilizer free of charge to peasant farmers in 1992–93. According to one farm-input supplier, free distribution of fertilizer in Gutu amounted to twice ordinary pre-drought sales (but Gutu may have received more than most other areas), while sales remained at about half the pre-dought level or the same as during the drought year. In 1993–94, promised government handouts were not forthcoming in time, and in spite of price increases, local sales in Gutu appear to have more than doubled relative to the pre-drought level. In addition to the existing farm-input suppliers, a local trader converted his clothing shop to the sale of fertilizer. Fertilizer sales appears to have continued to grow in 1994–95, although only slowly.

The reason for the rather dramatic increase in fertilizer sales is that the price of maize after the drought rose even more rapidly than the price of fertilizer. As a result, the fertilizer price in terms of maize equivalent fell to about half. However, this rapid increase in maize price has only benefitted larger communal farmers, small-scale commercial farms and resettlement farms producing a marketable surplus. Small communal farmers not producing enough for subsistence have been hit by price increases of both maize and fertilizer. The increased sale of fertilizer is therefore likely to have been concentrated on the larger farms. Their increasing incomes have resulted in increasing investments in farm implements (see above) and apparently also in increased production of chicken and pigs, and therefore increased sales of stock feed as well.

6.7 The network of rural business centres: three cases from Gutu district

Under the district service centres which are our main concern here, a carefully planned network of small rural business centres exist, located typically about 10 km apart. They play an important role in the distribution of consumer goods and the collection of cash crops, especially from the smallest communal farms. There are very detailed plans for these small centres, but few public investments have been made there. The network of centres was intended to comprise different levels of a hierarchy (Wekwete, 1991), and the centres also vary in size, but in reality most of them are dominated by general dealers.

In Makoni district (around the town of Rusape), Jansen and Olthof (1993) have made a survey of such rural business centres. They found that 167 business centres and 27 rural service centres in the district have on average three and eight enterprises respectively. Many of the business centres have only one or two shops, but the largest has 16, and there is no clear difference between the business centres and the rural service centres. In addition to these 194 rural centres, there is a small district service centre with 26 enterprises. Few people in the district live more than 3 km to the nearest centre. Out of the 862 businesses operating in the centres, 44 per cent were general dealers, 23 per cent grinding mills, 18 per cent bottle stores or beer halls and 8 per cent butchers. The last 7 per cent comprised restaurants, carpenters, metal workshops, warehouses etc.

Such rural service centre networks, characterized by a few large centres and a large number of rather undifferentiated centres, are found in many developing rural areas (Johnson, 1970). In an African context, Berg (1981) in Zambia and Musyoki (1987) in Kenya have described such rural service centres, which vary in size but not in function. However, there are few more detailed studies of such small rural centres and their businesses. In order to obtain a clearer picture of the small rural business centres and the way they function three such small centres in Gutu district have been surveyed. They are located along the road running eastward from Gutu centre, but at different distances from the centre.

Chisheche business centre, a relatively new centre, is located only 8 km from Gutu district service centre. The first activities there, a grinding mill and a general dealer shop, were established in 1976. The area for which Chisheche is the centre was largely evacuated in the 1950s because the nearby Gutu Mission wanted to set up a cattle ranch. The ranch was closed in the early 1970s and the original population was allowed to return. Many of the first shopkeepers in the centre belong to this group of return migrants.

The centre has developed as a midway centre between Gutu/Mpandawana and Mashayavanhu, an older business centre 15 km from Gutu/Mpandawana. It is also located close to Gutu Mission and draws a good many of its customers from the personnel at the mission's schools and hospital. Since its launch in 1976, Chisheche has developed into a small business centre with 18 different businesses run by 15 owners.

Gonya business centre is located 30 km east of Gutu district service centre. It has developed as a midway centre between Gutu and Basera, the second largest centre in Gutu communal area. Gonya had until recently the most businesses of the three centres, but it has now been overtaken by Chisheche. The first businesses in the centre, a grinding mill and a butcher's shop, were established in 1960, but the centre grew rapidly into 12 businesses by 1963. It then stagnated until the end of the 1970s, when it slowly started to grow again. In 1990, it contained 18 businesses run by 11 owners.

Finally, Mataruse business centre is located 75 km from Gutu centre, 20 km beyond Basera and only 10 km from the eastern border of Gutu district. It is the last stop on the bus routes from Gutu centre into the communal area. Mataruse is the smallest of the three centres, but also the oldest. The first business, a general store, was already established in 1950. From 1960, when it had four businesses, it grew until the mid-1970s to a size of eight businesses. By the end of the 1970s, the number fell to five to six shops, but by the mid-1980s, it rose again to the eight shops, which are still being run by six owners.

For the sake of comparison, some data on Basera, the largest rural business centre in Gutu communal area and the second largest centre after Gutu, are also presented. It is located a little more than 50 km from Gutu centre and close to a large mission station. It had 35 private businesses and 6 public services in 1994 (Mushauri, 1994).

The development of the three small business centres and their businesses

In both of the two old centres, Gonya and Mataruse, the first shop was set up by the same commercial farmer, who was of Greek origin. He opened a general store in Mataruse in 1950, which he ran until 1960, when he sold it to another white businessman with shops in many locations. He then opened a grinding mill, which became the first business in Gonya. Both of these businesses continued in white ownership until the end of the 1970s. However, since 1960, all new enterprises were established by African businessmen, in the beginning mostly people from Gutu district, but often not from the local sub-district. A number of these businessmen had shops in several rural business centres in Gutu district, e.g. Basera, Chitza, Dewure, Gonya and Mataruse. Up to the mid-1970s, more than half the businessmen in Gonya and Mataruse were non-locals in the sub-district the centre.

Since the mid-1970s, however, local businessmen gradually seem to have taken over more and more of the businesses, and although non-local businessmen continued to play a role, their importance has fallen significantly (see also Figure 6). In 1990, only four of 17 businessmen operating in Gonya and Mataruse were non-locals. Similarly, in Chisheche, which only started in 1976, almost all the businesses until 1989 were set up by local people or people who had been living in the local area for a long time. Since 1989,

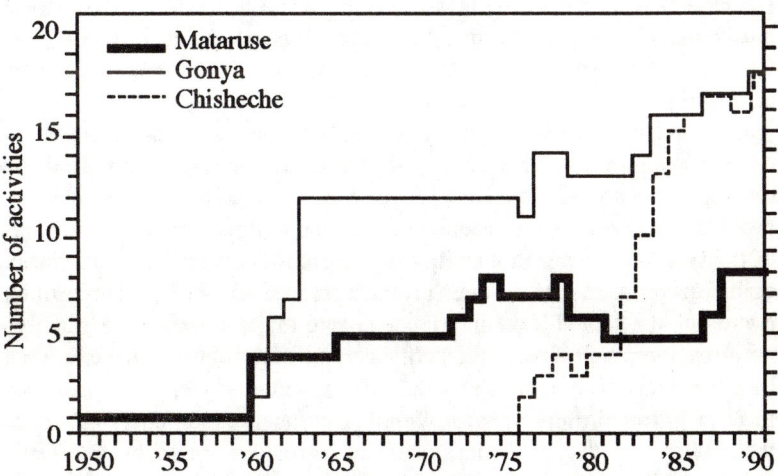

Figure 6   The development of activities in Chisheche, Gonya and Mataruse rural business centres

however, a number of the businesses have been taken over by businessmen from Gutu district service centre. The reason for this decrease in the 1970s in the number of non-local businessmen may be that the more successful businessmen have tended to move to the district service centres, where the markets have been more prosperous.

Although most of the businesses in the three small centres today are run by local people without businesses elsewhere, some of them run more than one business in their centre, typically a general dealer shop together with either a butchery, a bottle store or a grinding mill. Of the 17 businessmen active in Gonya and Mataruse, five run a total of 13 businesses.

There is also a considerable difference in the size of the individual businesses, especially in Gonya and Mataruse. The businessmen who run the largest businesses are typically those who have been running them for a long time. They have had longer to accumulate capital and therefore tend to be better stocked. Often, they have also been engaged in the grain trade (as approved buyers for the Grain Marketing Board). Due to a lack of both capital and transport, the smaller businessmen have only been able to do this on a very limited scale, if at all.

A large majority of the new local businessmen, especially before the mid-1980s, were active or pensioned civil servants. Of the 14 businessmen who have been active in Chisheche business centre before 1989, ten are or have been employed in the public sector or in the missions: one headmaster, three teachers, two boarding masters, a medical orderly, a railroad worker and a driver for the district administrator's office. In many cases, their wives are also teachers, nurses etc. There is only one communal farmer without a permanent job or other businesses. Of the last three, one was a driver and salesman before he opened his business in Chisheche, and the two others are mechanics who run garages in Gutu centre. Thus most of the businessmen in Chisheche have earned the money they invested in their businesses as wage earners, mostly in the public sector.

In addition to their jobs and businesses, all the businessmen also have smaller or larger communal farms. These farms contribute important additional income to the household economy, but they also tend to increase cash-flow problems, because capital resources are bound to these farms for a large part of the year and thus cannot be invested in commodity stocks. Thus chronic cash-flow problems are the main problem for most businesses. This problem could only be solved if credit were available to them, which it generally is not. However, even if they could obtain credit it is doubtful whether it would be a good idea to borrow under the existing circumstances. It would solve their cash-flow problems, but it would also increase their costs and reduce their ability to withstand the large fluctuations in turnover which are likely to prevail as long as the economies of the communal areas are so closely linked to agricultural cycles.

Most of the businesses in Chisheche are run by the owner and/or his family. Only a few other people are employed. In Gonya and Mataruse, some of the larger businesses employ two to four people in addition to family labour. Except in the grinding mills, which are considered men's work, most of the people who work in the shops are women.

Only a few producers or wholesalers bring their commodities directly to the shops, and especially in Gonya and Mataruse, most of the owners have to fetch commodities from wholesalers in Gutu centre or sometimes in Masvingo. This presents a problem because many of the shopowners do not have cars, or if they have, they are often old cars which breakdown frequently. In addition, many owners who work outside Gutu use their cars during the week. Consequently, goods are often transported by bus.

Of the 44 business activities located in Chisheche, Gonya and Mataruse in 1990, 25 were general dealers with very little specialization, and the specialized functions, butchers, bottle stores and beer halls, are probably specialized because the licensing regulations require it rather than for any economic reasons. The general dealers basically sell groceries, although some of them also have limited supplies of such goods as textiles and kitchenwares. In Chisheche, four of the 11 general dealers stock some textile goods, partly produced themselves or delivered by other small entrepreneurs in the family. Before independence, the number of general dealers was around 50 per cent of the total number of businesses in the three centres. After independence, the proportion of general dealers rose to about 70 per cent in the mid-1980s, but presently, this figure is declining: the number of specialized businesses continues to grow, while the number of general dealers stagnates (see Table 10).

The lack of specialization, in the usual sense of the word, does not mean that everyone sells the same goods and serves the same market. Rather, each shop tends to some extent to have its own secluded market, consisting of the owner's extended family and people from his home area or workplace who tend his shop first.

At the same time, the generally low level of cash flow, the frequent breakdown of transport facilities, and the limited in availability of goods in the wholesale stores all result in a very limited, unequal and fluctuating supply of goods in the shops, depending on which goods the individual shop has been able to obtain in a particular week.

Consequently, although most customers may have their preferred shops, they will in fact often need to circulate between the shops in order to buy what they need. Thus over time all shops receive their share of the market, at the same time as the many competing general dealers with different resources increase the probability of permanent supply in the centre. Thus although all

Table 10
The development of different types of activity in Chisheche, Gonya and Mataruse rural business centres

Year	Grinding mills	General stores	Butchers	Bottle stores	Eating houses	Beer halls	Clothing co-operatives	Total
1950	–	1	–	–	–	–	–	1
51	–	1	–	–	–	–	–	1
52	–	1	–	–	–	–	–	1
53	–	1	–	–	–	–	–	1
54	–	1	–	–	–	–	–	1
55	–	1	–	–	–	–	–	1
56	–	1	–	–	–	–	–	1
57	–	1	–	–	–	–	–	1
56	–	1	–	–	–	–	–	1
59	–	1	–	–	–	–	–	1
1960	2	3	1	–	–	–	–	6
61	3	5	1	–	1	–	–	10
62	3	6	1	–	1	–	–	11
63	4	8	3	–	1	–	–	16
64	4	8	3	–	1	–	–	16
65	4	8	4	–	1	–	–	17
66	4	8	4	–	1	–	–	17
67	4	8	4	–	1	–	–	17
68	4	8	4	–	1	–	–	17
69	4	8	4	–	1	–	–	17
1970	4	8	4	–	1	–	–	17
71	4	9	4	–	–	–	–	17
72	5	9	4	–	–	–	–	18
73	6	9	4	–	–	–	–	19
74	6	10	4	–	–	–	–	20
75	6	9	4	–	–	–	–	19
76	7	10	4	–	–	–	–	21
77	7	11	5	1	–	–	–	24
78	7	13	5	1	–	–	–	26
79	6	12	4	1	–	–	–	23
1980	5	13	3	2	–	–	–	23
81	4	13	3	2	–	–	–	22
82	4	14	3	2	–	1	–	24
83	4	18	3	2	–	1	–	28
84	3	23	3	3	–	1	–	33
85	3	24	4	3	–	1	–	35
86	3	24	4	3	–	2	–	36
87	4	25	4	3	–	2	1	39
88	5	25	4	4	–	2	1	41
89	5	25	4	4	–	2	1	41
1990	7	25	5	4	–	2	1	44

the centres are dominated by general stores, there is still a certain unplanned differentiation between both dealers and centres, but a differentiation caused by supply factors rather than demand factors. Differentiation arises not out of a decision to specialize, but rather from a lack of the financial resources to stock shops fully, insufficient transportation, and limited and unstable supplies, all of which prevent shop owners from acquiring the goods they would like to stock. Thus the general stores in the small centres do supplement each other to some extent.

Change and stability in business communities in the small rural business centres

Although we have been able to identify some changes in the business community in Chisheche, Gonya and Mataruse during the last 30 years, these changes have been slow, and one could well argue that the main characteristic of development has been a remarkable stability. Of the 30 businessmen who have been running businesses in Gonya and Mataruse during the 30-year period from 1960–90, 17 still operate in the centres. The 13 which have closed down during this period had been in operation on average for almost 12 years; and the 17 businesses still in operation in 1990 had been so for an average of more than 11 years. Four of them were more than 28 years old, and only four were less than 5 years old. In Chisheche, which developed mostly during the 1980s, the average age of the enterprises is obviously much lower than in the two older centres. But here too there have been relatively few changes in ownership.

This high degree of stability is quite surprising when one considers that the businesses have been operating in an environment with very large economic and political fluctuations caused by frequent droughts, commodity shortages, unstable deliveries, changing policies and the war of independence. The reason for this high degree of stability is found in the investment strategy and cost structure of businesses in the small rural centres, where:

– original investments are usually based on own savings and treated as sunken costs, so that no interest needs to be paid;

– current investments are often small;

– alternative income for the labour applied is often very low or even zero;

– the owner or his wife often have other sources of income.

As a result, most businesses are able to survive for long periods even with a very low turnover. If the shopkeeper has a large family, the wholesale discount which he realizes as a retailer for his family's own consumption may be enough to justify his keeping the shop open. In addition, there is a certain prestige in having a shop, and as costs are limited, it may be kept going even if incomes are low. On the other hand, the success of a businessman depends to a large extent on his ability to stock his shop. Businessmen operating at a very low level may well survive, but they are not likely to be able to stock their shops satisfactorily and will therefore have low turnover and income.

Often the old businessmen use their shops as a pension scheme, and thus gradually destock it until little more than the building is left. This life-cycle change of shops in the small business centres is one of the reasons for the very great differences in turnover of shops in most centres. It is probably also an important reason why so few of the businesses in these small centres are taken over by the children. In fact, in our three centres, there seems to be only one instance where a shop has been taken over by one of the owner's children. To take over one of the old shops and run it successfully requires considerable capital, partly because the new owner will have increased costs if he has to buy or rent the shop, and partly because a younger owner is likely to require a larger income. Consequently, the shop is likely to be either closed or taken over by someone with a larger capital who is better able to secure a larger share of the market.

Unlike to Gonya and Mataruse, which have been dominated by one or a few large shops, Chisheche until 1990 had a much more equal structure. The take-over of one of the shops in 1990 by a businessman from Gutu centre seemed for a time to change this. This new businessman was able to stock his shop much better than the old ones, and in 1992 it seemed that he would be able to take over a considerable share of the market from the other shops. This would have created a more skewed enterprise structure in Chisheche, similar to that found in Gonya and Mataruse. However, when we visited Chisheche in early 1995, the shop had been destocked and turned into a bar, which has a much more rapid turnover and therefore requires less operational capital. There were two reasons for this change. First, a serious traffic accident meant that the owner was unable to work for a long period and that he lost his file of debtors. Unable to reclaim outstanding debts, he lost his shop at his original home in a neighbouring district. Secondly, he had made large investments in renovating a restaurant in Basera, which earned much less than he had hoped due to drought.

Though these are very specific problems, experienced by an individual businessman in Chisheche, they are also typical of the problems of many small businessmen that make it difficult for them to expand their businesses. The example shows first that the businessmen's risks are not only the normal business risks, but also personal risks, which are high in the developing countries and for which there is no social security. Secondly, the example also illustrates an observation that I made in many more cases, namely the

104

tendency of many small businessmen to invest what they earn in fixed capital so that even small fluctuations in the economy leave them without sufficient working capital. As few small businessmen are able to obtain credit, this often forces them to reduce their activities.

The development of Basera, the largest rural business centre in Gutu communal area

Mushauri (1994) found that Basera in 1994 had 35 private businesses, or almost twice the number in Chisheche and Gonya, and in addition six public services; the smaller centres had none. According to the data presented in Table 5, this is only a modest increase from 28 private and public establishments in 1976, and almost stagnation from 40 in 1986. However, the data from 1976 are probably too large because they are based on licences rather than on actually existing enterprises, and therefore the real growth is probably larger than indicated by these figures. Thus Mushauri (1994) shows that 15 out of the 35 private businesses operating in 1994 were established during the 1990s, while only six date from before 1980, thus indicating either rapid growth during the first half of the 1990s or a rapid turnover of enterprises. The existence of five defunct shops in the centre points towards a considerable turnover. However, the sectoral composition of the new businesses established during the 1990s indicates that they are not just a continuation of the old, but represent a diversification of the centre away from general store and the retail trade. Thus while the five defunct shops were all general stores, only two of the 15 new businesses set up during the 1990s were retailers (both bottle stores). The rest were small one-person production and service enterprises dominated by four grinding mills and four hairdressers, in addition to a welder, fence-maker/carpenter, butcher, radio-repairer and hotel.

As in the small business centres, most of the entrepreneurs in Basera only run one business. In total, the 35 businesses are owned by 25 entrepreneurs, of whom five run 15 businesses, while 20 run only one each. Some of the large entrepreneurs who run more than one business in Basera also run businesses in other centres. Their businesses in Basera also tend to be larger than the average for Basera. Thus the five entrepreneurs who run more than one business in Basera employ more than half the 45 people working in all the businesses.

As we shall see, the trend away from general dealers towards the establishment of smaller and more specialized enterprises has also taken place in Gutu and Gokwe centres since the end of the 1980s; but as Table 10 shows, it has to a very limited extent taken place in the small business centres, although the grinding mills also appear to have increased in number here during the 1990s.

6.8 Market segmentation and the dynamics of the distribution system in the district service centres

Most attempts to develop service centres and distribution systems in the rural areas of developing countries have been based directly or indirectly on Christaller's central-place theory, formulated either in neo-classical market terms or as a centrally planned system of service centres. Christaller sets forth a theory of a demand-led service system. Supplies are supposed to be forthcoming whenever there is a demand, either through market forces or through a central planning agent. Specialized commodities and services are assumed to belong to sub-sectors which are homogeneous, i.e. a hardware store is a hardware store is a hardware store. Commodities and services are also ordered according to the minimum size of the hinterland necessary for economic operation. Commodities and services requiring only a small number of customers will be located in all centres, even the smallest, while commodities and services requiring a larger number of customers will be located only in the larger centres. Thus both services and centres are ordered in hierarchies which coincide. In a service-centre system governed by market forces, the order of activities and centres are determined by the market. In a planned service-centre system, the order is determined by decree. Activities located in the lower-order centres are supposed to be supplied by the necessary inputs from the higher-order centres, but they have a locational monopoly within their own local hinterland.

The system of service centres developed since independence in the communal areas of Zimbabwe, described above, is very different from the Christallian hierarchy, whether planned or market-based. The sub-sectors of the distribution system in the district service centres are not homogeneous but are typically served by several parallel channels of distribution. Thus locally owned specialized stores often compete with branch stores, general stores and small or large local producers. At the same time, they all compete with stores in the small rural centres and with suppliers in the larger towns. Even within the same type of outlet, the range of goods and services available may vary considerably from store to store and from time to time. Competition between the different channels is not based on price only, but on a market segmentation based on delivery services: credit, transport, availability of goods, size of consignment, and product quality. This segmentation is a response to scarce resources in the distribution system and to large instabilities in both supply and demand. This market segmentation does not mean that there is no competition between the different distribution channels, which compete over the delimitation of their market segments.

Contrary to neo-classical theory, which usually sees market segmentation as a sign of market inefficiency, I believe that under conditions of scarce resources in the distribution system, market segmentation will result in a better utilization of scarce resources in the distribution system, and in greater supply security than would be achievable by distribution systems based on perfect competition, total monopoly or Christallian local spatial monopoly.

A distribution system based on many competing distribution channels with access to different resources is likely to reach a larger, more diversified part of the total market. However, it does not guarantee that the most peripheral and thinnest markets are actually served. Also, the existence of several parallel distribution channels does not in itself guarantee that competition actually takes place or that profits are kept low. The system may dwindle into an oligopoly, where each distributor operates in his own closed market.

Since independence in 1980, the distribution system in the district service centres has experienced considerable growth. This growth has been driven partly by growing demand, but also by a changing supply structure. Demand has increased as a result of the increased commercialization of agriculture and growing wage employment, especially in the public and parastatal sectors but since the second half of the 1980s also in the private sector. At the same time, however, increased diversification of the supply of goods and services and reduced price differences between district service centres and the large towns have made it possible for district service centres to capture an increasing share of the rural consumption which earlier went to the larger towns.

The establishment of branches of large national retail chains has been instrumental in reducing the differences in the consumer prices of industrial goods because many of the chains have operated with fixed national prices. They have therefore forced local traders to lower their prices or leave the market. Another example of a policy which has led to reduced price differences is GTZ's support for the MCU, which has made it possible for the cooperative to improve its fertilizer distribution and not only lower its own fertilizer prices, but also force the private traders to lower theirs.

Notes

1   Such import was legalized as part of structural adjustment in the early 1990s. It often takes the form of semi-barter trade, where crochet work or other handicrafts produced in Zimbabwe are sold south of the border and industrial goods brought back (see also Brand, Mupedziswa and Gumbo, 1995).
2   The CARD programme is a large rural development programme run in Gutu district with support from the German development organization, GTZ.
3   This was supported by our own small survey of 21 farmers distributed throughout Gokwe district: none used any fertilizer.

7 Agricultural processing and marketing in district service centres

7.1 Agroprocessing and marketing in the national economy

Agroprocessing is one of the important industries in Zimbabwe. According to the census of production of 1988–89, the food, beverage and tobacco industry employed 40,000 people in 1988, corresponding to 22 per cent of total industrial employment. Most of the employment is located in the large towns, 75 per cent in Harare and Bulawayo alone. Organizationally too, the industry is concentrated in a small number of large parastatal and private enterprises. Until the late 1980s, employment was almost stable. From 1985 to 1989, employment in most sub-sectors grew a little, while employment in milling increased by 900, but decreased in tobacco by 1,000 and in canning by 400. During the early 1990s, employment must have gone down due to a lack of raw materials following the drought, a shrinking home market caused by both drought and structural adjustment, and increased competition from the small-scale sector, though we have no detailed information on this.

In addition to these formal industries, there are approximately 60,000 small food-processing enterprises (with less than 50 employees but an average employment of only 1.85) according to the recent the Gemini survey of small enterprises in Zimbabwe (McPherson, 1991). Almost 50,000 of these, however, brew traditional beer, while small butchers, mills and bakeries only make up around 12,000 enterprises with a total employment of probably around 20,000. Practically all the small enterprises in the sector are located in the rural areas.

Finally, there are a large number of rural vendors and retailers trading in farm products and livestock. According to the Gemini survey, approximately 75,000 enterprises have a likely employment of about 140,000, of which many may only be working part time. Most of these traders are located in the rural areas.

Although one should expect agroprocessing to play an important role in the economy of small towns, for historical reasons this has not been so. Until independence in 1980, agriculture in the communal areas was mainly based on subsistence. Very little of the agricultural produce grown in the communal areas was marketed outside the local rural area, and the market for processed agricultural products was even smaller. The bulk of commercially produced farm products were grown in the white farming areas and consumed in the larger towns. There was therefore a certain rationale in centralizing the processing industry in the large towns. However, this has changed since independence. The new government has attempted with considerable success to integrate the communal areas into the market economy by extending agricultural marketing, extension and financial services into the communal areas. As a result, more than half of all maize and cotton marketed was being produced in the communal areas by the end of the 1980s.

This growing commercialization of the rural economy, together with the extension of public services (especially education and health), has led to the growth of the small towns and the rapid expansion of demand for processed, commercial food products (and also other industrial products, especially clothing and building materials). In the district service centres and other small rural centres, this has led to a rapid growth in agricultural trade (both private and parastatal), but only slowly in processing activities. As a result, most agricultural products are transported to the large towns to be processed, while the small towns and rural areas are being supplied to a large extent with commercial and processed food products from the large towns. Thus Jayne and Chisvo (1991) estimate that 25 per cent of the industrially produced mealy meal during a normal year in the late 1980s was sold to rural consumers with a grain deficit; in a drought year it would be over 40 per cent. Also in other sub-sectors rural consumers are to a large extent supplied with food from the urban areas. Therefore, there should be a considerable potential for the development of agroprocessing industries in the district service centres.

The purpose of this chapter is to give a detailed account of the structure of the agroprocessing and marketing sector in Gutu and Gokwe district service centres and the constraints on its growth. The account is based on fieldwork carried out in 1990. Since then, great changes have taken place in the sector as a result of structural adjustment and the severe drought in 1991–92. These changes are discussed in the last part of the chapter on the basis of shorter periods of fieldwork carried out in November–December 1993 and February 1995.

7.2   Agricultural marketing and processing activities in Gutu and Gokwe centres, 1990

The agricultural marketing and processing activities in the two centres make up a very diverse set of activities. Table 11 gives an overview of the types and numbers of activities found in the two centres in 1990, and of their employment. The sector is more developed and differentiated in Gutu than in Gokwe, although the total employment in 1990 was almost the same in the two centres: a little more than 200. However, in both centres the number of activities is limited and the sector is not very integrated. The following description of the sector examines five sub-sectors: grain and oil seed, cotton, livestock, dairy, and fruit and vegetables. Figure 7 gives a breakdown of the actual and potential links within the agroprocessing and marketing system.

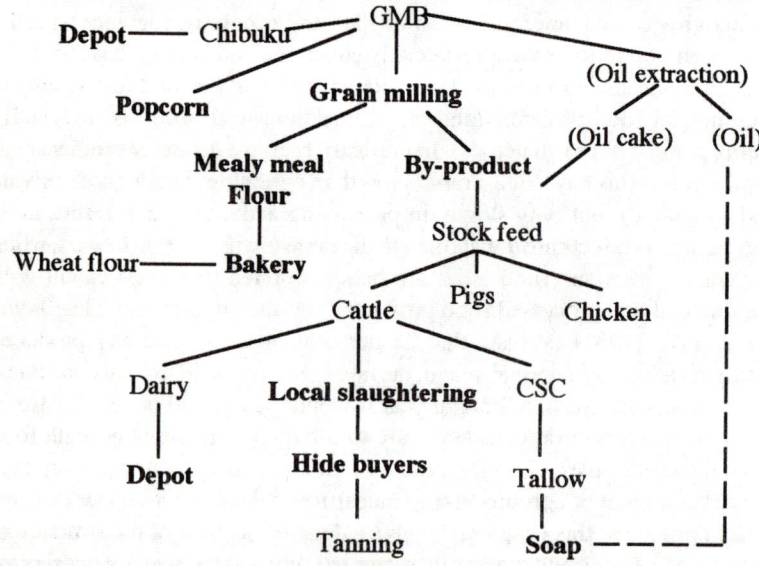

(Activities in bold are local small-town activities)

Figure 7   The structure of the agroprocessing and marketing system in Gutu and Gokwe

Grain and oil seed sub-sector

The grain and oil-seed sub-sector is the largest of the sub-sectors. In 1990 it employed about 100 people in both centres, a few less in Gutu than in Gokwe. This does not include employment by approved buyers, general stores and transporters. They play an important role in the sub-sector, but employment is difficult to isolate and also very seasonal.

Table 11
Agricultural marketing and processing activities in two district service centres in the communal areas of Zimbabwe, 1990

	Gutu			Gokwe		
	Locally owned enterprises	Branches	Total employment[a]	Locally owned enterprises	Branches	Total employment[a]
Grain and oil seed sub-sector						
Grain Marketing Board's depot		1	34		1	48
Small roller mill		1	12		(1)	
Grinding mills	3	1	8	4		6
Bakeries	(1)	1	32	1	1+(1)	53
Confectionery/take-away food	(1)			1		7
Rice-packing and distribution	1		2			
Popcorn production	1		2[b]			
Chibuku depot[c]		1	5			
Oil extraction	(1)					
Subtotal	*5+(3)*	*5*	*93*	*6[a]*	*2+(2)*	*114*
Livestock and dairy sub-sectors						
Butchers	9		18	4		8
Soap factory	1		35	1		6
Hide buyer				1		1
Dairy depot			5	(1)		
Subtotal	*10*	*1*	*58*	*4*	*2+(1)*	*15*
Fruit and vegetable sub-sector						
Market vendors	80		80	75		75
Wholesalers	2		2	1		6
Egg and chicken dealer				1		1
Subtotal	*82*		*82*	*75*	*2*	*82*
Total	**97+(3)**	**6**	**233**	**85**	**6+(3)**	**211**
Total without market vendors	17+(3)	6	153	10	6+(3)	136

Note: Numbers in parentheses show enterprises which are planned but not operating. They are not covered by the employment figures.

a   Permanently employed only. Most of the larger enterprises periodically employ casual workers, at the time of the interview probably around 30–40 in Gutu and 10 in Gokwe.

b   Employment in popcorn production is unknown. It is part of the soap factory and included there.

c   Chibuku is industrially produced traditional beer.

In both centres the depot of the Grain Marketing Board (GMB) is the largest enterprise in the sub-sector. However, in contrast to the national level, where the GMB plays a key role in the sub-sector, the local GMB depots in Gutu and Gokwe have few forward links with the local economy.

Besides the GMB depot, the sub-sector in Gutu consisted of a small commercial roller mill, four small grinding mills, a large bakery, a small popcorn production unit, a rice-packing and distribution enterprise and a depot for Chibuku beer (an industrially produced traditional beer). Another small bakery, a confectionery and an oil-extraction plant were planned. In Gokwe there were two bakeries, one confectionery and four grinding mills in 1990. A third bakery and a small mill to be run as both a commercial and a service mill were under construction.

Although the grain and oil-seed sub-sector is the largest of the agroprocessing and marketing sub-sectors in the two small towns, it is not very well developed when one considers the importance of the production and consumption of grain in the surrounding rural areas. A large part of the grain which is grown in the communal areas is used for subsistence consumption or sold locally to rural households with a grain deficit. Most of the grain which is both grown and consumed in the rural areas is also milled there by small grinding mills. These mills usually do not buy grain, but only perform a service function for local grain-growers. The grinding mills in Gutu and Gokwe perform the same service for grain-growers in the neighbourhood of the centres. Some of the grain consumed in the rural areas is used to brew traditional beer, although industrially produced beer appears increasingly to have taken over throughout the 1980s (Scott, 1995). Only that part of the grain which cannot be consumed or sold locally is sold to the GMB, either directly or through approved or non-approved buyers. How much of the harvest is sold to the GMB depends on the size of the harvest. Jayne and Chisvo (1991) show that in areas with a large grain deficit, most of the grain surplus is sold locally, while a larger share of the grain surplus is sold to the GMB in areas with larger surpluses and smaller deficits. This also means that the GMB receives a larger share of the surplus in good years than in bad years.

The grain bought by the GMB is resold to the large milling companies or other large-scale users in major urban centres. Very little of it is sold locally. In Gokwe, the GMB depot sells almost nothing locally, and in Gutu it only supplies maize to the local roller mill, which receives about 2 per cent of the maize delivered by the GMB depot, and to the very small popcorn production. In turn, the local roller mill supplies mealy meal to the local consumer market. However, it is difficult for it to compete even locally with the large urban milling companies, and it has hardly more than 20–25 per cent of the local market in Gutu centre for industrially processed mealy meal. The local mill also supplies the local bakery with 5–10 per cent maize flour, which it uses to stretch the wheat flour because wheat is often in short supply and more expensive.

All other inputs to the local grain sub-sector are brought in from the outside, wheat and rice because they are not grown in the district, and Chibuku beer because it is no longer produced locally.[1]

Of the oil seeds, cotton is by far the most important in Zimbabwe (see below), but sunflower has been growing rapidly in recent years (Mudimu, 1987; UNIDO, 1988). Sunflowers and groundnuts are grown in both Gutu and Gokwe districts. The production of sunflower has been increasing, especially on the drier lands of Gutu. Most groundnuts are consumed locally; some of them are first processed in the rural areas into peanut butter for local consumption (Makombe, Bernsten and Rorhbach, 1987). No oil extraction took place in either Gutu or Gokwe centres in 1990, but in 1991 oil extraction plants were set up in both centres.

In both grain milling and oil extraction, by-products are produced which play an important role in the production of stockfeed for livestock production. One of the serious consequences of the present lack of local processing is that these by-products – which could play an important role in developing the livestock sector in the communal areas – are transported out of the districts and instead fed into commercial livestock production in the vicinity of the large towns.

Cotton sub-sector

Practically no cotton is grown in Gutu district. In Gokwe district, on the other hand, it plays a large and growing role. However, cotton is grown in Gokwe in the peripheral parts of the district and not in the areas around Gokwe centre. The cotton is collected by the Cotton Marketing Board (CMB) at its depots in the cotton-growing areas and transported to ginneries in Sanyati and Kadoma. Thus the cotton largely bypasses Gokwe centre and has very little impact there.

At the ginnery, the cotton is divided into cotton lint, which goes to the textile industry, and cotton seed, which goes to oil-extraction plants in the large urban centres. In 1990 plans were made to set up a combined ginnery and oil-pressing plant in Gokwe. Employment for 2–300 persons was expected, much of which would be seasonal. By 1992, these plans had expanded into a large textile complex with both textile mill and clothing factories. Such a complex would more than double the population of Gokwe and require large infrastructural investments, first of all a large amount of water, which is not easily available in Gokwe. The government had therefore shelved the plans for the large plant by 1993.

Before structural adjustment, the meat industry was partially controlled by the Cold Storage Commission (CSC), which runs abattoirs in the large towns. The CSC bought most of its cattle from the large commercial farmers and much less from the communal areas. It had a partial monopoly on meat sales to the large towns, but at present the monopoly is heavily undermined by small private abattoirs operating just outside the towns. They buy cattle from farmers near the towns and thus have low costs. Therefore they can pay farmers more than the CSC and still be profitable. The CSC which has been expanding its production capacity rapidly since independence now has a market share of less than 50 per cent and as a result considerable over-capacity. At the same time, at the price level existing before structural adjustment there was a large unsatisfied demand for meat, and the CSC has regularly had to ration its deliveries. It has therefore been very keen on increasing its intake from the communal areas. It operates a livestock development scheme which finances the feeding of cattle from the communal areas for slaughtering.

The CSC is not represented in Gutu or in Gokwe, where meat is sold by a number of small butchers: in 1990 there were nine in Gutu and four in Gokwe. However, these butchers obtain most of their meat from the CSC. They also buy some cattle directly from commercial farmers, but very few from the communal areas, where cattle are generally of low quality. The butchers buy mainly from other sources when the CSC is unable to deliver, which happens regularly.

In addition to butchers, the livestock sub-sector includes soap factories. In Gutu in 1990, there was a relatively large soap producer (its soap production moved to Masvingo in 1994), while the Gokwe producer was very small and mostly out of production. It later closed. The soap factories base their production on tallow and caustic soda. Before trade liberalization tallow was in principle delivered by the CSC, which was, however, often unable to meet demand. Some tallow was imported, but deliveries were uncertain and the soap factories regularly found themselves short of input.

Finally, there is a hide buyer in Gokwe who buys hides from domestic animals for reselling to tanneries in the large towns. In Gutu there is no such enterprise, although mobile buyers travel the district.

Dairy sub-sector

There are no dairies in the communal areas; milk production there is limited and highly seasonal. The milk which is produced is either used for household consumption or sold unprocessed in the local area.

Until the early 1990s, the commercial dairy industry was almost completely dominated by the Dairy Marketing Board (DMB), which runs six industrial dairies in the large towns. It is based on milk produced by only 540 large commercial dairy farmers, of whom 530 are white. Until the 1960s the dairy industry only delivered milk to the low-density white areas of the towns, but as milk production expanded, milk was also marketed in the high-density African urban areas. Since independence, the policy has increasingly been to provide the rural population too with milk. This has led to a change from the production of fresh milk, which requires refrigeration, to sour milk, and to UHT milk with long durability, and recently also to milk powder, which is easier to distribute in rural areas without electricity.

This has also led the DMB to set up depots in a number of the new district service centres. Such a depot existed in Gutu in 1990 (it was closed in 1994) and another opened in Gokwe in 1991. These depots function as wholesale outlets for milk and milk products produced by the DMB. The depots do not actively distribute milk outside the service centres, but they do make it easier for retailers from the rural areas to obtain dairy products.

Since the beginning of the 1980s, the DMB has also operated an experimental dairy development programme for the communal and small-scale commercial farming areas. The DMB's interest in increased milk production has been limited, however, as it already has difficulties selling the milk it receives from the commercial dairy farmers. The programme has later been taken over by the Agricultural and Rural Development Authority (ARDA), and the goal has shifted from milk production to the broader and more farsighted goal of cattle development. At present, the programme is geared only towards the rural market, and it is likely to be a long time before it can deliver milk to the district service centres (NORAD, 1989).

Fruit and vegetable sub-sector

In both Gutu and Gokwe, fruit and vegetables are sold mostly by market vendors in the marketplace, although some general stores and supermarkets also sell them. In both towns, the district councils have built roofed stalls for the market vendors, but especially in Gutu, licensed market vendors also operate outside the stalls. In both towns, the number of licensed vendors is around 75, although there are probably a few more in Gutu. In addition, there are a number of unlicensed vendors who mostly operate in the residential areas.

In Gutu, locally grown fruits and vegetables only make up a limited part of the supply. Most of the fruits and vegetables sold in the market are brought from Harare by bus. Groups of three to five vendors often send a representative to Harare to buy for the whole group. In 1990, a fruit and vegetable wholesaler in Gutu also regularly ferried truckloads of bananas, oranges and other fruits and vegetables into Gutu to sell to the market vendors, and a second wholesaler was about to open. None of the wholesalers had transport of their own, and by 1994 both had closed again. In addition to the wholesalers, a white commercial farmer in Masvingo district regularly brought truckloads of cabbages and other vegetables to the market in Gutu as well as to other centres in the province.

In Gokwe too, many fruits and vegetables are brought in from Harare by the market vendors, or by a wholesale outlet established in 1990 (also closed by 1994). But here local produce covers a larger part of the supply than in Gutu. This is partly because of the climate in Gokwe, which is better for vegetable growing, but the characteristics of the market vendors probably also play an important role. In Gutu, the market vendors are all women, mostly single or divorced women living in the high-density residential area of the town, and without close relations with the potential vegetable growers. In Gokwe, a number of the vendors are male vegetable-growers from the nearby rural areas, and many of the women vendors also grow vegetables themselves. This guarantees a direct link between vendors and growers which does not exist in Gutu. If the local supply of fruits and vegetables to the markets in the district service centres is to increase, these links must obviously be developed. The new vegetable wholesalers in Gutu and Gokwe claimed that this was their long-run intention. At the time of the interviews, however, they were receiving all their supplies from Harare and from commercial farmers. Among the market vendors in both Gutu and Gokwe, there was considerable resentment toward the wholesalers, who were seen as competitors rather than as providing a service.

7.3 Agricultural marketing and processing enterprises: their size, organization, suppliers, markets and competitors

The enterprises in the agricultural marketing and processing sector in Gutu and Gokwe centres are generally small. If we do not include the market vendors, there were in 1990 in the two centres, 38 enterprises altogether in the sector, each employing an average of 7 persons each. Though all the enterprises are relatively small, there is a considerable variation. More than half the enterprises only employ one or two people, while the largest employ 48 (see Table 12). Of the 38 enterprises, 10 are purely marketing and trading enterprises, while 28 have some manufacturing function. Of these, however, 13 are small butchers with very limited processing, and in two of them, manufacturing is limited to packing operations.

About a third of the enterprises are not locally owned but are branches of national or other non-local enterprises. As they are larger than the local enterprises, they cover more than half of the employment. Many even of the locally owned enterprises are not independent, but part of larger conglomerates of local enterprises. This is especially the case for the butchers, which are mostly run together with a general store or supermarket, and often also other enterprises.

Table 12
Size of enterprises in the agricultural marketing and processing sector in two district service centres in Zimbabwe, Gutu and Gokwe (market vendors not included)

Number of employees	Number of enterprises		
	Locally owned	Branches	Total
1	4	2	6
2	19	1	20
5		2	2
6		2	2
7	1		1
12		1	1
17		1	1
32		1	1
34		1	1
35	1		1
36	1		1
48		1	1
Total number of enterprises	26	12	38
Total employment	120	169	289
Average employment	4.6	14.1	7.6

For most of the enterprises in the agricultural marketing and processing sector, the core of their market is either the local urban retailers or local consumers and bus passengers visiting the centre. From here, their market stretches in varying degrees into the rural hinterland. In Gutu, some enterprises also market their goods in neighbouring towns such as Masvingo, Chivhu, Chatsworth and Buhera. This is less the case in Gokwe, which has a more isolated location. Only a few enterprises attempt to reach the national market.

The ability of enterprises to reach both local and more distant markets depends not only on their own internal efficiency, but also on their competition. Competition comes from the large national (or other out-of-town) enterprises which are often better able to secure stable deliveries of scarce production inputs and foreign currency, and which often have a greater transport capacity and are therefore better able to reach the rural market. Competition is also offered by rural processing activities at the household or village level. This competition varies strongly from product to product. Thus grinding mills and rural beer brewing, which are based on local subsistence crops, are very competitive, while rural bakeries and soap production, which are based on non-local inputs often short in supply, generally are not. The ability of local enterprises to compete depends to a large extent on:

–   agricultural marketing and pricing policies;

–   administrative allocation mechanisms for scarce production inputs and foreign currency;

–   access to national economic, administrative and political networks.

7.4   The role of agricultural marketing and pricing policies in small-town processing activities

Until structural-adjustment policies were gradually implemented during the first half of the 1990s, the structure of the agricultural processing and marketing system in Zimbabwe was to a large extent shaped by agricultural marketing and pricing policies.

The staple crops, grains and oil seeds, which comprise the most important production in the communal areas, were regulated through the GMB. Local private trade was legal within the individual communal areas, but all grains and oil seeds sold out of communal areas or traded in the rest of the country had to be sold to the GMB, which bought crops from the farmers at a fixed panseasonal price at their depots and sold them again to large urban millers and other industrial or large-scale users at a fixed but higher selling price at the depot gate. Since independence, the GMB's selling price for maize has been about 15 per cent to 35 per cent higher than the buying price, with a tendency to increase. Although this difference was meant to cover costs, the GMB has had a considerable deficit in most years since independence.

Generally, GMB depots have not sold to local consumers or local traders. Instead, rural households with a grain deficit which could not be satisfied within the rural area have been forced to buy industrially processed mealy meal from the large urban mills. Jayne and Chisvo (1991) estimate that 25 per cent of the industrially processed mealy meal in a normal year has been supplied to rural households with a grain deficit, and that in drought years it has been more than 40 per cent.

This marketing and pricing policy has had two negative consequences for the development of agroprocessing in the small towns. First, it has made it very difficult for the small commercial mills to compete with the large urban mills. In milling as in most other agricultural processing, there are considerable scale economies in the processing itself. A small mill may still be able to compete because it has lower collection and distribution costs. However, with GMB's fixed selling price the small mill has not been able to exploit these lower costs. Indirectly, the fixed selling price has given the large millers a subsidy on their collection costs.

Secondly, the marketing and pricing policy has tended to keep the communal areas in a semi-subsistence economy because it has made it much more attractive to grow crops for subsistence than for the market, and very expensive for households with a grain deficit to buy supplementary food. In 1989–90 the GMB's producer price was 215 Z$ per tonne of maize, of which 15–30 Z$ should be deducted for transport, depending on the distance to the nearest GMB depot. On the other hand, the value of crops for subsistence, including the cost of local grinding (which was about 50 Z$ a tonne), must be set equal to the cost of the alternative, namely industrial mealy meal, which in 1989–90 was more than 450 Z$ depending on quality. Thus the substitution value of subsistence crops was about 400 Z$ or about double the price of marketed maize.

This large price difference would make it very difficult for urban processing industries to compete in the rural areas had they not enjoyed a virtual monopoly. It also made the rural processing of semi-subsistence crops such as service milling and rural beer-brewing more competitive than they otherwise would have been.

Similar centralizing processes as those described here for grain milling have existed for oil extraction, which are even more centralized than commercial grain milling.

7.5   The role of ministerial allocation mechanisms for scarce production inputs and foreign currency

Two of the main difficulties in developing of new enterprises in the district service centres have been:

–   insufficient allocations of scarce production inputs from the parastatals and other government controlled sectors (for example, tallow from the CSC, wheat and rice from the GMB);

–   a lack of foreign currency for the import of capital equipment and production inputs.

Such allocations are made by the Ministries of Commerce, Industry and Finance. Although considerable effort has been made to make allowances for small enterprises, administrative allocation procedures tend in general to favour large enterprises which are more stable and easier to identify than the many small enterprises which come and go, grow and decline. Small enterprises may well get into the allocation systems, but the systems tend to change slowly, and growing enterprises are likely to have their allocation increased only after considerable delay.

In sectors dependent on scarce inputs, such as bakeries and soap factories, it has generally been difficult to run small enterprises. In such sectors, rural enterprises have in general not been profitable, and in small towns, branches of national companies have had much better chances to obtain sufficient raw materials than independent local enterprises.

The other key problem is the allocation of foreign currency for investments in decentralized production capacity. Many of the large-scale industries, whether private or parastatal, have had a large unused capacity. There has therefore been an understandable reluctance to allocate scarce foreign currency to the establishment of new decentralized production capacity, although such new capacity might be more efficient and save foreign currency in the transport sector.

The central position of the administrative allocation systems has generally meant that branch enterprises and private entrepreneurs with close ties to either large enterprises or the national political-administrative system have had much greater prospects of success than local entrepreneurs.

7.6 Feedback between farmers and agricultural processing in small towns

Many balances must be secured if national agricultural production is to function efficiently. Different crops and livestock must be balanced with agricultural resources. Farmers must have a secure market for their products, and processing industries must have the necessary inputs to utilize their production capacity efficiently. Urban consumers must have the necessary supply to satisfy their demand. The agricultural development authorities and the marketing boards were originally established to secure some of these balances at the national level, and in Zimbabwe throughout the years both before and after independence, they have done this with considerable success. Seen from a rural and small-town perspective, however, the system has been problematic.

Since independence, agricultural development policies have succeeded in increasing the marketed production of maize and other crops delivered to the processing industries in the large towns, but they have still left many rural

120

areas with large grain deficits. At the same time, there have been few attempts to diversify agricultural production and marketing channels in the communal areas in order for communal farmers to take advantage of the growing food market in the communal areas. This local market, where the local farmer has a clear locational advantage, has therefore mostly been supplied at high cost with food from the large towns.

As we saw above, marketing and pricing policies have at the same time supported the strong centralization of the processing industries inherited from the colonial era. They have also led to a heavy extraction of agricultural resources from the communal areas, destroying the balance between crop and livestock production there. In the milling industry, maize is divided into mealy meal and a 20–30 per cent by-product, depending on the refinement of the meal. In oil extraction, the oil seed is divided into consumer oil and oil cake, which corresponds to 50–70 per cent of the original oil seed. These by-products, often together with other additives, are used in the production of stockfeed. As most of the maize and oil seed has been processed in the large towns, stockfeed production has also taken place there. Even some of the by-products from the roller mill in Gutu have been transported to Harare to go into stockfeed production there. Stockfeed is sold to livestock and dairy farmers, mainly as chicken- and pig-feed and supplementary cattle-feed. Stockfeed is a relatively cheap product which is very sensitive to transport costs. The price of stockfeed therefore increases rapidly with the distance from the large towns. Consequently, most stockfeed is sold to large commercial livestock and dairy farmers near the large towns.

Both prices and transport-cost allowances have been highly controlled in the grain sector. Thus the milling companies have been allowed to add a fixed transport allowance to their price of mealy meal corresponding to a transport distance of about 60–80 km. For stockfeed, however, the transport allowance has increased with distance to 46.80 Z$ a tonne at distances above 196 km. This means that the price of stockfeed in most communal areas becomes prohibitive. This has favoured livestock and dairy production close to the large towns, and constrained livestock production in the communal areas.

Of course, there are many other reasons for the failure to develop the livestock sector in the communal areas. Livestock here serve mainly as draft animals and savings, and will never be able to produce as much meat and milk as livestock on commercial farms. But if the maize (50,000 tonnes) and oil seed which are transported out of Gutu district each year were processed in Gutu and the by-product channelled to local chicken, pigs and cattle at marginal costs, this would obviously make a great difference.

According to Sunga *et al.*'s (1990) investigation of 759 communal farmers, the total herd of 3,280 cattle produced in one year 432 cattle for sale and 447 cattle for slaughter, while 1,248 cattle simply died of old age, illness, hunger or drought. Only 11 per cent of farmers purchased stockfeed. These figures indicate that even a marginal effort might be enough to improve the livestock situation to the extent that more cattle in the communal areas could be sold or slaughtered before they die.

7.7 The development of agricultural marketing and processing since 1990: the effect of structural adjustment and drought

Since 1990 the agroprocessing and marketing sector has undergone a series of dramatic changes, due partly to structural adjustment policies and increased liberalization of the sector, and partly to the drought of 1991–92 and the drought relief measures then introduced. These shifting policies have led to large-scale restructuring of the agroprocessing industries, a restructuring which has also had its effect on the small towns.

The devaluations and import liberalizations carried out as part of the structural adjustment policies initiated in 1990 started a series of price increases which were not followed by similar increases in wage levels (see Table 13; also Chipika, 1993a), and therefore led to falling real wages in the urban areas and consequently to a reduced flow of remittances to the rural areas. The severe drought of 1991–92 led to further price increases, especially on food, and reduced both money incomes and subsistence crops in the rural areas. As a result, consumer demand for many industrial goods fell dramatically, while at the same time the supply of inputs to the agroprocessing industry fell. This led in turn to a large drop in manufacturing employment during the drought, especially in clothing and agroprocessing. The longer term reduction in total formal urban employment appears so far to have been more limited, though serious enough in an economy with a rapidly growing labour force. The result has been a shift in the pattern of consumption. Clothing and other non-food consumer goods were replaced with food, and luxury food such as meat and bread with the most basic staple food, maize meal.

In Gutu and Gokwe, bakery sales dropped below half of 1991 sales, and production in general went down from 3 shifts to only 1 or 2 shifts. Although the harvest in 1993 was reasonably good, bread sales did not increase because prices continued to rise. In addition, the difficulties of two of the independent bakeries in Gokwe also appear to be caused by an acute lack of working capital, which means that they cannot buy sufficient flour. As a result, they have been working irregularly and at low capacity utilization. The weak market also means that they have to go further afield to sell bread, so that their distribution costs have risen, and competition with bakeries in neighbouring towns has increased. But there were apparently no problems in obtaining flour. While larger industrial bakeries have had difficulties, new small bakeries and confectionaries have been established in both town centres. They are mostly based on the sale of fresh bread within the town centre itself and also operate as cafeterias.

Table 13
Indexes for the development of consumer prices, urban wages and urban employment

	1990	1991	1992	1993
Consumer price index	100	123	175	224
Food	100	113	193	267
Clothing	100	123	162	186
Earnings in urban formal employment, total	100	108	133	152
Earnings in manufacturing industries	100	117	141	168
Formal urban employment, total	1000	1044	1037	1016
Employment in manufacturing industries	1000	1042	1000	952

Source: Quarterly Digest of Statistics, October, 1994. Harare: General Statistical Office.

Meat sales also dropped dramatically in 1992, and a number of small butchers appear to have closed. Sales did not increase much in 1993, not only because prices continued to increase, but also because the CSC had little meat to sell. Thus in 1993, the CSC ceased to deliver meat to Gokwe. At the same time, since it became difficult to buy cattle in the communal areas after the drought, most of the butchers that stayed open belonged to businessmen with cattle farms of their own. The CSC's increasing difficulties in delivering meat are not only caused by the drought but also by market liberalization, which has allowed the establishment of private abattoirs. In a few years, these have been able to buy a rapidly increasing share of the cattle sold for slaughtering by commercial farmers. As a result, the CSC's market share is now less than 50 per cent (Chipika, 1993a). Part of the fall in meat sales was caused by a shift in consumption to fish, which is cheaper. Since the drought, therefore, a number of traders have started to sell dried fish from Kariba and more recently also fish imported from Namibia.

In spite of structural adjustment and drought, the DMB has been operating without a deficit and has been one of the first parastatals to be privatized. However, in Gutu the DMB closed its depot in response to reduced milk consumption. ARDA NORAD-supported small-scale dairy projects also appear to have fared fairly well during the drought.

Although vegetable sales also must have decreased during the drought, the number of market traders with licences did not go down. But repeated attempts in the early 1990s to establish vegetable and fruit wholesalers in both Gutu and Gokwe to supply the market have all failed.

Although the consumption of more expensive food items went down, the sale of mealy meal exploded in 1992 after the drought, because few people in the rural area had grain supplies of their own. The grain which was imported as drought relief was distributed through the large milling companies, which were also administering the consumer subsidy on maize. As a consequence, the large roller mills and those small commercial mills which were able to get grain, were working at full speed to meet the demand, and general stores and supermarkets in the small towns were busy distributing mealy meal. The small roller mill in Gutu, which had been bought in 1991 by an African businessman, also got its share of subsidized maize and worked three shifts throughout 1992, while the small service mills had little to do.

In 1993, when the first crop after the drought was harvested, the maize subsidy was withdrawn and the grain trade gradually liberalized. This immediately led to large increases in grain prices and to a shift in demand away from industrially processed mealy meal toward raw maize, which consumers then had milled in small service mills. In Harare and other large cities, growing grain on open urban land, which was not tolerated before the drought, now became accepted (Drakakis-Smith, 1994). The transport of grain out of the communal areas by private traders and individuals became legal, and GMB depots became more open and expanded their sales of grain to local traders and individuals. A growing private market for raw maize developed in both rural and urban areas. The number of small service mills expanded, especially in the urban areas (Jayne and Rubey, 1993), and the production of the large urban mills fell dramatically. As a result, the large milling companies have closed a number of their roller mills in the provincial towns.

The 18–20 small commercial hammer mills (including the mills in Gutu and Gokwe) which were established during the late 1980s and early 1990s, partly with support from a couple of NGOs, used a technology which made it possible for them to operate both as service mills and as commercial mills (Chipika, 1993b). They now benefited from their greater flexibility and were able to get their share of the growing demand for service milling. As commercial mills, however, they ran into increasing difficulties, meeting stiff competition and a number of rather monopolistic trading practices by the large milling companies. The market share of these companies was rapidly declining, but they still had much better resources than the small local mills. Interviews with the small millers indicate some of the measures that the large milling companies use to compete with the small:

–   they offer retailers better credit facilities than the small millers are usually able to do;

– they operate with bonded sales. The larger millers operate as wholesalers not only in mealy meal, but also in a whole range of groceries, apparently threatening retailers with stopping delivery if they buy local mealy meal at a lower price than their own. The small local mills are therefore not able to compete on price;

– they try to buy up maize from GMB depots near the small mills so that the latter are unable to get any maize.

As a result, those small mills which do best as commercial millers are those which have their own retail or wholesale distribution or which have been able to develop a local institutional market (schools, hospitals, army barracks etc.)

At the same time as the small commercial mills were being established, a number of small oil extraction plants were set up in Gutu and Gokwe and other district service centres. However, in 1992, following the drought, problems arose due to a lack of oil seeds, and most of them had to stop production for a period. The increased availability of oil seeds in 1993 has in general not solved their problems. They seem to be up against the same type of competition from the large companies as the small mills and suffer from the same lack of working capital.

Although in principle both small millers and oil processors are now able to buy grain and oil seeds from local farmers at a much lower price than the GMB's producer price, most of them still prefer to buy from the GMB, where they can get credit and in addition distribute their purchases over the year. If they bought from communal farmers, they would have to pay cash right after harvest. In other cases, the small oil processors buy from the GMB because the local supply of oil seeds is insufficient and unstable.

In the long run, oil processors appear to have better prospects than small commercial millers because they operate on an expanding market, while the market for commercial milling has been shrinking. However, the profitability of both markets may well depend on their ability to collaborate on the use of their by-products in stockfeed production for a local market. Some of the more profitable enterprises therefore run a mill, an oil press, stockfeed production, and a piggery or chicken farm where the stockfeed can be used (Chipika, 1993b). Since the drought, there appears to have been an increasing market, especially for chicken- and pig-feed. This development in the market for stockfeed in the communal areas will be important for the development of small-scale commercial milling and oil-extraction.

Although in general the agricultural processing sector was hit hard by the drought of 1992, small-town activities in the sector appear to be picking up since then. Employment in the sector in early 1995 does not appear to be much lower than in 1990. The roller mill in Gutu has closed, but the small commercial mill and oil press which started just before the drought are still there, and a new small bakery has opened. The old bakery, which expanded its capacity just before the drought, is not able to utilize that expanded capacity, but it is still running with almost the same number of employees as in 1990. In Gokwe, the small mill which opened just before the drought was still closed in 1993, but that was apparently due to the death of the owner as much as to the market situation. The general stores and food traders were in general hit less hard by the drought than might have been expected because to a large extent they were able to shift from more expensive to cheaper food items.

Since the drought, the liberalization of grain marketing has resulted in a massive shift in demand from industrial mealy meal to raw maize milled on small service mills, and many of the traders who used to sell mealy meal now distribute raw maize instead. In the long run, the small commercial mills and oil presses are also likely to benefit from liberalization, although a lack of working capital makes it impossible at present for them to exploit benefits fully. Thus although they are surviving, small-town businessmen in general are disappointed with structural adjustment policies, which have not lived up to their generally positive expectations. These policies have made access to forex and imported goods easier, but they have also led to increased prices, higher interest rates and a shrinking market, which make it impossible for them to grow as they had hoped.

Note

1   A small white-owned Chibuku brewery existed in Gutu before independence.

8 The clothing sector in the district service centres

8.1 The clothing sector in the national economy

The clothing industry is an important manufacturing sector in Zimbabwe. Since a low point in 1984, when the sector employed about 15,000 people, it has been growing rapidly both on the domestic and export markets. According to Riddell (1990b), 10–15 per cent of domestic production is exported.

In December 1991 the formal industry consisted of 240 enterprises (with more than 5 employees) with a total of 24,000 employees. Employment was strongly concentrated, however, as 22,000 were employed in those 73 enterprises which were members of the Zimbabwe Clothing Council. These 73 enterprises thus had an average workforce of about 300, while the rest of the formal industry only had an average of 12. Only about 30 of the enterprises were exporters, and 10 of the largest enterprises were responsible for over 80 per cent of exports (Riddell, 1990a).

In addition to these organized industries, there are according to Riddell (1990b:45) '600 informal sector operators employing less than 30 employees' which are 'responsible for about 20 per cent of the total domestic production'. However, these 600 informal operators only make up the top of the informal sector. The Gemini survey (McPherson, 1991) reported that in 1991 there were an estimated 170,000 small enterprises (with less than 50 employees) in the clothing sector (tailoring, dressmaking and knitting) with an average workforce of less than 1.5 and thus a total workforce of around 250,000. However, the great majority of those employed are probably working only part-time. Little is known about the productivity and production of these small enterprises, but the average is surely very much lower than in the large-scale industry (see, e.g., Mugambiwa, 1989).

More than 90 per cent of those employed in the small-scale sector are women, while less than 40 per cent of the workers in the larger industry are women.[1] Since the end of 1991, employment in the clothing sector is said to have dropped by more than 30 per cent, and many enterprises have gone into liquidation due to the combination of structural adjustment policies and the drought (Zimbabwe Press Mirror, 1992).

Of the formal clothing industries, the majority are located in the urban areas. According to the 1988–89 census of production, 86 per cent of total employment in the sector was located in Harare and Bulawayo alone. Of the small-scale sector, about half is located in the rural areas (McPherson, 1991).

In addition to these manufacturing enterprises, there are also a large number of retail and wholesale businesses in the clothing sector. According to the Gemini survey, there are around 30,000 small clothing venders and retailers in the country, about one-third in the rural areas. However, especially during the last half of the 1980s, a number of large national and regional retail chains have spread networks of branch stores all over the country (see, e.g., Zinyama, 1990), and they are responsible for a large part of the retail trade. As a result of the dominance of the large manufacturing enterprises and retail chains, which tend to trade directly with each other, the wholesale sector is not very well developed and mainly serves small rural shops.

It is within this general trend that the clothing sector in the district service centres, and more specifically in Gutu and Gokwe, has developed. The account of this development to be presented in this chapter is based on fieldwork carried out in March, 1992 at a time when the impact of the 1992 drought was feared but not yet felt. The two towns were later visited in November to December, 1993, and Gutu also in January, 1995.

8.2   The structure of the clothing sector in Gutu and Gokwe

Retail trade

The supply of clothing to the small-town market is dominated by the retail trade, and local production plays a relatively minor role. The retail sector is dominated by the branches of large national and regional retail chains. In Gutu there are about 10 chain stores, and in Gokwe even more. However, there are also locally owned clothing shops, and many general stores sell some clothes and fabrics. Finally, a little is sold in the small open-air market, mostly pieces of cloth and low-quality dresses. Some of the branch stores specialize in clothes only, but many of them have a second speciality line, e.g. furniture, enamel kitchenware, shoes and records, towels and bedspreads, blankets and suitcases, or fabric and buttons.

There is a certain segmentation of the market, according to both income groups and types of clothes. Most chain stores cater to middle-income groups, but even so there is a visible difference between stores catering primarily to rural customers and others catering to more 'urban' customers, mostly civil

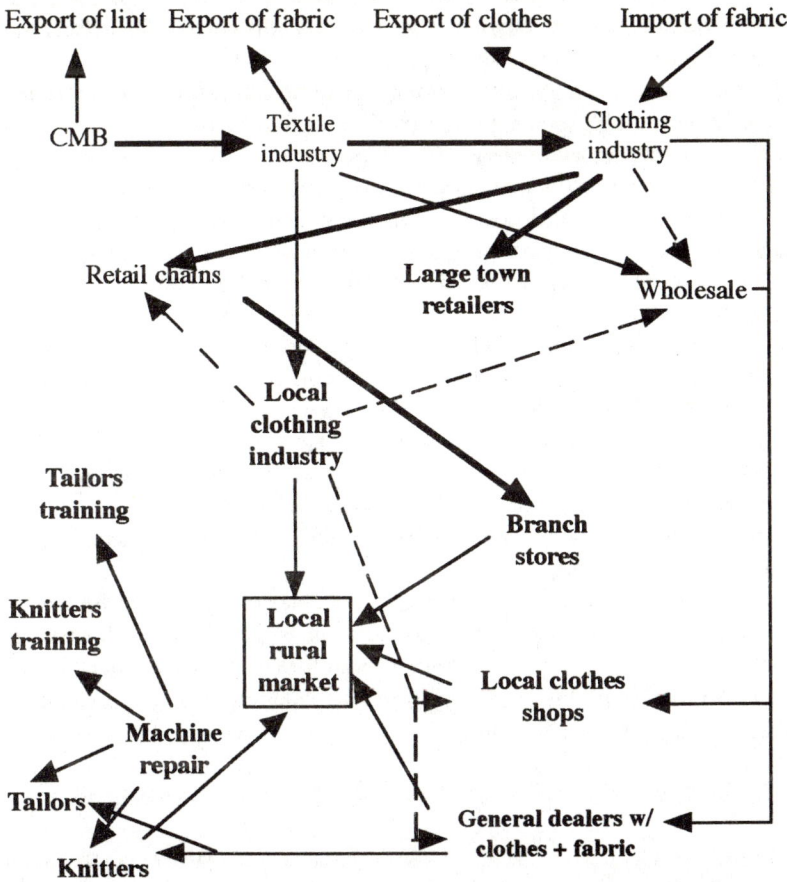

Export of lint   Export of fabric   Export of clothes   Import of fabric

CMB → Textile industry → Clothing industry

Retail chains   Large town retailers   Wholesale

Local clothing industry

Tailors training

Knitters training

Branch stores

Local rural market   Local clothes shops

Machine repair

Tailors

Knitters

General dealers w/ clothes + fabric

(Activities in bold letters are local small town activities)

Figure 8   The structure of the clothing sector in Gutu and Gokwe

servants. Some of the large chains operate with uniform prices all over the country, others with uniform prices except in Harare, where they tend to be cheaper. In general, chain stores do not give credit, but many of them 'lay-by', which typically means that the customer pays over three months but only receives the goods when they are fully paid. Some chains advertise nationally on radio or television. In Gokwe (which has a higher income level than Gutu) a few of the chain stores cater especially to high-income groups (civil servants and traders), selling higher quality goods at higher prices and typically giving credit. In Gutu, some of the locally owned shops perform this service. Many of the general stores and smaller locally owned shops cater mostly to middle- or low-income groups. In order to compete, they often give credit to known and trusted customers.

School uniforms are an important market segment which most shops try to serve, but in which one chain in particular has specialized. This chain has branch stores in both Gutu and Gokwe. It sells school uniforms and sports clothes of relatively high quality and high price. It tries to sell directly through the schools through campaigns and student competitions.

A special small market currently developing is the market for sports clothes. In Gokwe a very small retailer has specialized in sports clothes, which it tries to sell both to individuals and through schools and sports clubs. In Gutu, a new large book-binding enterprise with 30 employees rebinds old books for the schools and as a sideline prints school names and logos on T-shirts for the schools' sports teams.

The chain stores are supplied with almost all goods from their head offices. Local managers usually have no competence to buy on their own, although in the small regional chains especially they seem to have more room to suggest purchases of local products. Locally owned shops and general stores are mostly supplied by wholesalers and producers in the larger towns, although some of them, especially those catering to the low-income market, are supplied directly from small workshops, often through family relations in the larger towns.

Partly due to the dominant position of the chain stores, clothing wholesalers are not very well developed and mostly operate in the rural areas. Even here, the larger shops can often buy directly from the producer, and many of the smaller retail chains are in fact partly producer outlets for small or medium-sized clothing factories.

Clothing production and repair

Clothing production in the small centres consists of knitters, tailors and a few larger workshops which could be called industrial.

In Gutu there are three larger clothes-making workshops with 5, 15–20 and 30–35 employees, respectively. Their most important market is school uniforms. The smallest of the three (established in 1988) produces mostly school uniforms, but also dresses which are sold retail from the workshop. It does not attempt to secure larger orders, because with its present size it would not be able to fill them. The two largest workshops both attempt to reach other markets as well, because the market for school uniforms is highly seasonal. However, it is difficult for them to get into the local retail market because it is dominated by chain stores which have no competence to buy locally. In order to get into the local market, both large workshops have established their own retail outlets in Gutu centre (one of them also has an outlet in Buhera centre about 60 km away) and have salesmen travelling in the rural areas. However, the local market is not sufficient for either of the two enterprises and both attempt to develop specialities which can bring them into a larger regional or national market. This is made difficult by the lack of a well-developed wholesale sector.

The largest of the workshops, which at the time of fieldwork had only been in operation for eight weeks, had not yet developed clear product specialization, but tried to produce women's dresses of sufficiently high quality to be acceptable to the national retail chains. It started production just before the consumer market collapsed in 1992 due to the drought and structural adjustment, and was therefore not able to gain entry to the chain-store market to any great extent. Instead, like the other clothing producer in Gutu, it has ventured into the market for work clothes. It has also done some sub-contracting work for larger enterprises and in spite the crisis has apparently been doing quite well.

The second largest enterprise was established in 1985 as a shop selling off-cut fabrics from the wholesalers. It only started production in 1987 because some customers wanted the fabrics they bought to be tailored as well. The enterprise expanded to its present size in 1991. It has been diversifying from school uniforms into protective work clothes printed with company names for the enterprise market in Harare and other large towns and for the mines. It has been an advantage in this market that the large producers with which the workshop competes have often been so busy in export markets that they have long delivery times in the home market.

In addition to the three clothes-making workshops, there is the book-binding enterprise already mentioned, which does cotton-printing of school names and logos on T-shirts for school sports teams. It was established in 1990. This enterprise focuses primarily on the school market, but it can compete at least potentially on the cotton-printing market with the producer of work clothes, which also does cotton-printing.

In Gokwe, there are so far no larger clothes-making workshops. However, one of the largest industrial corporations in the country plans to establish a large textile complex in Gokwe based on the growth in cotton production in the district. The complex was originally supposed to comprise a ginnery, oil mill, spinning, weaving and potentially also clothing industries. Fully developed, this project would double the population of Gokwe centre. However, due to insufficient supplies of water and electricity the government has apparently proposed that only the ginnery and oil mill should be located in Gokwe, while the textile industry should be located in Kwekwe instead. There have also been competing plans for a smaller ginnery and oil mill in Gokwe proposed by a high-ranking civil servant from the district.

The small tailoring businesses running in the centres are mostly one-person enterprises run by men.[2] Some of them have rented a shop or part of one, while others are located on rented shop verandas. They do mostly repair work, but some of them also produce school uniforms. There are about five of these small tailors in both Gutu and Gokwe. They have no employees and mostly no apprentices (although some are training their own children or nephews). But at the time of the survey (March, 1992) one tailor in Gutu had recently started a six-month training programme with six paying apprentices, and more have plans to take on paying apprentices.

In addition to the independent tailors, some of the local shops selling clothes employ a tailor who mostly fits industrial clothing to customer size. Some of the knitting enterprises also do some dressmaking (see below). One woman in Gutu runs a small retail shop where she sells women's and children's dresses produced by two young women, and also secondhand clothes. In addition, she runs a hairdressing salon, while her husband has a dry-cleaning outlet. In Gokwe, one woman tailor specializes in bedspreads and cushions, while a man produces travel bags.

The small knitting enterprises which produce jerseys and sweaters on knitting machines are all run by women. In total, there are more than 15 knitting enterprises in Gutu centre but only half as many in Gokwe. Including the owner/manager, they employ from one to four people. The market for knitwear is highly seasonal, concentrated in the few winter months, and few of the women can afford to produce stock for the rest of the year. In order to counteract the seasonality of the market, some combine knitting with dressmaking, and many take in two to six paying apprentices at a time, who are typically trained over a three-month period. A few also run hairdressing salons, one together with her husband's radio, TV and watch-repair business. In Gutu, many small knitting enterprises are run by the wives of the larger general dealers in the centre on the shop premises. Knitwear is mostly sold from the shop or through saleswomen travelling in the rural areas. Only one of the enterprises interviewed in Gokwe sells some of its production through other retailers.

Finally, in Gutu (in the industrial area) there is a small (white-owned) general store cum day-old chicken seller cum pay-library, which also sells embroidery and knitwear, e.g. tablecloths, bedspreads and cushion covers. The products are produced by an embroidery business based on homework and run by a white woman, employing thirteen women working in their rural homes. She delivers the material, pays the work at a piece rate, and sells the product through the shop in Gutu and another shop in Masvingo.

In general, it seems to be easier for the small-scale knitters to compete with the retail sector than it is for the small tailors. The obvious reason for this is that the small knitters often produce jerseys of a similar or even better quality than the large industries, while the quality produced by the small tailors is usually lower. The tailors therefore have to compete on price to a much larger extent than the knitters. On the other hand, only a small proportion of the small tailors, dressmakers and knitters work in the business centre. Many more, especially women dressmakers and knitters, are likely to work from home. Thus the fact that some disappear from the centre may mean not that they have closed, but that they have moved their business to their home to save rent.

Both the large clothing workshops and the small tailors buy most of the fabric they use directly from the factories. Here, prices are often only half the prices in the local shops. On the other hand, for small tailors buying only small amounts of fabric, the time and cost of going to the factory is considerable. Consequently, they often depend on family members living near the factory to do the buying. In addition, textile factories do not usually give credit. This is a problem for the large workshops because their large buyers often require 30 days' credit. The small tailors all pay cash and mostly also sell for cash, although some of them do give credit to people they know (mostly 50 per cent down and the rest over two months).

In general, there are no difficulties in getting material, except sometimes imported synthetic fabric. However, there sometimes appears to be difficulty in getting material locally. The largest of the workshops has a forex allocation permitting it to buy imported material. When the workshops work for the large chains, these will sometimes deliver the imported material from their forex allocation. Small tailors often work on material bought by the customer.

Wool for the knitting businesses is either bought from local wholesalers or from wholesalers in the larger towns (in Gutu, from Harare; in Gokwe, from Kwekwe or Gweru). However, prices are much higher locally than in the larger towns, so people mostly buy locally when they buy small amounts. The price difference appears to be especially large in Gokwe, where one of the knitting enterprises has started to sell wool to the other knitters. In Gutu, the price difference seems to be smaller and more of the wool seems to be bought locally. However, here some of the knitting enterprises run by the wives of large businessmen are able to buy directly from the factories. Some of them even obtain credit, though most have to pay cash. Still, many knitting businesses do sell on credit. There are in general no difficulties in obtaining wool.

Dressmaking and knitting schools

In addition to the training in tailoring and knitting that takes place in the small production enterprises, a number of enterprises, especially in Gutu and to a smaller extent in Gokwe, offer training on a larger scale in dressmaking and knitting. These training centres are all run by women, mostly as private enterprises, but some are run by churches or cooperatives.

In Gutu, one private knitting school offers a three-month course in knitting for up to 45 trainees at a time, and four dressmaking schools (two private, one run by a church and one cooperative located six kilometres from Gutu Centre) offer a six-month course in dressmaking with the possibility of another six months in design and pattern-making. In Gokwe, only two schools (both church-run) offer similar dressmaking courses. The knitting school in Gutu had already started in 1973, while the dressmaking schools were started during the 1980s. Their capacity increased during the late 1980s. Altogether, at the beginning of 1992, the training capacity is estimated to have been around 150 knitters and 300 dressmakers in Gutu, and 25–30 knitters and 40 dressmakers in Gokwe in a normal year. Due to the drought many fewer were actually being trained during 1992, especially in Gutu.

Most of the trainees from these small training schools get jobs in small workshops, mostly in Harare, Bulawayo or the larger provincial towns, and until the drought of 1992 apparently with little difficulty. Very few start directly on their own because it requires both experience and capital to invest in a sewing or knitting machine. Still, many of the small knitting businesses and some of the tailoring and dressmaking businesses in Gutu and Gokwe are run by people trained locally.

The large industrial enterprises say that they cannot use trainees from the small training schools. They have their own internal training and claim that most of the trainees from the small training schools are not qualified even for this. One of the problems is that the small training schools operate with old household sewing machines which are much slower than the large machines used in industry.

The large enterprises recruit their workers from the smaller workshops and apparently have had no difficulty in finding qualified candidates, although employment in the industry has been growing rapidly during the second half of the 1980s. This indicates a career pattern in which trainees from the small training schools work some years in the small workshops. Many of them leave work when they get married, some start on their own, and others advance to the better paid jobs in the formal industry.[3] Thus although large industry does not find the small training schools satisfactory, the schools may play an important role not only in developing the small enterprise sector, but also in creating a recruiting base for the large enterprises.

Although neither of the two larger workshops in Gutu thinks very highly of the local training schools, they have employed a few people trained there. In general, however, they have had to train people themselves or employ people with several years of factory training. One of the workshops advertised nationally for people with at least two years' factory training and received 200 replies. Most of the people working in the two workshops come originally from Gutu or neighbouring districts.

Machine repair services

The newest element in the clothing complex in Gutu was a one-man 'Machine Centre' offering repair services for knitting and sewing machines and typewriters. The owner was originally trained in South Africa, but had worked independently since 1980 in different towns in Zimbabwe. He had worked in Gutu since 1985, but first established a small shop in 1992 (shared with a small local security firm). He had two trainees who were supposed to be in training for 1 1/2 years. Most of his customers were from Gutu centre, but some also from elsewhere, although in January 1992 he said he had enough business in Gutu. He served both the local businesses and private households. Earlier, some travelling repair men came to Gutu, but they could not compete with the local repair shop. Among the 15 enterprises interviewed in Gutu which could use his services, one-third said they did so, one-third said they or their husbands did their own repair work, and the remaining third had it done elsewhere, mostly in Masvingo. He sometimes had difficulty getting spare parts. He bought them in Bulawayo, where he could stay with his brother, whereas most of the knitting or tailoring businesses that buy their own spare parts go to Masvingo or Harare. He must have been hard hit by the crisis in the clothing sector; by 1995, he had closed his business and left town.

In Gokwe, where there is no local repair business, the tailors interviewed do the repair work themselves, while the knitters have a repair man who comes from Harare, Chegutu or Gweru. As they have to cover his travel costs themselves, some knitters try to order him at the same time so that they can share them.

8.3   Enterprises, entrepreneurs and managers in the clothing sector in Gutu and Gokwe

The headquarters of most retail chains are located in Harare or Bulawayo, but some of the chain stores in Gutu are branches of Mondera enterprises, and in Gokwe of enterprises in Kwekwe or Kadoma. They were all established between 1986 and 1991. Most of the national chains have white management, and at least one is foreign-owned (South African). Many of the regional chains are owned by Asian businessmen, only a few, mainly producer outlets for medium-sized clothing workshops, being owned by black businessmen. However, all the local branch managers are black and often very young (22–32 years old), mostly men (only two out of eleven interviewed were women) with a Form 4 or O-level exam, who after a few years training in the enterprise have been appointed branch managers. Their decision competence is quite limited. Few of them feel that they are part of the local business community, or that it would be possible for them to start their own enterprise. Some do, however, and a few others have quite definite plans to do so.

Almost all the branch stores are run from rented premises, although some of the chains are now planning to build shops of their own after it has become possible to obtain a title deed on land in the centres.

The local independent shop owners are in general much older (40–60 years) or in a few cases young second-generation owners. In Gokwe, however, some of the independent shops are owned by people living elsewhere and run by a manager who is often related to the owner. The creation of a job for a younger family member appears to be an important consideration behind some of these enterprises.

The relatively high age of business owners partly reflects the fact that many of the independent shops are older than the branches, but it also reflects how difficult it is to borrow the money to start a business. For most people, a new business has to be based either on their own savings or on money borrowed from or invested by other family members. Accumulating enough money can take a long time.

The chain stores play a larger role in Gokwe than in Gutu. The reason for this is to be found in the history of the two centres. Gutu is older than Gokwe. It has developed slowly since the 1950s and was already of a considerable size at the time of independence. As a result, Gutu has a number of large local businessmen who have had up to 30 to 40 years to accumulate and develop their businesses. By contrast, Gokwe was still a very small centre at the time of independence, with only a few local businessmen to take advantage of the rapidly growing market during the 1980s. But in Gokwe the market has been growing even more rapidly than in Gutu. This has attracted both retail chains and small businessmen from all over Zimbabwe. Thus while the local businessmen in Gutu are local people from the centre or its hinterland, many of the small businessmen in Gokwe are migrants or people living elsewhere who invest in Gokwe and often employ young family members.

Successful local businessmen in both Gutu and Gokwe have diversified from the original general stores into more specialized shops and services (e.g. restaurants, hotels, taxis, and real estate). In each of the two centres, one of the old businessmen owns a number of business premises which are rented out to other businessmen or branch stores. With very few exceptions, local businessmen have not invested in production enterprises.

The two large clothing workshops set up in Gutu have both been established by academic researchers (one at a parastatal research institute and the other at the University of Zimbabwe) who work in Harare in areas which have no immediate relevance for the clothing industry. However, originally both come from Gutu district and both have qualified family members involved in the daily management of the enterprise. One has, as foreman and cutter, two brothers with long experience in the industry, one as foreman in a clothing factory in Bulawayo, and the other as owner of a general store and a small school-uniform workshop in the rural area of Gutu. The other has as his daily manager a young cousin who has worked in the enterprise since it was started in 1985, later following a training course in business management in Harare.

Although one of the enterprises was already established in 1985, they both took advantage of the creation of the Zimbabwe Investment Centre in 1989 to apply for investment permission and forex allocation in order to establish and expand their clothing workshop in Gutu. In both cases, the projects were approved very rapidly (in one case within a month), while it took much longer to acquire the machinery and start production. The smaller of the two workshops built its present two-storey building in Gutu centre between March and October 1991, only then acquiring the new machinery (one cutting machine and 18 Japanese electric sewing machines). The second workshop was originally planned to be much larger than it is today. The plan involved a number of partners, among them one of the biggest local businessmen in Gutu and a foreign partner who would deliver the machinery. Therefore, they only needed forex for the operating capital. However, by the time the project was approved in 1990, the partners had withdrawn. The present owner then decided to go ahead alone and sent a new application for the present much smaller enterprise. He now also required forex for the machinery, and this was approved in only six weeks, but he was not able to start until January 1992. He has bought 32 sewing machines (of different types) and two cutting machines in Japan. He works from a building in Gutu industrial area rented from the Urban Development Corporation, which was built some years ago in order to attract small producers to Gutu. Both workshops are financed through a mixture of personal savings and bank loans.

The small male-owned tailoring businesses are all run at a very low level from small rented shops or verandas and with one or a few sewing machines often purchased second-hand. Many of the male tailors, especially in Gutu, are quite old (five of the eight tailors interviewed were around 50 years old, but one was only 17). Most of their businesses were established in the late 1980s, but in Gutu one dates from 1983 and one even from 1957. Most of the tailors have been in the tailoring business all their lives, either as an employee or as an independent tailor elsewhere. Three of the five older tailors were originally Malawians who migrated to Zimbabwe in the 1950s. The male tailors all started their businesses with their own savings, and none of them have obtained bank loans.

The women running knitting or tailoring businesses are younger than the male tailors; in Gutu most of them are in their late thirties, while in Gokwe four out of six are in their mid-twenties. They started their businesses in the late 1980s or early 1990s (especially in Gokwe), woring from rented shops or from their husbands' shops. They typically have one or two knitting machines and sometimes one or two sewing machines as well. The largest, who has a number of trainees, has seven knitting machines. While the male tailors tend to run a traditional tailoring business, many of the female tailors and knitters tend to be more innovative, on the one hand trying to specialize (children's wear, travel bags, bedspreads etc.), and on the other hand, combining their knitting activity with other trades and services (e.g. hairdressing).

While the male tailors have all had to finance their businesses out of their own savings, many of the women have been financed either by their husbands' businesses or by other family members. In Gutu, many of the small knitting businesses are run by the wives or daughters of local businessmen in the centre. These knitting businesses are typically financed by money earned in the husband's or father's business and run from his shop, where the woman also works. In Gokwe, where there are fewer local businessmen, small knitting enterprises are more often run by younger women as independent businesses. But often their establishment has been supported by the mothers or fathers or is owned by family members living elsewhere in Zimbabwe. It may also have been easier to borrow money in the official system in Gokwe than it is in Gutu. The only two micro-enterprises in our sample to have obtained loans are two knitting enterprises in Gokwe, one from a bank, the other from the Small Enterprise Development Corporation (SEDCO) (the only enterprise in our whole sample to receive a loan from SEDCO).

Finally, another reason for there being more independent small knitting and tailoring businesses in Gokwe than in Gutu is that there are a larger number of small cheap shops for rent in both private and council premises. A number of old private buildings in the centre have been split up into small shops, and the council has built a new house near the bus stop with 16 small shops for rent. This has made it relatively easier for women to establish themselves in Gokwe than in Gutu, where such small premises for rent are scarce.

8.4 The effect of drought and structural adjustment on the clothing sector in Gutu and Gokwe

The falling real incomes resulting from the drought and from the structural adjustment policies in 1992 reduced the sale of clothing in the shops in Gutu and Gokwe to between 20 per cent and 50 per cent of pre-drought sales. In early 1995, it was still well below the pre-drought level. Shops selling more expensive, high-quality goods were worst hit. One locally owned shop which specialized in expensive women's dresses before the drought shifted during it to groceries; after the drought it shifted again to trading in fertilizer, cement and other heavy goods. At the same time, however, one of the largest local businessmen opened a new shop with expensive women dresses.

Many of the clothing shops shifted during the drought to cheaper goods, and a few started to sell second-hand clothes. One of the effects of structural adjustment has been a trade liberalization leading to a rapid increase in the import of second-hand clothes, which has resulted in the market for second-hand clothes becoming very important in the large towns. However, in neither Gutu nor Gokwe does trade in second-hand clothes play any significant role. This appears to be partly because district councils have been reluctant to issue licenses to second-hand clothes dealers in the district service centres themselves. Trade in second-hand clothes seems to play a much larger role in the rural areas, where travelling traders apparently often exchange second-hand clothes for grain. Therefore, although trade in second-hand clothing plays a limited role in the district service centres themselves, it may have contributed considerably to the reduction of trade, especially among the retail stores and small tailors.

None of the branch stores in the two centres have been closed; rather, a few new ones have been opened, mostly branch stores of small regional chains selling cheap goods. However, some of the small shops owned by local women which partly sell their own production have been closed. Some of them may now be running from home in order to reduce costs. Some of the independent tailors and many of the small knitting businesses based partly on apprenticeship fees appear to have closed, at least temporarily. The dressmaking and knitting schools have also been running at a very low level because people have not been able to afford the fees. However, in early 1995 the number of students appeared to be rising again. The sewing machine repairman who had opened a shop in Gutu before the drought had moved away again.

Surprisingly, all three larger clothing workshops in Gutu survived the drought and in early 1995 were still running with the same workforce as before and apparently doing reasonably well. The smallest had even moved into larger premises and increased its workforce from five to six. The largest of the workshops did not succeed in its plan from before the drought to specialize in women's dresses for the chain-store market. Instead, it has been producing protective work-clothes and school uniforms like the other large workshop in Gutu. The market for work-clothes is a niche with limited competition from the large factories, but often resulting in sufficiently large orders to be attractive for medium-sized workshops. In addition, the production of work-clothes and school uniforms does not compete with second-hand clothes.

8.5   The effect of retail chains on the development and restructuring of the clothing sector in the district service centres

The development of the clothing sector in the district service centres has been heavily influenced by the establishment of branch stores of large retail chains during the latter half of the 1980s.

Many of the national retail chains have operated with fixed prices all over the country. This has forced local traders to reduce their prices and has set in motion a process of restructuration and specialization in the clothing sector. The general dealers' clothing sales have probably gone down, while some locally owned, specialized clothing shops have been opened. While most of the chain stores cater to the middle-income market, locally owned clothing shops have tended to cater to the higher income market of civil servants and business people. Some of the small general stores, on the other hand, sell low-quality goods, often supplied from informal workshops owned by family members.

The reduced price differences between the district service centres and the large towns have made it possible for the small towns to recapture an increasing part of the rural market, which was formerly supplied directly from the large towns by labour migrants. As a result, the local market has increased much more than rural incomes. The branch stores have also produced increasing competition for the small local tailors, who have been left with little more than the market for repair work.

The dominance of the clothing market by large retail chains has also reduced the local market for the larger local producers. The retail chains obtain their goods nationally and operate as their own wholesalers. As a result, local branch managers usually have no competence to buy goods locally. Local producers therefore tend to have a very limited local market and are forced to go directly to the national market. The dominance of the retail chains on the national market also means that the wholesale sector for clothing is not very developed. The larger local producers therefore either try to sell their products through their own retail shops or through travelling salesmen in the rural areas, or to produce for the enterprise or institutional market where small to medium-sized orders can be obtained.

Notes

1   According to the National Union of the Clothing Industry, it had been 45 per cent, but has dropped since the introduction of three months' paid maternity leave.

2   There are only a few dressmaking enterprises run by women in the two business centres; however, more dressmaking and knitting enterprises are most likely run in the residential areas of the towns, which have not been investigated.

3   Wages in the small workshops vary from 150–250 Z$ per month, while in the formal industry they are around 375 Z$.

9 The construction sector and building-material production and trade in the district service centres[1]

9.1 The building sector in the national economy

Throughout the latter half of the 1980s, the formal construction sector employed 30–40,000 people (Central Statistical Office, 1988–89). Of these, 20–25,000 were employed in the private sector and the rest in the public sector. Public-sector building activities grew rapidly after independence, but in the latter half of the 1980s employment fell from 16,000 in 1985 to only 8,000 in 1988, as public-sector building activities were increasingly contracted out to large-scale private construction firms. Part of the public involvement in the construction sector took the form of building brigades consisting of former guerillas and unemployed youth. These building brigades built low-income housing and smaller public buildings, and produced building materials, especially cement blocks. However, by the late 1980s not many brigades were left, their members often becoming small private entrepreneurs or public employers.

The formal private construction sector, i.e. enterprises belonging to the Construction Industry Federation of Zimbabwe, consisted of 246, mostly very large enterprises in 1989. Of these, 91 were general contractors, 140 were building specialists/sub-contractors and 15 were members on probation. These large enterprises are almost all white-owned and highly concentrated in the large cities. Of the general contractors, 78 per cent are located in Harare and Bulawayo, though they operate throughout the country.

In addition to the construction sector as defined in the *Census of Production*, considerable employment is found in formal-sector building-material production and trade. However, it is not easy to obtain a precise picture of the size of this employment because building materials cannot be isolated from other production in the industrial statistics. They belong to a number of different sub-sectors such as saw-milling and wood products (employing 5,355

141

in 1988), paints etc. (678), structural clay products including bricks (2,881), glass, cement etc. (5,724), and metal products (16,907). In total, formal building-material production probably employed around 20,000 people in 1988, mostly organized in a relatively small number of enterprises which operate in monopolistic or oligopolistic markets: for example, there are only two cement factories, one producer of roofing material, four producers of burned bricks, one window-glass factory, two enterprises producing fittings, three large producers of steel frames for windows and doors, and a handful of medium-sized producers, including three producers of tubes and pipes. In addition, these enterprises are often interwoven in terms of ownership.

Besides this formal building sector, there is a large, almost entirely black-owned small-scale building sector. According to McPherson (1991) there are around 35,000 small construction enterprises with less than 50 employees, together with around 45,000 carpenters, welders, brick-makers, masons and hardware dealers, mostly engaged in the building sector. Most of these enterprises are located in the rural areas and in small towns. Together, they probably employ around 150,000 people, or more than twice as many as the formal sector.

In the early 1980s, the government attempted to promote some of the more experienced and better equipped black contractors by offering them contracts, especially on school and clinic buildings, without the normal tendering and security presentation, the projects instead being monitored technically and financially by the government. Altogether around 60 African building enterprises benefited from this policy before it was halted in 1984 because no clear results could be shown and misappropriation of funds was discovered. In the late 1980s, the Ministry of Construction began a policy of reserving 5 per cent of its work for tenders from small black-owned contractors. In 1989, 104 small contractors were on the ministry's pre-qualification list, though only 20 of them were actively tendering.

In spite of these failed policies, however, the number of emerging black contractors apparently grew during the building boom of the late 1980s. In 1989, the National Employment Council for the Construction Industry registered around 550 (most likely black) contractor/building specialists in addition to the 246 formal large contractors. It is probably this larger and growing number of enterprises which is reflected in the employment figures presented in the *Quarterly Digest of Statistics* (Central Statistical Office, December 1991). Here, employment in the construction sector is said to have stood at 45,000 in 1985, rapidly increasing to 59,000 in 1988 and 80,000 in 1991. These larger figures do not include small rural building enterprises and probably not small urban ones either. At the start of the 1990s, 220 of these black contractors founded an association of their own, the Zimbabwe Building Contractors Association. This new organization works for the registration of more black contractors and for the reservation of all public tenders below 10 million Z$ for the emerging black businessmen (see also Section 11.5).

9.2   The structure of the building sector in Gutu and Murewa

The building-sector enterprises located in the small towns consist of:

– local, mostly small, registered contractors;

– local builders and building cooperatives;

– a number of different specialized artisans: plumbers, electricians, painters, carpenters, welders, brick-makers and masons

– local hardware and general stores selling building materials; and

– branches of non-local building material merchants.

Table 14 shows the number of enterprises active in the different sub-sectors of the building sector in Murewa and Gutu district service centres according to Rasmussen's (1992) survey, carried out in 1989. In evaluating the figures in Table 14, however, one should bear in mind that most of the small builders and artisans operating in the centres reside outside, and if they do not have a workshop in the centre, they only work there as long as they have contracts there. Secondly, there is a considerable overlap between the different activities, e.g. draughtsmen are mostly also merchants, carpenters or public employers, several merchants are also manufacturers, and some brick-makers are also contractors. Finally, many of the enterprises perform other tasks in parallel with their building-related activities.

At the same time, the local building market is not only supplied by local enterprises, but also by large non-local registered contractors and non-local building-material producers or merchants distributing directly to the small towns and their rural hinterland. And in the rural areas, the small-town contractors and builders compete with small rural builders and artisans.

In terms of numbers employed, the builders' merchants are the largest enterprises, with an average workforce of 25, while the building specialists are small artisan enterprises with an average workforce of only 2. The welders, who generally engage in more permanent production, are a little larger with an average of 5, and the contractors and builders are larger still, with an average of 8. However, there is a relatively large variation in size within the group of contractors and builders, and some of the smallest builders have very few people permanently employed.

143

Table 14

Number of enterprises operating in the building sector in Murewa and Gutu, 1989

Type of activity	Murewa	Gutu	Average employment in enterprises interviewed
Registered contractors	2 (2)	6 (3) }	
Builders	9 (4)	24 (2) }	8
Carpenters	6 (2)	12 (4) }	
Plumbers	2 (1)	3 (1) }	
Electricians	3 (1)	6 (1) }	2
Painters	4 (1)	5 (1) }	
Draughtsmen	2 (–)	4 (–) }	
Welders	6 (4)	4 (3) }	5
Brick-makers	1 (–)	2 (–) }	
General builders' merchants	3 (3)	6 (6)	25
Other manufacturers		1 (1)	
Total	**38 (18)**	**73 (22)**	

Note: The number of enterprises interviewed is shown in parenthesis
Source: National Employment Council for the Construction Industry; information from enterprises and clients

In addition to this normal employment, some enterprises employ apprentices, though not in the formal sense of a government-approved apprenticeship programme of four to five years (probably none of the enterprises would qualify for that). These are informal apprentices who are supervised for two to three years and then apply for a trade test with the National Employment Council. There seems to be considerable unused training capacity, especially in the welding enterprises. The total employment relating to the building sector exceeded 300 in Gutu and 100 in Murewa. This corresponds in both cases to about 6 per cent of total employment in the centres.

A more detailed presentation follows of four of the more important sub-sections of the building sector, namely builders' merchants, welders (producing door and window frames), carpenters (producing wooden items and occasionally constructing parts of buildings) and building construction. Construction specialists (plumbers, electricians etc.) are not dealt with separately.

Builders' merchants

Builders' merchants are a recent phenomenon in Gutu. Before 1983, materials were only obtainable from a white farmer's store, but then two larger branches of town-based enterprises (one multi-national, one Masvingo-based) were established. In 1986, a big local businessman increased supply by opening a hardware shop close to his other shops. Recently, another Masvingo-based trading firm has added some key building materials to its general stock at its Gutu branch.

Local competition is fierce. The three major merchants are fully equipped with all materials, with the exception of some specialized electric devices and glass, which only one firm supplies. Being marginally cheaper and with no expenses for delivery service, the branch of the Masvingo firm competes on price. This attracts price-sensitive low-income households. In the case of larger complete orders (from drawings to delivery), delivery is arranged directly from Masvingo. The largest branch, owned by a multi-national firm, had its best period in the mid-1980s, when school construction boomed and local competition was limited. It now competes on delivery service to the rural hinterland, using its lorry fleet to deliver materials within a range of 50 km, as far as roads allow. The local businessman competes on his reputation for good service to steady customers. Old customers are treated favourably, and materials can be ordered and delivered through his outlets in three small rural business centres

Despite harsh competition from nearby Harare, the building-material trade has also expanded in Murewa during the 1980s, although only one locally owned large trading enterprise has become a complete supplier. Until 1987, timber was unobtainable in Murewa and glass has only recently appeared on the local market. Only paint, electrical devices and piping and tubing are still unobtainable. Two branches of Harare-based firms sell some basic building materials as a (very small) part of their total stock, but not timber or glass.

None of the suppliers are particularly cheap. Ironically, they seem to cater mainly to lower income customers, who lack transport, while richer families stock up directly from Harare. Moreover, salesmen from Harare-based companies frequently visit the rural area, especially schools and larger institutions, searching for bulk orders which they can supply directly from Harare. Only the locally owned supplier operates an (erratic) delivery service to the rural hinterland or uses some of his small local branch outlets for distribution.

In all localities, welding enterprises produce copies of many standardized industrial products, as well as a wide range of their own products. In contrast to what has been claimed in other studies (e.g., Moyo *et al.*, 1984:60), these producers are often specialized. All welding enterprises are small owner-operated businesses (average workforce of the enterprises interviewed is five). They all produce window and door frames which are 10–30 per cent cheaper than the industrial products sold by the merchants.

In Gutu, steel manufacturing is a relatively recent phenomenon. The largest welding workshop concentrates on producing scotchcarts for farmers and car repairs, with additional activities in fencing, burglar bars, and iron pillars for verandas. One small independent welder rents some space on his premises for open-air window-frame production. Another old welding enterprise deals mainly with car repairs and only produces window frames and fences in times of low demand for its car repair service. One enterprise was set up recently as an offspring of a smaller welding business in Kwekwe, owned by an old Gutu resident. It produces primarily window frames, but also burglar bars and metal doors, and does various repair work, directed mostly towards town families and shops.

In Murewa, only a couple of enterprises operated in 1981, and they clearly disliked the later appearance of four newcomers. However, the strong competition has created a larger degree of specialization than in Gutu. The largest old workshop specializes in scotchcart production and vehicle repair, but has added window frames and burglar bars to its assortment. As the sole owner of a bending machine, the owner of this workshop specializes in metal bending; relying on his technical skills, he also produces axle bolts. In Murewa, another smaller welder combines welding and carpentry in a unique production of durable steel-reinforced school furniture in addition to the production of stoves, hoes, harrows, gates, window frames and burglar bars. Scotchcarts are less important here. Both enterprises cater mainly to rural customers.

One welder concentrates on a more simple product range: window frames, burglar bars, gates and scotchcart repair. The Mission and the District Council are important customers for window frames, to which he attaches burglar bars. A welding cooperative, established with the assistance of the Ministry of Youth, produces mainly window frames, burglar bars and fences for the District Council, which has taken the cooperative under its protection. Finally, one welder specializes in radiator- and aluminium-welding, several other welders referring customers to him for such repairs.

Carpentry

All carpentry enterprises in the district centres are owner-operated units, very small, and technologically quite simple.

In Gutu, only two carpenters have workshops, while four others operate in the backyards of their houses or in rented rooms. Except for the well-equipped District Council school furniture workshop, all these carpenters also take on construction jobs, as do six other carpenters working regularly in Gutu. Their product range is relatively uniform, mainly supplying low-income market demand for cheap copies (doors, chairs, wardrobes). One of them adds a limited specialization by making coffins and wooden forms for brick making

Finally, Gutu also has a 'high quality carpenter' who does not have a workshop but carries out all the more sophisticated carpentry work in building construction (roofs on larger shops, internal plywood covering, shop-fitting and some kitchen units and furniture in times of low demand) and combines this with drafting. He deliberately sets his prices high and serves the market of better-off local shopkeepers.

Murewa has three carpentry workshops in addition to some mobile carpenters involved in construction only. The most successful enterprise combines production of relatively good-quality furniture with sawing trusses for own carpentry work in building construction. The two other workshops produce roughly the same type of furniture (school benches, wardrobes, tables) but of lower quality, although one has added shop-shelving as an additional specialization. This production is also combined with occasional construction work. All three workshops cater mainly to schools and rural families, and in the case of the latter two, they compete on price.

Building construction

Building construction in the district centres is carried out by the following enterprises: the Ministry of Construction, local registered contractors, external registered contractors, and a number of non-registered builders. Except for one Gutu contractor, none of them are able to undertake full contracts.

In Gutu, the Ministry of Construction only operates with three to four workers engaged primarily in maintenance. The largest local contractor, who is also one of the large businessmen in town, differs from the other five contractors in undertaking full contracts, which he can do because of his technical skills and equipment (trucks and concrete mixers). He operates in the whole district as well as in the neighbouring towns of Masvingo and Mvuma. The other contractors confine their areas of operation to Gutu district, where they build shops, high-cost houses and schools. Some Masvingo-based contractors also operate in Gutu mostly in the same market as the local contractors.

In the early 1980s, like many other districts, Gutu had established a building brigade which in the mid-1980s successfully built 25 per cent of the low-cost housing built in that period. However, by 1989, it had been reduced to a small private contractor and a brick-making brigade which was partly protected from competition from other brick-makers by a bureaucratic quasi-monopoly.

The competition is fierce among the numerous builders. The bulk of their work is in Gutu town or in rural business centres constructing small shops, low-cost housing and school extensions. There is considerable flow into and out of this segment of the building sector. Many previous builders now sub-contract or simply work for registered contractors.

The largest building enterprise in Murewa is the Ministry of Construction, which employs 20 skilled workers (mainly from the provincial head office in Marondera) and 50 temporary workers (mainly local). They undertake the bulk of construction work in Murewa town such as medium-cost housing, a hospital extension and a new training centre. Two local contractors also operate in Murewa, one simultaneously running a retail shop. The biggest of them undertakes all kinds of larger jobs in the district and sometimes outside (large schools, clinics, big shops), and is recognized for his long experience. The other contractor undertakes slightly smaller jobs within the district (schools, larger shops etc.).

In addition to the construction of ordinary houses, some of the builders in Murewa also participated in the construction of larger buildings. For example, the largest on-going private building construction, a large hotel, was managed fully by the owner but carried out by local builders. Some builders work only for the District Council and must be considered semi-employed workers, although they formally have to bid on tenders. Finally, builders based in Harare undertake a number of jobs which are often obtained through personal acquaintance with the customer.

9.3   Market segmentation in the building sector

Building construction

Housing construction is basically a commercial activity even in rural Zimbabwe. All the houses surveyed were built with at least some professional assistance. In the few examples found of self-built houses, the houseowner was himself a professional builder or was closely related to one. In most cases, the builder/contractor also takes care of the carpentry work, primarily roofing, either by himself or by hiring a carpenter for the building team. About one-fifth of the houseowners hired independent builders and carpenters and a mere 2 per cent hired a carpenter only for roofing. Other construction specialists like plumbers, electricians, painters and draughtsmen are used to varying degrees, but especially in the district centres. In the rural areas, specialization is less pronounced.

There is considerable segmentation inthe building market, where different types of builders/contractors tend to serve different market segments. The market can roughly be divided into four such segments:

1   Central government and parastatal building activity which requires public tenders is practically always carried out by large non-local contractors or public building companies. The same is true of most of the shops and office buildings built by large non-local enterprises. Here, the contractor will usually manage both the building materials and the construction work and deliver a complete building. Although some of the small local contractors might technically be able to carry out some of these larger projects, they are usually unable to provide security for the often large amounts of capital needed. In addition, during periods of unstable supplies, they will often be unable to purchase the building materials required for such contracts.

2   Shops and modern high-cost housing are mostly built by local contractors. The contractor organizes and manages the labour, but the client typically organizes the building materials. However, much of the high-cost housing built for public or parastatal civil servants during the 1980s was built by large non-local contractors because they were tendered out in large projects. Although local contractors might technically have been able to carry out such large projects comprising a large number of houses, they did not have enough resources to manage them financially.

3   Low- and medium-cost housing, district council building and rural shops and schools are mostly built by informal builders operating in the district centres. They will usually provide only labour, the client managing the building work and organizing the building materials.

4   Finally, especially in the building of rural houses but also of some urban low-income houses, the client may also contribute a considerable part of the labour himself.

Figure 9 attempts to give a breakdown of the structure of the building sector which results from this market segmentation. The market segmentation is based not only on the technical construction work itself, but also on the necessary services, such as financing, work organization and procurement of building materials and transport. Large-scale contractors are formally classified on the basis of their financial strength rather than their technical ability, although these are of course often related. Large contractors usually organize both work and building materials, sub-contract building specialists, and deliver a turn-key building.

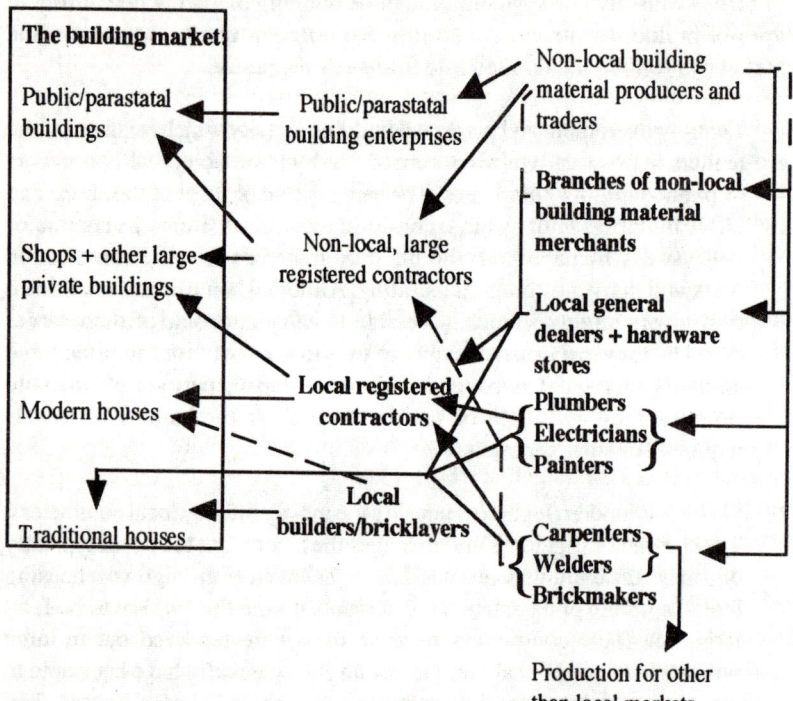

Note: Activities in bold are local small-town activities

Figure 9   The structure of the building sector in Gutu and Murewa

The small contractors and builders usually have few funds of their own and operate on a market where building loans (both official loans and private/family loans) are rare exceptions, so that building is therefore mostly carried out on a cash basis. This lack of finance is important for the way the work of the small contractors and builders is organized. The customer often supplies the building materials himself, which he may often have collected over a long period of time. This is advantageous because building materials have tended to increase in value more rapidly than inflation. In addition, since they have often been in short supply, they need to be bought when available. As the small contractor or builder is not usually able to obtain supplier credit and has no motorized transport, he has little to offer the customer in terms of material procurement. The customer may also organize the labour and sub-contractors himself, even supplying part of the labour.

About two-thirds of the house owners interviewed by Rasmussen (1992) found that acquisition of building materials constituted their biggest problem because of high prices and shortages. As a rule, materials such as cement were increasingly difficult to obtain throughout the 1980s.

While building construction is almost by definition executed locally, building materials can be bought over long distances. Local producers and distributors of building materials therefore have to compete with non-local producers and distributors. The most simple and bulky items, such as bricks, sand and gravel, are mostly obtained locally. Buildings in Gutu are mostly constructed with cement bricks or blocks, while rural burnt-clay bricks not requiring scarce cement are commonly used in Murewa. In Gutu, the local council has prohibited the use of such burnt-clay bricks – which require large quantities of scarce firewood – for environmental reasons (and in order to protect the local building brigade's cement-block production). Unburned clay bricks are considered unacceptable for building in both Gutu and Murewa. Industrially produced burnt-clay bricks are rarely used for whole buildings (banks and parastatal offices are exceptions) but frequently as 'face bricks' for store fronts. Such bricks are only produced in large towns. Most cement blocks are produced locally. However, in Gutu some consumers (15 per cent) buy their cement blocks in Masvingo, because they consider them to be better. They are also cheaper when transported in bulk together with other building materials. Sand is not commercialized in the two district centres nor in the rural areas, while in the two centres gravel and stones are bought from quarries in Masvingo and Harare respectively.

Wooden materials and steel frames manufactured locally are used in both Gutu and Murewa in only 15 per cent of the cases interviewed. In Gutu centre and its hinterland, most of these goods are bought from local retailers, primarily in Gutu centre; but 25 per cent of the customers have bought them from retailers in Masvingo or Harare, from where migrant workers bring timber and steel frames home on the top of the bus. Locally produced timber is used especially in rural areas, and timber for some of the largest buildings was obtained directly from saw mills in the Eastern Highlands. In Murewa, local building-material retailers only play a minor role, and most timber and steel frames are bought in Harare.

Steel frames for windows and doors weigh heavily on the building budget. Other iron and steel products are burglar bars and gates. Consumers who prefer locally produced frames mostly take the cheaper prices and more favourable terms of payment into account, but there was widespread dissatisfaction with the quality of locally produced frames which often do not have the correct measurements and close badly.

Other commonly used products, such as cement, roofing, glass, paint, plumbing and electrical devices, are all produced industrially in the larger cities. In Gutu, these products are bought from retailers in Gutu centre in about 75 per cent of cases, and in Masvingo or Harare in the 25 per cent of cases. In Murewa, local retailers only supplied about 25 per cent of these materials, while 75 per cent were bought in Harare.

In general, the dominance of city-based manufactured products is clear in all important categories of building materials, and even district centre retailers of urban products have a hard time competing with retailers in the larger towns. Of the consumers who obtain their building materials in the large towns, 45 per cent mention lower prices as the primary reason, followed by 28 per cent who stress availability. An additional 8 per cent, all in the rural areas, state that it is easiest to organize the whole procurement from the town in which they or their husbands work.

Few customers, not even in the rural areas, mention transport as their major problem. Nonetheless, competition and segmentation between different groups of suppliers seem to be partly based on transportation services or location. Thus the small contractors and building-material producers who have no motorized transport serve mainly the urban small-town market, while the larger building-material merchants, who often have a truck at their disposal, supply both the rural and urban areas.

9.4 Strategies and management of enterprises in the building sector

Small-town enterprises operate in rural markets, which tend to be very unstable in both seasonal and annual terms. Markets fluctuate especially with the agricultural seasons and the climatic swings in rainfall. More than half of the enterprises interviewed are significantly influenced by seasonal changes. Building-material producers and merchants are especially affected, while the builders/contractors appear to be less seriously affected, probably because they use casual labour or sub-contractors to a large extent.

Annual fluctuations are more pronounced and felt by almost all enterprises. They are especially caused by droughts and swings in public-sector demand. The late 1980s were generally considered good business years compared with the early 1980s, which were characterized by frequent droughts. Dissatisfaction with the late 1980s was caused by material shortages and high prices rather than demand constraints. This has clearly changed again since the main fieldwork was carried out in 1989, a result of the drought and structural adjustment policies of the early 1990s.

In this uncertain and fluctuating market, enterprises have to pursue flexible strategies. In general, they are forced to reduce their fixed costs by minimizing their permanent labour force and fixed investments and by paying investments out of their own savings and treating them as sunken costs. However, different types of enterprise pursue different strategies.

The smallest and simplest enterprises (e.g. small builders, painters or plumbers) are both run and managed by the owner and employ at most a few people. At the bottom end, these enterprises may be what Rasmussen (1992) calls 'workers/farmers in disguise', who own neither major tools nor the workshop and to whom the enterprise only serves as a secondary source of income. In times of low demand, such enterpreneures tend to seek other employment or retreat to peasant farming, although some also produce for stock. If they employ casual labourers, these are obviously the first to be sacked.

In the intermediate category of somewhat larger enterprises comprising building specialists and enterprises where the owner functions mainly as manager, the entrepreneurs rarely retreat to farming or wage labour. Although most possess some land, they do not seem to depend on it. Instead, they try to keep the business going by reducing employment, producing for stock, expanding their market into the rural areas outside the district or into neighbouring towns, or diversifying into other business activities which they might already own.

Finally, the enterprises managed by a manager rather than by the owner, which also tend to be the largest, try to adapt to declining demand mainly by reducing the workforce.

When demand is high, the majority of enterprises expand activities by employing additional casual labour. Other enterprises prefer to cope with increased demand by working overtime. This applies especially to enterprises which require skills which casual workers cannot perform. Only a few said that they referred customers to other enterprises in busy periods, and none collaborated with other enterprises in order to meet demand. This indicates fierce local competition without much of a network or mutual trust between enterprises, with enterprises attempting to capture the market on their own when it is there.

In building, sub-contracting is important. Most of the registered contractors use sub-contractors, and many of the smaller contractors, building specialists and builders serve as sub-contractors or even work occasionally as labour for the larger contractors. However, there is little relationship among the production enterprises. The evolving market segmentation has not been accompanied by a significant division of labour between the production enterprises. They also buy their materials separately, even though they could save considerable amounts of money and time by common bulk purchases. The few entrepreneurs who have tried to organize bulk purchases have met with resistance and mistrust from the other entrepreneurs.

The structure of the material supply system may be an important reason for this lack of cooperation. Under conditions of material scarcity, a stable relationship between the enterprise and its supplier is crucial. The larger owner-managed and manager-managed enterprises therefore rarely change suppliers. By staying with the same supplier, they are guaranteed a fairly continuous access to materials during shortages too. Usually, they also receive supplier credit (typically 30 days). On the other hand, the smaller enterprises seldom enjoy these stable supplier benefits and therefore change suppliers according to price fluctuations, the availability of materials and transport opportunities.

In such an unstable environment, many of the small building artisans and producers develop clientilistic relations with some of the larger builders and material merchants in order to secure themselves sub-contracts or material supplies. Some also rent premises in town from larger businessmen.

Most contractors, builders and building specialists use only hand tools. Only the larger contractors need imported compactors and vibrators in order to undertake jobs demanding a certain quality. But carpenters need machine-saws and planes, electricians need drills, and welders need welding machines. In total 29 per cent of the enterprises interviewed use machinery of some kind. Most of this machinery can be obtained in Zimbabwe, but it is mostly old and obsolete and requires frequent repair and maintenance. It is therefore a major problem that qualified repair services are not available in either Gutu or in Murewa and have to be obtained 90 km away in Masvingo or Harare.

Business services, other than banking, did not exist in Gutu and Murewa centres at the time of the investigation in 1989. But both centres had banks, and all but two of the enterprises interviewed had bank accounts (although not all of them in the local banks). But only the larger and more sophisticated enterprises enjoy borrowing rights or overdrafts, while most of the small owner-operated enterprises are excluded from formal lending. On the other hand, many of those without borrowing rights are not very interested in taking out bank loans at the given interest rate. Due to the considerable business uncertainties, they consider it very risky to commit themselves to high regular repayment rates which in case of default can deprive them of their house or other critical assets. Many enterprises therefore explicitly prefer to save rather than borrow.

Knowledge of the Small Enterprise Development Corporation (SEDCO), which in principal provides substantial loans and other assistance to small enterprises, is very limited. Only half of those small enterprises eligible for loans knew that SEDCO existed. A couple of the enterprises interviewed had applied for SEDCO loans, but only one (a welder) had received one.

In addition to their own financial problems, building enterprises are also heavily influenced by the lack of building financing in the district centres and rural areas. Until the early 1990s, it was not possible to own land in the small towns or rural areas, and prospective building owners have generally not been able to provide collateral for building loans. As a result, most owners have paid cash for their buildings out of their own savings. Builders and contractors have often therefore not been paid in time (if at all), and the building process has been stopped for long periods due to a lack of building materials or cash-flow problems.

In spite of the very unstable market in which building enterprises in small towns operate, most enterprises are surprisingly stable: 16 out of 32 enterprises interviewed were more than ten years old at the time of the interview, i.e. dated from before independence, while only five were less than two years old. This stability is partly due to the strategy of operating with very few fixed costs, which makes it possible for enterprises to survive for long periods at a very low level of activity. But at the same time it is virtually impossible for an enterprise to go bankrupt, because banks and other creditors are generally not willing to take over enterprises in the district service centres. An example is a window- and door-frame manufacturer who started production in Gokwe in 1992. He rapidly expanded production and after two years was employing 160 people. He also started to invest in a large factory. But as a result of the economic crisis of 1992 demand for his products dropped, and he was not able to pay his material suppliers, so they would no longer supply him. He was forced to stop production, although his debt was apparently quite limited compared to his assets and sales. He still owns the factory, however, and hopes to be able to start production again.

9.5   Entrepreneurs in the building sector

Training and accumulation

To start an enterprise in the building sector (as well as in other sectors) requires skills and experience, networks and capital. Very few entrepreneurs have therefore started right after leaving school or vocational training. In fact at the time of the interviews, the most frequent age group for entrepreneurs was 45 to 50 years old. This rather high age conforms with other studies of entrepreneurs in the rural areas and small towns (Helmsing, 1987; Göttlicher, 1986), but is slightly higher than that found in studies of informal entrepreneurs in large towns. When they started their enterprises, entrepreneurs were of course younger, on average 33 years old, but with considerable spread; the average age of contractors was 39 when they started their enterprises while smaller entrepreneurs such as welders and carpenters were only 28.

All of the entrepreneurs interviewed have a relatively high basic education. All but one completed at least five years of school and most attended school for nine years. In addition to basic school education, almost half of them attended a year or more of vocational training, although almost as many only followed short informal training courses. Most of the entrepreneurs with a more formal training attended mission schools or Domboshawa Training

Centre (near Harare), often before independence. In general, there seems to be a relatively high correlation between the complexity of the enterprise and the education and training the entrepreneur.

In addition to training, the entrepreneur also needs capital and practical experience to start a business. The possibilities to obtain these in the rural areas and small towns are limited, as there are few qualifying jobs and generally no possibilities to borrow money from the banks. Although private loans are more frequent, they are also scarce. Half the entepreneurs interviewed obtained both capital and experience by working in their profession in the large cities, where two-thirds of them had worked for more than ten years. Contractors, builders and welders especially have gained experience and saved capital by working in their profession in the cities. On the other hand, carpenters and other small entrepreneurs requiring little capital have never had urban jobs in their profession, though a few of them have been trained and worked in their profession in local enterprises before starting on their own. Yet others have worked in non-farm jobs outside their profession. Less than 10 per cent started with only a farming background.

Rural linkages

In spite of the long time many entrepreneurs have spent in the large towns, more than 80 per cent of them come from the local district. More than half of them state that their main reason for locating their enterprise in the district centre is that it is near their rural home; almost 30 per cent say it is because they have lived there most of their lives; and only 20 per cent say it is because they found a good job or market there.

Although the market in the district service centres is rather restricted compared to the large cities, it is large compared to the rural areas, and a small-town location has a number of other advantages: work can more easily be combined with other sources of income, especially farming, and housing expenses are minimized by the family living together in the nearby rural areas.

Thus more than 90 per cent of enterprises interviewed were involved in activities other than building. About 70 per cent was engaged in farming and more than 40 per cent in other non-farm activities. However, a large majority received their principal income from the building activity investigated.

Farm income and other additional incomes are not only a matter of economic necessity for the smallest entrepreneurs. Large entrepreneurs are engaged in farming and other business activities to the same extent as the small entrepreneurs. It is rather a general strategy of spreading risks in a strongly fluctuating economic environment. The difference between the small and large entrepreneurs' involvement in farming is that while the land of the small entrepreneur is tilled by his wife and himself, the large entrepreneur employs farm labour.

The other advantage for local entrepreneurs with a district centre location is that they can reside in a rural dwelling almost without cost, and about half of the entrepreneurs in fact live with their families in their rural homes. This home can be up to 25 km away, from where they walk, cycle or take a bus to town every morning. The other half lives in town, but most of them also have a rural home. Only 15 per cent are urbanized in the sense that they do not possess a house in the rural area.

In total, more than three-quarters of the entrepreneurs in the district centres live together with their wives and children. This is much more than is found in most rural areas, where labour migration is high and deciding to work in the district centre is likely to be an additional incentive for entrepreneurs.

Many of the entrepreneurs living in the district centres expressed a desire to move back to the rural areas when they retire. This was especially true of the small entrepreneurs, while many of the entrepreneurs who were better off and had a house in town wanted to remain there. Besides a house in town, many better off entrepreneurs have a range of income opportunities (e.g. trading and house-letting) which can continue after they retire from the building sector and thus secure their standard of living.

Family succession

As discussed above, most entrepreneurs in the building sector have obtained the experience and capital to start their businesses by working in their profession mostly in the large cities. Few have inherited their enterprise. Of the enterprises interviewed, less than 10 per cent have the same profession as their father and only two had inherited the business.

There are several reasons for this. The building sector, like other non-farm activities, has been growing since the 1950s, and about half of all the entrepreneurs are the children of communal farmers or farm labourers. In many of the smallest enterprises, incomes are so small that there would not be work for more than one person. Therefore, the family is seldom involved. In total, families assist in about half the enterprises. In half of these, it is the wife and children who assist; in the other half, it is other family members, especially brothers and uncles. In the larger businesses, family involvement is more common. However, the better-off entrepreneurs who can manage it usually prefer their children, especially their sons, to have an academic education and enter formal-sector employment. In general, artisan and technical training have until recently not been held in high esteem, and only 15 per cent of entrepreneurs recommend their children to take up their own profession.

However, the trend may be changing. At the time of the interview about half the entrepreneurs with adult sons had at least one child working either in the family enterprise or in some other enterprise in the same profession. And almost half of the entrepreneurs had advised their children to learn some technical skill (e.g. mechanics, architecture, draughtmanship) which would make them independent of formal jobs, which had become increasingly difficult to obtain. However, 30 per cent of entrepreneurs, especially the less educated, still advise their children to get as much formal academic education as possible.

The low rate of family succession may also be reinforced by the often very patriarchal family structure which causes many children deliberately to seek a way out of the father's sphere of control. At the same time, the long tradition for labour migration also means that sons who remain at home tend to be regarded as failures and thus incapable of taking over the business. And given the very centralized economic system in Zimbabwe, this may well be true. Family succession in small-town building businesses is therefore not likely to increase rapidly.

9.6   The district council and entrepreneurs

The district councils play an important role in the building sector as market regulator, customer and competitor.

As a regulator, the district council plays an important role in the building sector through its administration of town plans and building regulations, which affect both the operation of building enterprises, and the demand for building materials and construction. Although the different district councils administer the same rules and regulations, there appear to be considerable differences in the way they do it.

In Gutu and especially in Murewa, there has been an almost permanent under-supply of small stands for small-scale producers and artisans. On the other hand, there is a large unused supply of large industrial stands, originally designed for decentralizing manufacturing companies and branch plants, but which have not been occupied at the rate expected. Also in the commercial centres, there is an under-supply of small stands. In contrast, Gokwe has been much more active in providing both small stands for local artisans and small shops for local traders.

At the same time, building and zoning regulations have tended to make it very expensive for small enterprises to build if they are lucky enough to get a small stand. Strict zoning regulations prohibit mixed land use. Entrepreneurs are not allowed to live at the commercial or workshop stand, even though this would reduce establishment costs. The situation is aggravated by local building regulations which in 1989 required a minimum value of 15,000 Z$ for a building on a small stand. This is much more than required by the Department of Physical Planning (2,000 Z$ for small service industries and 8,000 Z$ for commercial building). Thus the small entrepreneur is precluded from building a shed, locker or toilet amounting to a few thousand Z$, which is often all he needs.

Similarly, alternative building materials such as earth bricks, which have a minimal content of cement, are not allowed or are discouraged, despite the desperate cement shortage. In Murewa, shop owners in the town centre are even pressured to use expensive and scarce face bricks on the front of the shop in order 'to create uniformity' for all shops.

The supply of especially low-income housing in the district service centres has been very restricted. In Murewa, it is almost impossible to find a residence, and the minimum value for residential building is 15,000 Z$, or almost double the price of a low-cost house in larger towns such as Masvingo. Low cost self-help or site-and-service schemes have not even been considered.

In Gutu, 200 low-cost housing units were built with support from the World Bank in the mid-1980s, but since then little has been done to accommodate the growing population. This has led to increased density of the villages around the town. This development has not been acceptable to the district council and has led to a conflict between the council and the chiefs (who traditionally had and still have some rights to allocate land in the rural areas) about who has the right to allow the building of new huts or houses in the villages. As a result, in the late 1980s the council burned down huts in the surrounding villages which it had not permitted itself.

In Gokwe centre, which has been growing very rapidly, the housing situation is even more catastrophic, with people living on shop verandas in the centre and many businessmen commuting daily the 140 km to Kwekwe or Kadoma.

The district council also plays an important role as the customer of building-sector enterprises. About 30 per cent of enterprises mention the public sector as their most important customer, which to a large extent (especially for the smaller enterprises) this means the district council. However, the relationship between local enterprises and the authorities has been somewhat ambivalent. Especially in Murewa, many of the small entrepreneurs found that the council was very rigid and slow and had too high planning standards. In the early 1980s the attitude towards the private sector was generally negative and the local authorities favoured the formation of building cooperatives, brigades and local/central government-owned enterprises. But the building brigades formed just after independence have slowly withered away because local government has not been able to sustain them with a continuous flow of tasks. The Gutu Council building brigade successfully constructed a quarter of the 200 low-cost houses built in the mid-1980s, but at the time of the investigation in 1989 it had been reduced to a brick-making brigade protected by a bureaucratic quasi-monopoly. Gutu Council also runs a carpentry workshop which produces school furniture in competition with private carpenters. Similarly, Murewa Council runs a welding cooperative. These activities gave raise to much less complaint from the private entrepreneurs, as they apparently operated on a more or less competitive basis. They also carry out some training of young people.

Although the official rhetoric had not changed much by 1989, larger entrepreneurs and private businessmen especially were gaining respectability in public-sector offices, perhaps partly because an increasing number of civil servants were themselves becoming businessmen. There seem also to be increasing informal contacts between local civil servants and especially the larger businessmen and registered builders, and a considerable number of businessmen complain about alleged shady procedures when the council announces new contracts.

The introduction of structural adjustment policies in 1990 undoubtedly led to an even more positive view of the local private building sector. Donors, NGOs and banks increasingly focus on support for developing small enterprises, and the association of emerging black businessmen (IBDC, Indigenous Business Development Centre) has been lobbying for small enterprises with considerable success. However, these new activities have mainly been concentrated in the large cities and have spread only slowly to the district centres and rural areas. In addition, both the banks and many donors have tended to focus especially on the largest of the small enterprises which dominate the emerging businessmen's association. In the building sector, the Zimbabwe Building Contractors' Association (an associate of the IBDC) presses for registration of its members and distances itself from the small builders, who cannot be registered and whom it sees as a threat (see also Section 11.5).

There is thus a very real risk that a new alliance will develop between the council/civil servants and the larger local businessmen, not only against the large non-local white-owned enterprises, but also against the smallest local enterprises.

Note

1   This chapter is mainly based on Rasmussen, 1992.

10 The dynamics of district service centre growth: external forces

10.1 Introduction

Being part of the rural areas, small rural towns are influenced by the seasonal and climatic swings of the rural economy. They are also part of the urban system and are influenced by economic cycles and changing policies in the larger national and international economy.

In this chapter and the next, I argue that since independence the Zimbabwean district service centres have passed through three development phases which have been formed by external forces to a large extent, but which have also been the result of local reactions to those external forces. Focusing on the external forces, the following section presents the three development phases; Section 10.3 presents a more detailed account of the effects of structural adjustment and drought during the early 1990s; and Section 10.4 concludes on the role of the external forces. Chapter 11 focuses on the internal forces: entrepreneurs, managers and local policies.

While chapters 6 to 9 analyse the structure and development of individual sectors in the small-town economy, chapters 10 and 11 rather attempt to present a picture of the small-town economy as a whole. These two chapters function partly as a summary of chapters 6 to 9, but they go further in presenting data on enterprises and activities from other sectors than those presented in the earlier chapters.

10.2 Three phases of development in district service centres in Zimbabwe since independence

The economic basis for the development of the district service centres is growth in rural and small-town money incomes caused by increasing:

- agricultural cash incomes;

- rural non-farm economic activities;

- labour migration and remittances;

- rural and small-town wage employment.

Agricultural cash incomes have increased rapidly in most of Zimbabwe's communal areas during the 1980s as the size of the marketed crop has grown. However, agricultural cash incomes have fluctuated widely both seasonally and yearly, depending on rainfall. They have also been concentrated on a relatively limited number of households. Non-farm activities, remittances and local wage labour have at least partly supplemented agricultural cash incomes, although they have hardly reduced income differences. Remittances and especially public-sector wages have also tended to stabilize the economic base, at least until the early 1990s.

This growing rural economic base has been a prerequisite for the growth of the small rural towns. However, small-town growth has also been supply-driven. The sector studies already presented indicate that the development of the district service centres is the result of a series of growth waves set in motion after independence by public policies and the growing economic base.

The first of these waves consisted of the establishment of agricultural and public services and infrastructure, parastatal depots and public administration. This development benefited the traditional rural traders (primarily general stores, bottle stores and butchers), which grew in number. This public-sector-driven growth dominated during the first half of the 1980s, but continued during the second half, albeit at a slower rate.

The second wave, which dominated the second half of the 1980s, was carried by a number of large national and regional retail chains, which in order to exploit the growing rural market (and partly invited by the government) established branch stores in many of the larger district service centres. These retail chains operate especially in clothing (see Zinyama, 1990), but also in hardware and other sectors. Many of the national retail chains operate with fixed national prices, thus forcing local shops to reduce the often considerable price differences on industrial goods which existed earlier between rural and urban areas. The expansion of retail chains into the rural areas has led to increasing competition in the retail sector, reducing many general dealers to grocery stores and forcing others to develop more specialized shops, especially in clothing, furniture and hardware. Local wholesalers serving rural general dealers were also established during the second wave.

Reduced price differences have made it possible for the small rural towns to regain a large part of the rural buying power which had been spent earlier in the large towns. The total turnover in the small towns has therefore increased, and except for small tailors, the number of local stores and artisan workshops appears to have grown.

The third wave, which started slowly during the last half of the 1980s, is carried by a still small but growing number of medium-sized manufacturing enterprises with about 20–40 employees. In Gutu in 1995, there were seven such enterprises: a bakery, a grain mill, an oil mill, two clothing workshops, a book-binder also printing exercise books and T-shirts for sports teams, and a scotchcart producer. In addition there was a soap factory with a small production of popcorn and popsicals, which has, however, recently moved its soap production to Masvingo, and a small roller mill, which has been out of operation for some time.

In Gokwe, an almost similar number of enterprises have been established and more have been planned. However, when we visited Gokwe in 1994 only two bakeries and an oil mill were operating. A third bakery was said to be working irregularly; a grain mill had closed after a short time because its owner had died; a large building-material producer closed due to lack of capital after a short period of rapid growth and left the unfinished frame of a large building; and a factory for electrical supply equipment to be opened in a large building finished several years ago never started operation. Thus although plans and visions for Gokwe have been more ambitious than for Gutu, developments seem to have been less solid.

Parallel to the development of these medium-sized industries, since the end of the 1980s there has also been a growth in the number of small enterprises. Many of these are very small specialized retail or service enterprises based primarily on the consumer market (e.g. photography, records, women's dresses, hairdressers and dry-cleaner outlets), but also increasingly on the producers' market (e.g. training courses and small-enterprise consultancy, debt collectors, legal services and security firms). Others are small producers (e.g. dressmaking, welding, carpentry and fence-making). However, not all the new service enterprises are small. In Gutu, a new security firm has developed into what is probably the largest enterprise in Gutu, employing about 140 young men and women as guards and largely out-performing the non-local security firms which used to serve the town.

The introduction in 1987 of a number of tax concessions on investments in growth points and larger district service centres (Moyo, 1995) and the new investment code marking the start of the structural adjustment programme in 1989 (Gibbon, 1995b) may have been instrumental in initiating the third wave of small-town development which was on its way around 1990. But the wave has been delayed at least temporarily by the current crisis caused by drought and structural adjustment.

10.3 The effect of structural adjustment and drought on the development of district service centres

The structural adjustment programme, which has gradually been carried out since 1989 in order to transform the Zimbabwean economy, has also influenced small-town economies. Unfortunately, the negative impact of the structural adjustment programme in 1991–92 coincided with the impact of one of the worst droughts of this century, so it is difficult to distinguish in detail their respective effects. After a partial recovery in agriculture in 1993 and 1994, Zimbabwe was again hit by a drought in 1994–95 which in part of the country appears to have been worse than the drought of 1991–92.

Here, we attempt in more detail to disentangle the impact of structural adjustment and drought on the small towns primarily on the basis of data from Gutu obtained during visits in March 1992, November, 1993 and January, 1995. Gokwe was only visited in March, 1992 and December, 1993.

The first phase of the structural adjustment policies in Zimbabwe was a change in government policies during the late 1980s towards foreign and local private investment in Zimbabwe. The focus of this policy change was primarily the attraction of foreign investments and encouragment of export-oriented production, but it also made it more attractive for local capital to invest in production for the home market. The new policies made it easier for small and medium-sized enterprises to obtain foreign currency for the import of machinery and production inputs. At the same time, the Investment Centre was created as a 'single window' facility which simplified application procedures for investors. Most of the medium-sized production enterprises established in Gutu around 1990 appear to have taken advantage of these new policies. Thus these new investment policies have at least promoted the third wave of development, even if they have not initiated it.

These changing policies were partly the result of a changing attitude towards small and medium-sized black entrepreneurs. Into the 1980s, the socialist government in Zimbabwe continued the pre-independence industrial policies which favoured large-scale, mostly white-owned urban industries. In the rural areas, small non-farm activities, cooperatives and women's groups were supported, but the attitude towards small and medium-sized black businesses was rather negative for both economic and political reasons. Economically there was a widespread belief in large-scale production, and politically the socialist government was not keen on developing an African entrepreneurial middle class. By the end of the 1980s, however, African businessmen were strong enough to form the Indigenous Business Development Centre (IBDC), which has been an effective lobby for the development of small and medium-sized businesses and has undoubtedly been instrumental in changing official attitudes.

The second phase of the structural adjustment programme consisted of gradual devaluation and trade liberalization. On the one hand, trade liberalization, which made it possible for industries to obtain production inputs and spare parts which were earlier only available in limited quantities, was intended to lead to increased capacity utilization. On the other hand, devaluation resulted in large price increases which reduced buying power. Increases in consumer prices were further aggravated by the drought, which resulted in an explosion of food prices and a fall in real incomes in 1992. As a result, consumption fell dramatically, and capacity utilization in industry did not increase as expected, but rather decreased further.

Consumption was especially depressed in the rural areas. The district service centres were therefore severely hit. In clothing, which was one of the sectors to be worst hit, the turnover in many shops decreased by between 20 per cent and 50 per cent of the pre-drought level. In building materials, the reduction in sales was apparently smaller (50 per cent or less). Many businessmen who could afford to do so appear to have engaged their excess workforce in building and repair work when the usual level of activity dropped during the drought.

On the other hand, many general stores and grocers maintained their turnover or even increased it by shifting from selling a varied assortment of food products to selling only mealy meal to peasants who in normal years would be self-sufficient, but due to the drought were forced to buy mealy meal. Bread sales fell dramatically. Many butchers had to close, not only because of weak demand, but because no meat was available. Instead many consumers shifted to dried or fresh fish, which is cheaper than meat, and new fish shops were opened in the small towns.

The commercial grain mills, like the small roller mill in Gutu, which received their share of the imported food relief grain, worked three shifts during the drought, while the service mills closed because people had no grain of their own. The new oil mill had to close due to lack of oil seed. Lack of grain also prevented rural beer brewing and favoured the consumption of industrial beer in spite of its higher price.

After the grain trade was partly liberalized, private grain trade from and among the communal areas was legalized. GBM depots started to sell unprocessed grain to local traders and consumers, and most general dealers now sell unprocessed grain as well as industrial mealy meal. As a result, the large millers have lost their virtual monopoly on supplying communal areas which have grain deficits. Even in urban areas, the large mills have lost market share. Many urban dwellers now bring grain from their rural home area. Also grain farming on open urban land, which used to be prohibited, is now allowed. As a result, the capacity utilization of the large industrial milling companies fell to below 50 per cent, and they have closed many of their smaller roller mills in a number of provincial towns. Instead, small rural service mills flourish, and many new service mills have been opened in the urban areas.

The new small commercial mills established in the district service centres since the end of the 1980s have generally survived because they use a technology which allows them to operate both as service and commercial mills. As commercial mills, however, they have difficulty in obtaining access to the retail market because the big industrial mills, which are also grocery wholesalers, attempt to practice bonded sales and are also often able to offer retailers better credit terms. The mills which are doing best are those run by businessmen who have their own wholesale or retail stores, have been able to enter the local institutional market, or are producing stockfeed for their own chicken or pig production.

The large advantage which the small commercial grain and oil mills in the small towns should have gained from the liberalized grain trade, because they are now able to buy grain and oil seeds cheaper directly from the communal farmers, appear to have been mostly countered by a lack of capital and rapidly increasing interest rates. The small commercial millers therefore still seem to buy most of their grain and oil seed from the GMB.

When the grain market was partially liberalized in 1993, prices remained controlled but increased dramatically. This benefited those communal farmers who, in the first years after the drought, grew a market surplus, especially because much seed and fertilizer had been distributed free of charge by the government during the drought year. The prices of fertilizer and farm implements also rose, but much more slowly than the price of grain, so that the price in terms of grain actually decreased. As a result, sales of fertilizer, farm implements and also building materials rose rapidly again after the harvest of 1993.

Communal farmers without a market surplus did not benefit from the raising grain prices, and farmers with a grain deficit (probably close to 50 per cent of farmers even in good years) suffered severely. The opportunity to buy unprocessed maize instead of expensive industrial mealy meal has partly reduced their loss, but rural income differences have undoubtedly increased.

An important element in the structural adjustment programme has been the gradual liberalization of imports of consumer goods. In the district service centres, this has been most visible in the establishment of a number of small kiosks selling cheap radios, watches, jewellery and other industrial goods. Most were imported informally, first from Botswana and later mostly from South Africa.

Trade in imported second-hand clothes, which now plays an important role in the large towns, is not very visible in the district service centres. This is at least partly because the local councils have been hesitant to licence second-hand clothes dealers in the centres. However, second-hand clothes are sold by travelling traders in the rural areas and thus may still be contributing to the decrease in sales in clothing shops in the district service centres. On the other hand, the local clothing workshops do not appear to have been hurt much by second-hand clothes because they have specialized in work clothes and school uniforms, for which there is no second-hand market. Although the national clothing industry suffers from the large import of second-hand clothes, prices of second-hand clothes are so much lower than prices for new clothes that consumers save money which may be used to buy goods from other sectors, which will thus benefit.

In total, both structural adjustment and drought have had severe a impact on the economy of the small towns. However, there have been counter-mechanisms which have made the negative impact on small-town businesses less than one might expect. Few enterprises appear to have closed, and many have found ways to counter the crisis, at least partly.

Most small-town businessmen were originally in favour of the structural adjustment programme, which they hoped would result in easier access to scarce products and foreign currency. In general, this was achieved, but interest rates and prices increased markedly, and the rural market contracted. These effects were not forseen or appreciated. Therefore, although in general they fare much better than one might have feared, they are not satisfied with the outcome of the structural adjustment policies.

10.4 External forces in district service centre development

The rapid development since independence of trade and services in the district service centres has been triggered by external forces. The government's policies of decentralizing the state administration and developing agricultural and social services in the district service centres have led to increases in money incomes and a growing market in the rural areas. And the decision of the national retail chains to establish branch stores in the larger district service centres has reduced the price differences between the rural and urban areas and allowed the district service centres to regain a large share of the rural buying power which was earlier spent in the large towns.

At the same time, however, the very centralized and monopolistic structure of trade and production inherited from the pre-independence period has been a hindrance to the development of small and medium-sized industries in the small towns. Industrial policies throughout the 1980s continued to favour the large-scale, mostly white-owned industries, e.g. in allocations of foreign currency and of scarce production inputs. The dominance in many sectors of large retail chains and the high integration between large-scale producers and wholesale distribution channels made it difficult for new industries to enter even the local markets in the small towns.

Only with the structural adjustment policies of the late 1980s and early 1990s has the very centralistic industrial structure come under attack. As a result, the industrial system is now undergoing rapid restructuring. Structural adjustment was originally expected to increase capacity utilization because access to spare parts and scarce production inputs would be improved. However, in many sectors large-scale industries have been losing market share and experiencing falling capacity utilization. This is especially the case in food-processing, which earlier was highly controlled, but it is probably also the case in clothing, although some of the large enterprises have been able to expand into the export market.

The beneficiaries of the restructuring process have mostly been the very small informal activities in both rural areas and small towns. The future development of the small to medium-sized industries in the district service centres is still uncertain. However, most of them seem to be surviving so far in spite of the very contracted market resulting from drought and structural adjustment and the high interest rates, which especially hit new enterprises with recent loans and limited capital accumulation.

11 The dynamics of district service centres: internal forces

11.1 Changing groups of entrepreneurs, managers and administrators

The three consecutive waves of activity in the district service centres described in chapter 10 have been triggered by external national and international policies and institutional decision-makers, but local capital and changing groups of local entrepreneurs, managers, administrators and politicians have played an important role in the process.

The first wave of growth following independence was carried by public administrators and parastatal managers who had typically made their careers in their organizations and were transferred to the small towns relatively late in life. Loyalty to the national organization was more important to them than the development of their local branch. They saw themselves as administrators rather than as entrepreneurs or businessmen, and few had plans to start businesses of their own. Some came from the district or a neighbouring district, and they may have applied for their job in order to be closer to 'home'.

The private businesses which developed in the wake of the public and parastatal sector were dominated by traditional rural traders operating general stores or bottle stores, and by builders and small artisans. Some of them had been operating in the centres since the 1950s or 1960s, but were now expanding; others were new people who opened shops in order to benefit from the rapidly growing market. Some came from the rural areas; others were returning from the urban areas. In Gutu, most were local, but in Gokwe, many were immigrants from outside the region. Some of the old traders and builders had been able to accumulate considerable capital before independence, while many of the new traders and especially artisans started with very little.

The branch stores which carried the second wave brought new people to the small towns. Many of the stores were managed by very young people, often not more than 20 to 25 years old, bright O-level students who after a few years of training at head office were stationed as branch managers in the district service centres. Although for the most part they have only limited decision-making competence, they do run their branches in a much more business-like way than the administrative managers, and they will be in a much better position to start businesses of their own if circumstances compel them to do so. At present, however, only a few see themselves as independent businessmen, at least partly because they cannot see how they can acquire the necessary capital. Most of them are non-locals at the centre, and if they were to start businesses many would most likely start elsewhere.

The spread of chain stores during the second wave increased competition and led to differentiation among local traders. Many of the general stores were reduced to grocery shops, while some of the more successful ones diversified into more specialized trade and services not provided by the chain stores. This shift from general stores to more specialized trade represents a shift in business strategy. For the old general dealer, his stocks were his savings and his capital. What he did not sell this year, he would sell next. He would earn a good deal of his profit on seasonal and annual swings in prices. With the chain stores, this changed. The shirt which is not sold this season may be out of date next, and it ties up scarce and expensive capital. Competition has reduced the profit level, and this can only be compensated for by increasing turnover or by borrowing more capital, which leads to expensive interest charges, if it is available at all. Therefore, the new entrepreneur has to limit his stock to fewer commodities with a more rapid turnover.

Successful local businessmen who have excess capital to invest usually diversify into different trade and service activities within the town or in the small rural business centres. The largest have bought commercial farms, and a few have invested on a larger scale in commercial buildings at the centre. In both Gutu and Gokwe, many buildings in the commercial centre are owned by a few large businessmen. Many of these buildings are rented out to the retail chains, which in general have not wanted to invest in the small towns because they could not obtain title deeds to land. Local businessmen have been willing to invest with informal security consisting of local political connections, and they are undoubtedly profiting from the present distribution of title deeds. To some of the old traders, investments in commercial rental buildings have served as a retirement scheme.

None of the large local traders has invested in production enterprises. The few medium-sized production enterprises established in Gutu and Gokwe before the mid-1980s were set up as branches of large national or regional enterprises or by local builders or artisans. However, since the late 1980s, most of the larger production enterprises have been established by what one might call 'academic entrepreneurs', people with university or other higher education (sometimes in economics or commerce, but often in a subject unrelated to their business). They sometimes have work experience from the public or large-scale private sector, and often a larger national or even international network than the rural traders. Most also have a family background with connections both in the district and to the national economic and political elite. Some have been able to borrow at least part of their money with collateral in their public-sector wages or an urban house; others are linked up with larger family enterprises.

It is these 'academic entrepreneurs' who have carried the third wave of small-town development into the 1990s. They have done so together with a larger group of often younger entrepreneurs investing in small enterprises, mostly specialized in trade and services, but sometimes also in production. These young entrepreneurs usually have very little capital, but most have a secondary education and varying degrees of vocational training (limited for many). Some have been able to borrow part of their start-up capital from the family. In other cases, family members (fathers, uncles, brothers, sisters etc.) appear to have set up enterprises in order to create jobs for their younger kin.

In contrast to the other groups of small-town entrepreneurs, which consist mostly of men, there are many women in this group of young entrepreneurs. However, while women tend to dominate among small entrepreneurs in the rural areas (Daniels, 1994), this is not so in the small towns, where in general enterprises are larger and more capital intensive. In Gutu, most of these young entrepreneurs are from the local district or a neighbouring one. In Gokwe, there are more immigrants from other parts of the country.

The different groups of entrepreneurs and managers have different qualifications, partly as a result of the educational system in the district service centres and in Zimbabwe in general. This is investigated further in Section 11.2. The different groups also have different access to capital and networks, and they are influenced differently by local policies to support or restrict small enterprise development. These are the subjects of Sections 11.3 and 11.4 respectively.

To improve the local environment for economic development, there is a need for increased interaction between local government, the local business community and other interest groups in the district. Local government must change from being an administrator of rules to becoming a partner in local development, and the business community and other local interest groups must organize themselves in order to be able to negotiate with local government and each other. This is discussed in Section 11.5, while Section 11.6 is a conclusion on the local actors of development.

11.2 Vocational training and the small-town labour market

Education and training at the national level

The new groups of entrepreneurs which have entered the small-town economy are partly an outcome of the educational system which has been developed in Zimbabwe since independence. At the time of independence, education for the black population in Zimbabwe was not very highly developed. Primary education was not that low by African standards, but black youth had very limited access to education beyond that. Secondary and especially higher education were primarily reserved for white youth. Even the formal apprenticeship programme, which trained people to a high level for formal industry, was basically reserved for whites. More traditional forms of non-formal apprenticeship as existed in many other African countries were not very highly developed in Zimbabwe. In the last years before independence, the white government made some limited attempts to organize vocational training at a low level for black labourers. These attempts were largely discarded after independence as sub-standard training (see, e.g., Zvogbo, 1986).

After independence, one of the first goals of the new government was to develop a system of universal primary and secondary education. New schools, especially secondary schools, were built all over the country. In the primary schools, enrolment rose from 870,000 in the mid-1970s to about 2.2 million in 1990 (Närman, 1991; Republic of Zimbabwe, 1991a). According to Närman (1991) around 90 per cent of a cohort are enroled in primary education, but 5–15 per cent of them do not complete it. Around 300,000 students have been leaving primary school annually since the end of the 1980s.

Secondary education has grown even more rapidly, from around 70,000 students in the 1970s to 677,000 in 1990, and the enrolment rate has increased from 10–15 per cent to around 45 per cent of a cohort (Närman, 1991; Republic of Zimbabwe, 1991a). The annual intake in Form 1 is about 200,000, while the number of students leaving Form 4 was only 122,000 in 1989, but increasing. Thus many students leave secondary school after Form 2 with a Junior Certificate, and many drop out. Only about 8,000 continue to the advanced secondary school in Forms 5 and 6. Due to drought and structural adjustment, enrolment in both primary and secondary education has decreased again during recent years, especially in rural areas. From 1991–93, enrolment in secondary schools declined by about 10 per cent (Government of the Republic of Zimbabwe, 1993).

To accommodate the growing number of secondary school graduates, enrolment at the university and colleges (agricultural, technical and teachers training) has also grown rapidly from 8,000 in 1980 to around 50,000 in 1990 (including 15,000 evening students at the technical colleges) (Republic of Zimbabwe, 1991a; Secretary for Higher Education, 1991). However, the annual intake is probably still less than 15,000 and highly concentrated in the large towns. In addition, there is considerable in-service training in government ministries (e.g. health), parastatals (e.g. Agritex and PTC) and some of the large private enterprises, especially in the service sector (e.g. banking and insurance). There are also a large number of private colleges and correspondence institutes which offer training at various levels from simple secretarial training to full professional courses. In 1990, 108 private colleges were registered, graduating some 1,200 students a year (Republic of Zimbabwe, 1991a). However, in spite of the rapid increase in tertiary education since independence, it has only been possible to satisfy a small part of the demand from the exploding number of graduates from primary and secondary schools. In the early 1990s, only about 4 per cent of a cohort of youth left the educational system with a post-secondary education, less than 10 per cent left with a completed O-level, nearly 40 per cent with partly completed secondary education and nearly 50 per cent with only a fully or partly completed primary education (Government of the Republic of Zimbabwe, 1993).

As a result of the increasing pressure, entrance requirements to tertiary education have become very high and left a growing number of young people looking for vocational training. However, official policies for the development of vocational training have been much less expansive. Although some technical subjects (such as commerce, agriculture, fashion and textiles and secretarial studies) have been introduced into the curriculum, the secondary schools have remained rather academic. It is important that secondary school students are now introduced to practical subjects, but it is not enough to bring the students up to a professional level. In addition, many of the technical courses are only available in the larger towns, while most rural schools only offer a few subjects, due to a lack of qualified teachers and teaching materials (World Bank, 1992; McGrath, 1993).

The official apprenticeship programme still focuses on very high-level training, and only a few, usually large enterprises in the large towns are accepted as eligible for taking on apprentices. Furthermore, the number of new apprentices dropped rapidly during the early 1980s to 1,000–1,200 per year, because many private industries withdrew from the programme when the government insisted on controlling the intake in order to increase the number of black apprentices. Therefore, most apprentices are now trained by the parastatals. The annual intake was around 1,500 in 1990 (Republic of Zimbabwe, 1991a).

Several new programmes combining training with production were set up in the early 1980s:

–   The Zimbabwe Foundation for Education with Production (ZIMFEP) was established in 1980 to provide 'education with specific vocational training programmes in order to prepare the students for the world and make them self-reliant' (Närman, 1991; International Foundation for Education with Production, 1990). There are at present twelve such schools, all located on farms. According to an evaluation of 1987, the 'traditional curriculum is still dominant', and although these were intended to initiate a change of the curriculum (Närman, 1991), neither qualitatively nor quantitatively have they offered a solution to the vocational training needs of the small enterprises. In spite of increasing capacity, enrolment has decreased during the 1990s. In total, they only graduated 5,200 young people between 1983–90 (Government of the Republic of Zimbabwe, 1993).

–   Most districts, both rural and urban, set up building brigades which were expected to carry out public building activities in the district and at the same time train young people in the building trades. By the middle of the 1980s, it became clear that in most districts the brigades could only be maintained with heavy subsidies which the districts could not afford. Most of the brigades have therefore either been dissolved or turned into small private or cooperative enterprises (Rasmussen, 1992).

–   The Ministry of Youth, Sports and Culture (later the Ministry of Political Affairs) has been establishing youth projects in many districts, in order to train young people to establish their own production cooperatives. The ministry also operates fourteen Youth Training Centres throughout the country, to give young people vocational training. However, these centres only graduate a total of around a thousand trainees per year (Republic of Zimbabwe, 1988, 1991a). Originally, the centres offered a two-year course for youth with limited schooling, but since 1987, the training period has been increased to three years and the entrance requirements have been raised to O-level (Republic of Zimbabwe, 1988). The training capacity of the youth projects is also quite limited, for example in Gokwe district, which has around 300,000 inhabitants, the ministry operates seven projects with a total of only 100 participants.

These programmes were originally established for the purpose of reintegrating young ex-combat soldiers from the liberation war with limited schooling into civilian life, but they now have a more general enrolment. However, as elsewhere in the educational system, entrance requirements have been raised.

In addition to these larger schemes, there are several government and NGO vocational training centres which offer both pre- and in-service training. However, the total number of openings into tertiary and vocational training falls far short of the demand from students leaving primary and secondary education.

Educational policy in general seems to have favoured the development of very high-level education for people to be employed in the higher or middle echelons of the public sector or the large private or parastatal enterprises. It has focused much less on training for the lower layers of the large enterprises and for the small formal or informal enterprises. This is partly because the large enterprises train their own workers on the job. Many small-town entrepreneurs, especially older ones, have thus had years of work experience and training in the large enterprises before starting their own businesses, and they have also often earned their starting capital there. However, with a stagnating formal sector and a rapidly growing number of young people entering the labour market each year, this career pattern has become less common. The result is that today there are very few formal training or job opportunities for young people without a good secondary education, either at A-level or at a high O-level. Such young people increasingly have to work in one of the many small informal enterprises, which today have a considerably larger total employment than the formal public or private sectors.[1] Therefore it is unfortunate that the on-the-job training opportunities which actually exist in the small enterprises are badly utilized, partly because they are said not to live up to some technical requirements set by the large enterprises, and partly because the strict administration of minimum-wage legislation in Zimbabwe has made it difficult to operate informal apprenticeship schemes (King, 1989) like those existing in many other African countries.

Vocational training in the district service centres

In the rural areas and small towns which especially concern us here, the situation is even worse because colleges and training institutes have been highly concentrated in the large towns. Except for correspondence courses, formal vocational training is generally not accessible to youth in the rural areas and small towns. The concentration of training institutions also means that it is impossible for people from the small towns to combine practical work with in-service training at evening classes, as is possible in larger towns.

One of the difficulties in developing vocational training in the small towns is that the labour market has tended to be very closed. The two largest groups of job opportunities in the small towns are shop assistants in local and branch stores and secretaries in public and parastatal offices. Most shop assistants in private stores are family labour (mostly wives and daughters), while shop assistants in the branch stores are usually hired at head office. Secretaries in public and parastatal offices were until recently hired nationally. Therefore many of the local job opportunities have not been open to local youth.

It is thus interesting that especially since the late 1980s, vocational training has been established in the small towns such as Gutu and Gokwe. Most of these training initiatives have been established as private businesses, and except for some church organizations and a small local cooperative, NGOs have not been involved. In Gutu and Gokwe, the first of such courses were established in knitting and dress-making (see chapter 8). But since 1990, private schools offering O-level courses and courses in secretarial and business studies have also been established in both Gutu and Gokwe. They offer courses of up to twenty months leading to the British Pitman examinations. In Gutu, the mission has also started a small school for nurses, and there have been attempts to set up vocational training courses for mechanics, including sewing-machine mechanics. Due to difficulties in getting official acceptance and also to the pressing economic situation in 1992, the mechanics' course was never started. Enterprises offering secretarial and business courses also offer business consultancy and help small enterprises to register. It is interesting that it is possible to offer such services at the same time as international donors and NGOs are increasingly offering similar services and courses, often with large donor support.

In total, in early 1992 the capacity of private vocational training had expanded to offer training from three months to two years for up to 500 trainees in Gutu and close to 100 in Gokwe, most of them in knitting and dress-making. Thanks to the drought, the number of trainees actually trained in 1992 was considerably less than this. However, since 1992 training activities have further diversified and the number of trainees has again increased, although knitting and dress-making have not reached pre-1992 levels.

Private teaching and training institutions are not new to Zimbabwe: private colleges and correspondence courses have existed since the 1950s (King, 1989). But the new institutions are much smaller and less formal than the old ones, and even located in the small rural towns. The attitude of Zimbabwe's administrative and political system towards these small private informal training institutions has been very sceptical, not to say negative. Since the introduction of the Economic Structural Adjustment Programme (ESAP) in 1990 (Republic of Zimbabwe, 1990; 1991b), the attitude towards the informal sector has generally become more positive. The employment and training programme which the government has initiated as part of the adjustment policies recognizes the importance of the informal sector (ILO/Southern African Team for Employment Promotion, 1991; Government of the Republic of Zimbabwe, 1993). However, with respect to vocational training, the government's action plan for poverty alleviation (Government of the Republic of Zimbabwe, 1993) still builds on the very limited capacity of the Youth Training Centres alone. There is no recognition of the importance of the training going on in the small formal and informal enterprises themselves or of the possibilities for upgrading this training, for example through the establishment of semi-formal apprenticeship schemes and small local technical evening schools based on locally available classrooms and teachers organized by and among local businessmen, teachers and others.

Present government initiatives are not likely to satisfy the demand for trained youth for the growing labour market in the rural areas and small towns. The small private training initiatives now developing in the district service centres and elsewhere should therefore be recognized as serving an important function for the development of the small enterprise sector in Zimbabwe. They train people at a cost, which from a societal point of view is much less than the cost of training at government institutions.[2] In spite of the fee that has to be paid for private training, the cost to the trainee also appears to be lower because she can stay at home. On the other hand, there is an understandable and justified concern about the quality of training. Many of the small training centres in the district service centres at present provide training of an undoubtedly low standard. They are generally run from premises which would not be accepted in the larger towns, and they use mostly very old machinery. Training in dress-making is carried out on old household sewing machines,which are much slower than the industrial machines used by industry. Secretaries are often trained on very old typewriters. This is partly due to a lack of capital, but an equally important reason is that the small training centres have not been eligible for foreign currency allocations and therefore have not been able to buy new machinery. However, these conditions are not so different from the conditions under which many of the small enterprises which will employ the trainees operate.

The Ministry of Higher Education in Zimbabwe presently has plans to introduce a new vocational training structure with five standardized levels of certification. It may be useful to introduce such standards because this will force the private training centres to deliver training of a specified quality. On the other hand, it is important that the standards are not set too high. Standards which are achievable within the limited means of the small training centres may motivate them to improve quality, but standards which are prohibitively high will close the training businesses and stop the initiatives under way.

Private vocational training institutions in the district service centres which have developed to meet local conditions can make an important contribution to the future development of the small towns and rural areas. In general, the attitude towards such local initiatives has been more positive in the district council than in the Ministry of Education, and the local councils and administrations should be allowed to play a larger role in their development than is the case today.

11.3 Capital and entrepreneurial networks in the small town

Most local businessmen have started their businesses on savings from wages earned in the urban areas or less often from agriculture. Some have been able to obtain loans from family or friends, but very few businessmen, mostly the largest, have been able to borrow money from the formal financial system. It is also mostly the large enterprises which are able to obtain supplier credit; the small generally have to pay cash.

Small-town businessmen who want to borrow from the formal financial system are up against very centralized organizations, where decisions about loan applications are usually made at headquarters rather than locally. In recent years many banks have created specialized small-enterprise offices, which should make it easier for small enterprises to obtain loans. According to a joint statement published by the Bankers Association of Zimbabwe and the Finance Houses of Zimbabwe (*Herald*, 16/12/1993), 20 per cent of all loans and overdrafts provided to the private sector by the members of the two organizations went to black businessmen. However, the banks' small-enterprise offices have all been located in the large towns and have so far had little impact on the small towns. Detailed information about the entrepreneur and the project which a local decision-maker might have considered would be unknown to the central office and therefore not taken into account. Therefore decisions have tended to be based almost exclusively on collateral.

This disadvantage for the small-town businessmen is aggravated by the fact that they have not been able to use their rural and small-town property as collateral. Until recently land in the district service centres (as still in the rural areas) could not be owned, but only leased on a one-year basis and could therefore not be used as collateral. Since the early 1990s, this has gradually been changing. It is now possible to obtain title deeds to land in the district service centres. However, it is still uncertain to what extent title deeds can actually be used as collateral. The use of title deeds as collateral rests on the assumption that the property can be taken over by the bank if the loan is not serviced regularly. It still seems to be uncertain whether it would be politically acceptable for the banks to do so, and we have not been able to find cases where a bank has actually taken over land in a district service centre. However, this may also be because it could prove difficult for the banks to sell defunct small-town property during the present period of stagnation. Entrepreneurs who have to close their businesses due to cash-flow problems seem to be able to keep their property, even though they are in dept. Thus the provision of title deeds on small town land may not in itself solve the financial problems of local businessmen.

In the unstable economic environment of small towns in marginal agricultural areas, it is very risky for a businessman to base his enterprise on investment capital borrowed against high interest rates, and many of the small businessmen we interviewed would not take a loan even if it were offered. However, the unstable rural economy badly needs working capital to finance the economy from harvest to harvest and through drought years. Most enterprises therefore suffer from recurrent cash-flow problems. To finance working capital on transactions with a relatively short turnover may also be much less risky. The focus of many donors and NGOs on investment capital rather than working capital does not therefore seem very logical.

We found a conspicuously large number of entrepreneurs who seem to have 'over-invested', either in too large a production capacity or in too many different activities. As a result, they were left with no working capital when the economy tightened up, and had to reduce production or close altogether. There appear to be a number of different reasons for this tendency to over-invest. First of all, unstable supplies of building materials and increasing prices since independence have made it advantageous to invest savings in buildings and building materials. Secondly, pressure from family members to redistribute profits from the enterprise is much smaller when the profits are invested. Thirdly, in Zimbabwe there has been an excessive belief in the importance of the large scale. However, changing attitudes to scale economies and increasing interest rates during the 1990s may gradually change the tendency to over-invest.

Many of the small enterprises not only start with family savings, they also rely at least partly on family and kinship for both labour and market relations. Family and close social relations may offer social security which is important for small entrepreneurs with few resources of their own. However, they may also serve as a mechanism for the redistribution of resources, which may make it difficult for the entrepreneur to accumulate. The system suffers from what Hydén (1983) calls the economy of affection, and Evers and Schrader (1994) call the trader's dilemma between the moral and market economies. The more successful entrepreneurs often feel exploited by family labour and family customers who think they have a customary right to credit or a share in the surplus. As the enterprise grows, many entrepreneurs try to free themselves from family labour and family dependence or limit it to the core family.

For the large enterprise, local family relations are also less likely to offer sufficient network, resources and security to guarantee its survival. Therefore, the entrepreneur with a growing enterprise will often be forced to replace the family network with clientilistic relations to large local or non-local businessmen or politicians.

11.4 Local-government restrictions on support for local enterprise development

Since independence, considerable decentralization has taken place to the district level, partly to decentralized offices of government sector ministries and partly to the district councils. However, decentralized government is still dominated by central government. The district council has elected members from each of the wards in the district, but the government district administrator is the chief executive officer and chairman of the council; and the District Development Committee, which is responsible for district planning at the local level, is not a committee of the council, but of local field representatives of the sector ministries chaired by the district administrator, in which the council is also represented.

In the district service centres, the role of elected local government is even smaller. Moyo (1995) writes:

> Currently, growth points are owned and managed by the government through the Urban and Rural State Land Office in the Ministry of Local Government, Rural and Urban Development. Government owns the land, which it plans and surveys, issues leases for occupation of land, provides finance for the development of infrastructure, hires contractors to develop the infrastructure, collects revenue from leases and maintains the infrastructure. All this government does in consultation or partnership with local authorities.

However, the district service centres are generally not well represented in the local authorities. The district service centre may correspond more or less with a ward, thus having its own Ward Development Committee and an elected representative in the district council. However, with only one representative in a council that is completely dominated by rural areas, the diverse and often conflicting interests of different groups in the small towns are not well represented.

The dominance of central government administrators in local government and the limited funds available mean that to a large extent, local government administers state regulations and policies rather than initiates local development on its own. Nonetheless, local government still has an important independent role to play in developing the local economy. In practice there may be a considerable degree of freedom in administration, which can be used to support specific local development strategies. This is demonstrated by the large differences in administrative practice between the different centres.

There are two areas especially in which local authorities in Zimbabwe are empowered to regulate economic activities within their jurisdiction: control over land use and building regulations; and health and other regulations and the licensing of business activities (Stewart, Klugman and Helmsing, 1994). Many of the current planning practices and by-laws originated before independence, when they served to restrict the development of informal economic activity and protect the larger established and often white-owned businesses against competition from street hawkers and other small businesses. Recent restrictions in respect of the second-hand clothes trade in the district service centres seem to serve a similar purpose. Many restrictions are, of course, justified for health, environmental or other reasons, while others appear to be unnecessarily restrictive. Licence fees are generally reasonably low and hardly a hindrance to enterprise development.

Urban land-use plans for the small rural business centres appear to be excessively detailed, and zoning regulations in the district service centres are also unreasonably rigorous. While it is reasonable to have rigorous zoning of large-scale industrial areas, it is less understandable why it is necessary to forbid artisan households to live at their stands in the small-scale industrial areas. As a result, they must either live in the rural areas, or spend money on a residence that could have been invested in the enterprise. It may also force the owner to pay for a night guard.

At the same time, excessive building regulations often require entrepreneurs to spend large amounts of money on a high building standard of little practical relevance, money which might have been better used for machinery or working capital. This is especially a problem in a situation where building loans are not available and most buildings have to be paid for in cash.

To make sure that expensive developed urban land is also utilized, people who are allocated an urban stand are usually required to present a bank account with enough money to build. This is obviously reasonable. In spite of this, many stands, especially in the large-scale industrial areas of Gutu and Gokwe, remain poorly developed and appear to be held primarily for speculative purposes.

In order to support the development of small businesses in the district service centres, it is important that small stands, or even better small rooms for rent, are available both in the business centre and in a centrally located small-scale industrial area. In Murewa, this was not the case when Rasmussen (1992) made his investigation in 1989. The post office had just been allocated all the small stands originally set aside in the centre for small commercial businesses. Conversely, Gokwe appears to have followed a policy much more favourable to small enterprise development. Many small enterprises have been housed in an old building in the centre, and as part of the bus station, the council has included a large building consisting of small shops for rent. In addition, a large area has been reserved for small artisans and producers. In Gutu, there has been much less room for small enterprises to develop. The focus has been rather on the development of larger enterprises.

In Gutu, a new industrial area with about a hundred industrial stands has recently been developed and serviced. Most of the stands appear to have been taken as soon as they were developed. However, with the present rate of development, it is likely to take many years before they are actually utilized. At the same time, many of the existing medium-sized industries in Gutu are located just outside the town boundary on stands still unserved by hard-surface roads.

Large housing areas, both high and low density, have also been developed recently in both Gutu and Gokwe. These large development projects have been financed by the central government and carried out by outside contractors. There is undoubtedly a large need for these new housing areas. There has been a large housing deficit in both towns for some time, especially but not only for low-cost housing. In Gutu this has resulted in a gradual increase in the density of the rural areas and villages around the town (in spite of serious attempts from the council to avoid it); and in Gokwe, poor people have been sleeping on shop verandas, while some businessmen have been forced to commute daily from the nearest large towns 140 km away. However, in spite of the large need for housing, one can speculate whether a more gradual development controlled by the local council and carried out by local contractors would not have been more beneficial to the two centres.

Local authorities play an increasing role for local enterprises as institutional buyers, not only of buildings, but also of food, work-clothes, school books, furniture etc. Most of the small new industries in the centres rely to some extent on the local public sector as a market.

One explanation for the different policies towards small enterprise development in Gutu and Gokwe may be that the old traders who have tended to see new small businesses as competitors to be avoided have had a much stronger political position in Gutu than in Gokwe, where branch stores with little influence on local politics dominate much more.

11.5 Collaboration between local government and business: the organization of the business community

Local government as a vehicle for communal area development

In the present era of liberal policies, the negative features of local government regulations have tended to be over-emphasized. At the same time, budget cuts have made it increasingly difficult for local governments to deliver satisfactory local services. Although land-use and building regulations in Zimbabwe often appear to be unnecessarily strict and ought to be liberalized, they are hardly the very serious constraint to local business development which they are sometimes claimed to be.

However, the weak resource base of most local governments points to new functions of local governments and administrations which are assuming increasing importance, namely their ability to support and collaborate with local private business and NGO initiatives to develop new local institutions, and their ability to lobby for resources with the region, the state, donors, international NGOs and other outside actors on the development scene.

All over the world, local economic development is increasingly seen to depend on interaction and collaboration between local authorities, businesses and civil society. However, in Zimbabwean administration there is little tradition for such interaction. In addition, there has been no representative business or other organization to cooperate with. As a result, interaction easily degenerates into a collaboration between top administrators and the largest local businessmen. Such a collaboration is likely to reinforce the already existing pattern of political patron-client relations and may not serve to develop a wider spectrum of local businesses and institutions.

In an investigation of the local government reform presently under discussion in Zimbabwe, Roe (1995) found that many local administrators and politicians are worried about the integrity of local government if it becomes more politicized. However, Roe also claims that the local government reform, which will amalgamate local government in the commercial farm areas and the communal areas, will also strengthen local political power vis-à-vis central government, and is likely to change the perception of local government from being a primarily administrative organization to being a vehicle for local politics and communal area development.

Organization of the business community

During the 1980s, a number of attempts were made to establish national associations of small entrepreneurs. The most important of these has been the Zimbabwe National Chamber of Commerce (ZNCC). However, it has only been able to attract a few members in rural areas and small towns such as Gutu and Gokwe.

The establishment of the Indigenous Business Development Centre (IBDC) in 1990 seems so far to be the best bid to launch such an organization. The IBDC is a national membership organization of black businessmen working for the development of African-owned businesses in Zimbabwe. It also acts as an umbrella organization for other sector-specific organizations of businessmen, e.g. the Zimbabwe Building Contractors' Association. It won recognition by the political establishment at an early stage, and it has been quite successful in lobbying for a redirection of policies and state resources away from the large-scale industries towards smaller black-owned enterprises. As a result, in 1993 the government adopted the so-called 'affirmative action programme' (National Economic Planning Commission, 1993), which should guarantee that government building tenders below a certain size (originally 10 million Z$ but later reduced to 3 million Z$) are given to black contractors, and that large contractors winning large public tenders should sub-contract part of the work to smaller black entrepreneurs who are members of the Zimbabwe Building Contractors' Association. There appears to have been some resistance to the affirmative action programme in the public administration, but it seems to be working in the state sector, though less so in the parastatal sector. Some large contractors are said to have attempted to hire black businessmen as front-men in order to avoid sub-contracting.

The IBDC has also been able to attract support from NGOs and donor organizations for small-enterprise support programmes. It is IBDC policy to work for the upgrading and registration of black businesses so that they can gain market share from the large-white owned enterprises. However, the strong focus on the upgrading and formal registration of enterprises also seems to be a defence against competition from the growing number of informal small businesses.

Although the IBDC has been more successful than earlier attempts to organize small businesses in Zimbabwe, its individual membership still tends to be concentrated among the larger black businessmen in the urban areas (Business Extension and Advisory Services, 1992). It has been less able to attract members from among the smallest businesses, especially outside the large towns. For the small rural and small-town businessmen, the membership fee is quite high (100 Z$ in 1992), and they expect to get some tangible benefits from their membership in the form of, for example, training courses or loans (Grierson and Moyo, 1993). The indirect policy benefits gained through the IBDC's lobbying activities are seldom felt to be enough, and the loan schemes and management courses which have been organized so far have seldom reached the rural areas and small towns.

Local development organizations

In Gutu, a group of local businessmen established the Gutu Business Development Association in 1995 in order to promote business development in Gutu centre. The initiative for the new association came from the new group of small industrialists, the 'academic entrepreneurs'. Members of the association are not only businessmen, but also civil servants, teachers and others with an interest in local economic development. So far, its members have been drawn especially from the top levels of the local society, but the stated policy is to try and reach the wider business community. The new association seems at least partly to be an attempt by the new industrialists to take over the dominant position in the local business community and on the local political scene, which is presently held by the old traders.

To announce its establishment, in March 1995 the Gutu Business Development Association held a large and successful development conference in Gutu, which attracted not only participants from the district but also national politicians and administrators and donors. According to the organizers, the conference had demonstrated to them the present lack of communication between the local business community and the local administration. However, the conference may also have served as an opening for that more open communication and collaboration between local actors which is a prerequisite for more rapid local development. If the increased communication and collaboration is not open, there is a real danger that it can lead to increased corruption and misuse of power and resources. To avoid this, it is important that such business associations (and they are also being formed in other district service centres) are counterbalanced by local organizations of other groups in civil society.

11.6   Local development actors

The development of the district service centres has to a large extent been structured by external forces: government policies and institutions, parastatals and national retail chains. But the actual development that has taken place has been just as much the result of the local response to those external forces by managers, administrators and, most importantly, entrepreneurs (both locals and migrants, often return migrants), who have invested their energy and savings in the development of local enterprises and institutions.

Throughout the 1980s, new groups of people have been involved in the development process. Many of the traditional general traders have been reduced to grocery stores, others have been able to establish more specialized stores, mostly in clothing, hardware and furniture, and a few have been able to expand into large commercial business complexes. Of the traditional rural artisans, a few have grown into small construction enterprises, a few, mostly welders, have been able to establish small production enterprises, and one has diversified into one of the largest business conglomerations in Gutu, but many entrepreneurs survive as sub-contractors with a status not much different from casual labourers.

Since the end of the 1980s, a new group of entrepreneurs, mostly young people with secondary education and varying degrees of vocational training but often very little capital, have established many small enterprises often serving narrow niche markets. At the same time, a smaller group of what we have called 'academic entrepreneurs' have established a number of medium-sized production enterprises. They are typically highly qualified, well connected to national economic and political institutions, and with sufficient collateral outside the communal areas to be able to borrow enough to invest in a relative large enterprise.

In the branch enterprises, the older 'administrative managers' of the parastatal branches have been complemented by a new group of often very young 'business managers' in the private branch stores.

In this development process, the inward-looking rural patron-client system that existed before independence has gradually been replaced by a more outward-looking system which secures access to national/government economic resources and political decisions. Although government was partly decentralized after independence, control has very much remained with central government, and local government has remained more administrative than political. Still, the large differences in policy towards small enterprises show that local government has had possibilities to support specific local development strategies and has had an important impact on local economic development.

For local government to play an active role, however, it has to have local representative organizations to respond to, organizations which make demands on behalf of their members, and with which local government can negotiate. It is also important that there is more than one such organization. Different groups of entrepreneurs have different requirements, and their requirements differ from those of peasant farmers, labourers and civil servants. Different groups also provide different resources to the development process, for example personal qualifications and savings, which may remain unused if the groups are not allowed to act.

The different groups of small-town actors may well unite in their common fight for a larger share of national resources. But locally, conflicts may be waiting just below the surface. Rural traders, new industrialists and young small entrepreneurs have different resources and make different demands. At the same time, the old family-based labour market is gradually giving way to a new labour market in the small towns based on qualified wage labour and emerging conflicts between labour and larger entrepreneurs.

Notes

1   According to the *Statistical Yearbook* for 1989, there are around 1 million people employed in the formal sector in Zimbabwe. The Gemini study (Daniels, 1994) estimates the small enterprise, non-farm sector to employ about 1.5 million people.

2   According to figures in the annual report for 1989 from the Secretary of Higher Education (1991), the monthly cost per trainee at the government's Youth Training Centres and Technical Colleges is at least two to three times higher than the monthly fee at the small private training centres in Gutu and Gokwe.

Part III
THEORETICAL AND POLICY CONCLUSIONS

12 Instability, flexibility and the structure of competition and collaboration among enterprises in small African towns: strategies for small-town development

12.1 Introduction

In this book we have been inspired by the theories of flexible specialization, enterprise networks and industrial clusters to study the dynamics of small rural market towns in Africa. However, the African rural market town is not an industrial cluster. It is differently structured and usually much smaller, but resembles the industrial cluster in being an agglomeration of enterprises operating under unstable economic conditions, often even less stable than those of the industrial cluster. As a result, there are important similarities, but also differences, between the strategies followed by businessmen in industrial clusters and in rural market towns.

The theories of flexible specialization, enterprise networks and industrial clusters describe the strategies which small and medium-sized enterprises may pursue under unstable market conditions caused by rapid technological change in order to survive in an environment dominated by large enterprises. Their response to the unstable environment is specialization in order to exploit market niches, and collaboration with other enterprises in order to secure their access to resources and new technology.

In small rural towns in Africa, enterprises also operate under unstable conditions. However, the instability is not caused primarily by technological change, but by instability in agricultural production, production inputs and capital. As in more industrialized economies, the response of the enterprise is to attempt to create specialized segmented markets and to form networks which can secure their access to scarce resources. However, both specialization and networking tend to be of a different kind. Specialization and market segmentation is not primarily based on product differentiation, but on differences in distribution services; and networking is not based primarily on collaboration among specialized enterprises, but rather on family and social networks and patron-client relations.

In this final chapter, I shall examine the small rural market town as a special type of enterprise cluster and use the theory of industrial clusters to improve our understanding of the dynamics of the small rural market town. Section 12.2 presents a brief outline of the theory of industrial clusters. Then, based on the empirical studies, Section 12.3 describes the structure of the rural market town as a cluster of enterprises. The small-town enterprise operates in a very unstable economic environment. We believe this instability is the most important key to understanding the structure of the small-town economy. Section 12.4 summarizes the investment and networking strategies which businessmen and -women tend to follow in their attempts to counteract instability. The magnitude of the instability causes these strategies to be rather defensive. Section 12.5 looks at the causes of growth and stagnation of the small rural towns. Finally, Section 12.6 discusses the strategies needed to make the small towns grow more rapidly.

12.2   The industrial cluster

The *raison d'etre* of the industrial cluster is its ability to function efficiently in an environment which is rapidly changing due to innovation and technological development, or what Schmitz (1990, 1995b) has called collective efficiency. This collective efficiency is based on interdependence and cooperation among specialized clustering enterprises or between the specialized enterprises in a cluster and their suppliers and customers outside the cluster.

A cluster of enterprises may be based on vertically or horizontally specialized enterprises or a mixture of both; it may comprise the whole chain of vertical specializations in the production and distribution chain from raw material to consumer, or it may be specialized in a single or a few links of the chain; and it may be horizontally broad, comprising many different sectors, or narrowly specialized in a single or a few sectors. However, most discussions of industrial clusters and collective efficiency have focused on clusters based on small vertically disintegrated enterprises within the same broad sector or filiere.

Enterprises in such clusters pursue strategies of flexible specialization and networking as a response to unstable market conditions caused by rapid technological change, and in order to secure their access to resources and new technology.

The collective efficiency achieved in industrial clusters is derived from:

– collaboration between vertically specialized enterprises in the form of flows of goods, services and information between the enterprises. Such vertical collaboration may take place among small enterprises or entail sub-contractual relations between large and small enterprises. The benefits of such vertical collaboration within an industrial cluster include the ability to exploit scale economies beyond the size of the individual enterprise, the ability to specialize and diversify in order to attract a wider range of customers, and a more rapid diffusion of innovation through forward and backward linkages and labour mobility among the enterprises;

–   horizontal collaboration between small enterprises in order to service large orders, develop diversified private and public services, labour markets and markets for second-hand capital equipment, or form more formal small-enterprise organizations for the purpose of lobbying for government or donor resources and legal/political rights. These forms of horizontal collaboration are based on common interest and not on horizontal specialization between enterprises. Such horizontal specialization and market segmentation within clusters are not discussed much in the literature on flexible specialization, although many empirical studies show that it plays an important role (e.g., Schmitz, 1995a and b; Knorringa, 1995; Pedersen, Sverrisson and van Dijk, 1994);

–   family and social networks play an important role in the formation of more institutionalized enterprise networks;

–   local government, local offices of central government and civil organizations play an important role as partners, in both forming and running such enterprise networks.

The full-blown successful industrial cluster exploiting the maximum of collective efficiencies and developing along what has been called the high road (Sengenberger and Pyke, 1992) probably requires the cluster to comprise and control the whole or at least a large part of the links in the vertical production chain. However, some industrial clusters which have not been able to expand beyond a single or a few links in the production and distribution system may develop along the low road into clusters of simple sub-contractors or petty commodity producers (see also chapter 4).

12.3   The small rural market town as a cluster of enterprises

While industrial clusters are characterized by vertical specialization among enterprises, market towns are rather characterized by horizontal specialization. In Christaller's (1933) classical central-place theory, traders or small-scale producers from different sectors co-locate in the market town in order to exploit agglomeration economies. These agglomeration economies are not

191

based on the increased efficiency of the enterprises themselves, but on reduced transport and search costs for customers, and they therefore attract more customers than the individual enterprise would have been able to do. However, this larger flow of customers might make it possible for the individual enterprises to exploit economies of scale and thus increase their collective efficiency.

According to classical central-place theory, the market town is characterized by horizontal specialization among sectors, while individual sectors are assumed to be homogeneous and without overlap. Therefore, all enterprises within a sector are alike, and competition among them is purely price competition, where there is no room for collaboration between enterprises within a sector. Supplies of goods and services for the enterprises in the market town are assumed to be unproblematically supplied by enterprises in larger, higher order towns, either by a perfectly competitive market or by state administration. At the same time, the market town is assumed to have a spatial monopoly within its own hinterland. Thus hierarchies of enterprises and urban centres are merged into one and the same.

However, these assumptions about homogeneous markets and strictly hierarchical supply systems fit badly to the reality of the small African towns. Here, enterprises from all levels of the urban and organizational hierarchies often compete for the same local market. Small rural traders and small-scale producers may compete with larger traders, branch stores, small-town producers, retail shops in the larger towns selling to labour migrants, or large urban producers distributing directly to rural farmers. These different distribution channels may be locally owned or externally controlled. They may be operated as private businesses, cooperatives, NGOs, parastatals or government institutions.

NGOs, cooperatives, parastatals and government institutions are often discussed as if they served closed non-competitive markets. This is seldom the case. NGOs and cooperatives mostly serve quite limited niche markets and have to defend the borders of their markets. Even state and parastatal institutions operating with a formal monopoly most often have insufficient resources to serve the entire market satisfactorily and have to compete with black-market traders. However, this may not only be a disadvantage, because it means that NGOs, cooperatives and public institutions are important not only in their own market niche. Even fairly small organizations may also be able to influence neighbouring market segments, as shown by the example of cooperative fertilizer sale in Gutu presented in chapter 6.

The position of the small rural town in this system of parallel competing distribution channels varies from sector to sector and over time. We find examples where small rural businesses gain market shares, and others where large-town businesses win the competition. The small towns may gain market shares both from the small rural businesses and from the large urban enterprises; they may also lose market shares to both rural areas and large towns. However, it often seems possible for small towns to compensate losses to the large towns by gaining market share from the rural areas or the other way round.

The markets of the different channels of distribution and collection are typically segmented. In the industrial world market, segmentation is usually discussed in terms of product differentiation and quality. Market segmentation in the small African towns may also be based on product differentiation and product quality, but is more often based on the availability of scarce products or production inputs, on specialized sources of capital and labour, and on differences in delivery services, such as credit, transport, size of consignment or proximity.

Such market segmentation is a result of scarcity in the supply and distribution systems (e.g. lack of credit, transport or wholesale outlets) and can be seen as an attempt to overcome such scarcities. Contrary to neo-classical economics, which sees such market segmentation as an expression of market imperfection and therefore as a sign of inefficiency, we see it rather as an expression of collective efficiency based on horizontal specialization. Market segmentation leads to better utilization of scarce resources from a more diversified set of sources than one would find in homogeneous markets, under both free competition and parastatal monopolies. The segmented markets are able to draw on diversified supply of, for example, production inputs (industrial products, informal products, by-products, waste products), credit (banks, NGOs, suppliers, own savings) and transport (trucks, buses, cars, bicycles, walking), much of which would remain unused under assumptions of homogeneous markets. The competitive segmented market is therefore likely to reach more consumers than either the perfect market or the parastatal monopoly operating under similarly scarce resources in the distribution system. However, just like the monopoly operating under insufficient resources, it is unlikely to reach the poorest and most marginal consumers.

The horizontal specialization and market segmentation found among small-town enterprises thus result in collective efficiency, but a collective efficiency which is not based on direct collaboration among the enterprises but rather on a process of competition and mutual adaptation.

The fact that enterprises operate on segmented markets does not mean that they do not compete. Enterprises may obtain a partial monopoly in the core of their market segment, but they still compete over the delimitation and size of the segment. The borders of their market segment may shift as a result of, for example, innovation, increasing efficiency, changing input prices and government policies.

This process of market segmentation contrasts with the petty commodity theory, which tends to see small enterprises as duplicating one another rather than creating diversification. This duplication results in cut-throat competition and low earnings in the small enterprises. In terms of products, such duplication of activities clearly does take place. However, our investigation in chapter 6 of general dealers in the small rural centres shows that enterprises which seem to duplicate one another may in fact complement one another's limited resources. Due to a lack of transport, unstable commodity supplies and, most importantly, recurrent cash-flow problems, they cannot themselves guarantee regular supplies and provide the credit which many low-income households need. From a consumer point of view, activity duplication therefore often serves an important purpose.

12.4 Entrepreneureal strategies to counteract economic instability and grow

The structure of instability

The small rural towns function as intermediaries between the rural areas and the larger urban system. Thus they are hit by both rural and urban instabilities. On the one hand, they are part of the rural areas and depend on agricultural production and small rural non-farm activities, heavily influenced by seasonal and climatic swings. Financing the harvest and the storage of produce from harvest to harvest and during drought years swallows large amounts of capital and savings and leads to large seasonal capital shortages. As a result, most rural and small-town enterprises suffer from recurrent cash-flow problems and large swings in the market. On the other hand, small towns are also part of the urban system, if its most marginal part, to which instabilities caused by economic cycles and shifting national and international policies are channelled and often multiplied through unstable prices, cyclical employment and labour movements, and swings in public service provision.

Finally, individual incidents, such as family illness, traffic accidents, theft and fire, have much larger impact on the enterprises than in the industrialized countries where their effect has been reduced to a large extent by insurance and social-security systems. Small towns and their businesses therefore operate in a very unstable economic environment, where both product markets and access to resources are unpredictable and cash-flow problems endemic. I believe that this instability is the most important key to understanding the structure of the economy of small African towns.

Investment strategies

The ability to withstand economic instability depends on the one hand, on the fixed costs and obligations that one has to meet, even at the lowest turnover, and on the other, on the amount of capital that one can command with relatively

194

short notice as a buffer in times of crisis. Poor households therefore tend to be more sensitive to instability than rich ones, and small enterprises with few resources are often more sensitive than large ones. Thus the ability of an entrepreneur to withstand economic instability partly depends on social status and enterprise size, because the higher social classes and larger enterprises are likely both to command more capital and to be able to invest in the most profitable and stable sectors. However, the ability to withstand economic instability also depends on the strategies of the individual entrepreneur and his ability to collaborate and pool resources with other people, enterprises or organizations. The study shows a number of different strategies which small entrepreneurs choose in order to spread risk, reduce fixed costs and increase liquidity:

– most small entrepreneurs treat investments as sunken costs in order to reduce the fixed costs of interest and depreciation. They therefore hesitate to borrow money against interest for long-term investments because this would increase their fixed costs. They often find it less risky to borrow short-term money to cover operational costs, even though interest rates are higher;

– small town businessmen and -women tend to diversify into different sectors rather than expand their first business to non-local markets. This is partly to spread the risk, but also to be able to stay within the local market where local networks can be utilized and where it is easier to control the business. However, within each sector businessmen attempt to find niches where they are at least partly shielded from their competitors. Such niches may be based on specific groups of customers, on specific sources of raw material, capital or labour, or on specific combinations of delivery services (e.g. transport, credit, or size of consignment);

– many small-town businessmen have spent years as wage-earners in the large towns or locally before they started their businesses, and many keep their wage labour as a security against the large swings in the rural economy. This, of course, also means that they only invest part of their time in the business;

– small businessmen look for market segments where they can utilize their own specific combination of resources (rather than abstract capital) to create at least a partial monopoly. To successful businessmen, the market is only partly determined by external structural forces. It is to a large extent created though entrepreneureal strategies;

- most small-town businessmen prefer to invest in commodity stocks which are easy to convert into liquid capital and may even increase in value during crises. On the other hand, few small-town businessmen have been interested in investing in production machinery, which is much more difficult to convert into cash in case of crisis;

- entrepreneurs investing in industrial production appear in many cases to have over-invested in fixed capital, and as a result have ended up with insufficient working capital. This may be because they, often having an urban origin, have tended to underestimate rural market instability;

- the dominance of large retail chains and monopolized parastatals has meant that the wholesale sector in general is not very developed. This has made it difficult for small enterprises to expand in the national and international markets, and reinforced the tendency for local businesses to remain in the local market.

Networking strategies

To the small enterprise, networking is a strategy to obtain access to resources other than one's own in order to counteract the negative impact of instability or to grow. The small enterprise may participate in a number of different types of network. These networks may either be household-based, family/social networks or clientilistic relations, or they may be enterprise-based production and distribution networks or broader business associations. Most small businessmen participate in and rely on household-based family networks and clientilistic relations to overcome swings in the economy. Enterprise-based networks are much less frequent, although household-based networks may also function to some extent as enterprise networks.

Household-based networks can be seen as an insurance against instability in the environment. The family/social network gives members a certain guarantee against crises, but it also requires a redistribution of resources which may make it difficult for small businessmen to accumulate and invest. Many of the more successful businessmen therefore attempt to reduce their responsibility to the family/social network or limit it to the core family. However, this is a dilemma for the small businessman because the family/social network not only represents a guarantee against crises, but also an important part of the market.

However, the ability of a local family network to offer support during crises, especially among poor people, is quite limited (Fafchamps, 1992). It may offer support against individual casual events, but it is unlikely to offer security against larger seasonal and annual swings which tend to hit everybody in the local network at the same time. During such general crises, there simply will not be any surplus in the network to redistribute. In order to overcome such general crises, households usually attempt to develop family/social networks with members in both rural and urban areas. The rural poor tend to form households which have not been able to develop such urban-rural linkages in their social network. These are often female-headed households or women with husbands who do not earn enough to remit anything to them. In the absence of a state social-security system, poor households are forced to rely on patron-client relations. Thus in spite of the exploitative nature of most patron-client relations, it is in poor people's interest that some people have been able to accumulate enough wealth (or establish access to state or donor resources) to support others during major crises. In general, the poorer the people and the larger the instability, the more wealth patrons need to collect to serve their purpose. Patron-client relationships therefore represent a sort of negative sub-optimal equilibrium which is difficult to shift. The family/ social network is clearly not a possible substitute for the patron-client relationship. Rather, they complement each other. In most developing countries, attempts to let the state take over have so far had only a limited success.

The patrons are most often local big businessmen. For many small businessmen, the patron also makes up an important part of the enterprise network as a main supplier or distributor. For the somewhat larger businessmen, the local patron may be substituted by non-local suppliers or distributors, either large urban-based enterprises or small, often informal, business links. However, in an economy characterized by frequent commodity scarcity and lack of capital, stable contacts to large enterprises which can provide supplier credit and guarantee deliveries become very important.

Networks of small enterprises as they are found in industrial districts in Europe, and increasingly also in southeast Asia, have therefore had difficulties developing in Africa; and where they are found, they tend to be rudimentary (Sverrisson, 1993; McCormick and Pedersen, 1996). Due to a lack of resources, knowledge and external contacts in local, small and medium-sized enterprises, networks of small local enterprises mostly have too little to offer compared with links with large enterprises. Therefore, many of the links between small enterprises in the small towns have not been links between local enterprises, but family-based links between small-town enterprises and small enterprises in the large towns. The most pressing problem for small-town enterprises seems to be access to external resources, services and markets, which networks of small local businesses do not solve.

Broader national associations of businessmen have also attracted few members in the small towns. Such associations have been lobbying for small and medium-sized enterprises in general, but for the most part they have had little impact outside the large towns. Therefore, the present attempt to establish locally based development associations organizing not only businessmen but also other groups in local society may prove to be more successful, because they will lobby more specifically for more resources being given to the local area.

12.5 The causes of small-town growth and stagnation

In order to grow, small rural market towns, like all other enterprise clusters, require a growing market. For small rural towns, such market growth may come from various sources:

– the local small-town market may grow because money income in the small town and its hinterland increases. Due to increasing commercialization of the rural economy, many small towns have been able to grow for this reason, even where total rural production in the hinterland has decreased. Small-town enterprises may benefit from such growth without increasing their efficiency relative to external suppliers in the large towns or rural areas;

– the small town may also increase its share of the total local market in competition with external suppliers. This requires small-town enterprises to increase their individual or collective efficiency relative to external suppliers. They can do this either through horizontal specialization and diversification of the locally available supplies, or through vertical specialization and collaboration with non-local or local enterprises, which make them able to deliver goods and services at lower prices, on more favourable terms and with greater variety or better quality. Many small African towns, such as the Zimbabwean district service centres investigated here, have also been able to grow for this reason, primarily through horizontal specialization and diversification both between and within sectors;

– finally, the small town may expand into non-local/export markets. However, this requires small-town enterprises to increase their individual or collective efficiency in absolute terms, primarily through vertical specialization and collaboration with other large or small, local or non-local enterprises. Few small-town enterprises have been able to do this, and as a result few small towns have been able to expand into the national and export markets.

This contrasts with the successful industrial clusters which have usually expanded for all three reasons and have therefore been able to grow much more rapidly than the small rural market towns. More rapid growth of small

198

towns requires increased vertical specialization into production and specialized services, and an expansion into non-local markets. However, few local businessmen have the resources to invest in local industrial production and marketing for the non-local market; and those large local traders who would have sufficient resources to do so have with few exceptions (and probably for good reason) considered such investments too risky and preferred to diversify into other local trade and service sectors.

Those relatively few businessmen who have invested in small industrial plants in the small towns have generally been businessmen who only partly rely on the unstable rural market, for example branches of large urban enterprises, businessmen with well-paid urban wage employment, or local businessmen with strong family ties with the urban areas and often close family ties with the national political and economic elite.

The expansion of the small-town economy into manufacturing and non-local markets seems to require a shift in the structure of rural-urban links from personal links based on rural traders-cum-patrons and family/social relations into a more diversified and partly institutionalized system of inter-enterprise links. The prevailing very unstable and risky economic environment in the small towns has not been conducive to such a shift, nor have rural development policies in most African countries.

In the rural distribution system inherited from the colonial period by countries in eastern and southern Africa, rural-urban links were dominated by a hierarchy of rural traders-cum-patrons. They were only met with competition from the family or social network, which was based on migrant workers and the commodities they could carry back with them from the large towns. This gave the rural trader an almost monopolistic position in the local market, especially vis-à-vis the poorer households. On the other hand, the rural trader often had little control over his urban links, especially if he was African. Thus in Zimbabwe, African traders were legally restricted from carrying out most business activities in the urban areas. In many cases in Africa, rural traders have been dependent on local patrons controlling external contacts, which has made it difficult for them to operate outside their local area, because that would require them to shift to a larger regional or national patron.

After independence, European or Asian traders-cum-patrons were typically replaced by monopolistic parastatals or African traders-cum-patrons without changing the basic structure. In Zimbabwe, the growing commercialization of agricultural production in the communal areas togehter with increased labour migration and rural wage labour all led to a rapid increase in rural trade and in the number of rural traders. The establishment of parastatal grain- and cotton-marketing depots in the new district service centres and the resulting increase in produce trade especially benefited the larger rural traders who had enough capital to become certified buyers for the marketing boards.

199

However, the monopoly of the marketing boards also forced the rural traders to remain within their local area, and their pricing policies made it almost impossible for them to invest in local agroprocessing. In many countries, parastatals appear to have merged with patron-client relations without changing the basic structure of the distribution system.

Agricultural policies have also tended to limit the development of agroprocessing activities in the small towns. Most African governments have tended to favour the expansion of large standardized commercial crops in order to secure export incomes, inputs for large-scale processing industries, food for the growing urban population and a taxable level of production. Conversely, many donors and NGOs have focused on the expansion of subsistance crops in order to combat rural poverty and hunger. However, little has been done to secure a diversified agricultural production for the growing food market and small-scale agroprocessing in the rural areas and small towns. As a consequence, these markets are often supplied expensively from the large towns rather than from the local rural hinterland. Such diversified agricultural production would require collaboration and coordination between the small farmers and the growing number of small processing industries and market outlets in the small towns. In our Zimbabwean case, the lack of such coordination appears to be a major problem for the small local oil mills and also for the supply of vegetables to the market.

12.6 Strategies for small-town development

The development which has taken place in Zimbabwe's district service centres since the end of the 1980s can be seen as the beginning of a process of substituting personal patron-client relations and family networks with enterprise-based networks. However, it is still too early to tell where this process will end. I suggest three possible outcomes of this process of transformation:

1   In the optimistic scenario, the small town develops into an industrial cluster specializing in a broad sector which could be agroprocessing, but in Gutu, for example, could also be clothing. A large number of both vertically and horizontally specialized enterprises would develop within the sector. Thus the cluster should not be too narrowly specialized but be able to shift between alternative local, national and international markets in competition with large enterprises. Many of the enterprises would operate in markets with high transaction costs which they would attempt to reduce by internalizing some of them within the cluster. They would react to instability in input and product markets through the flexibility of their own production system and their ability and willingness

200

to exploit each other's excess capacities and technological capabilities. They would also collaborate over the development and aquisition of new resources and production capabilities. Collective efficiencies would be derived from enterprise collaboration both within and outside the cluster.

2   In the second scenario, the small town develops into a sub-contractor cluster based on narrow vertical and horizontal specialization, both of individual enterprises and of the cluster as a whole. Many of the enterprises, especially the largest, will be dependent on and, as sub-contractors or even as branches, linked to one or a few large enterprises. These large enterprises may be located within or more likely outside the small town. By linking themselves as sub-contractors to large enterprises, small enterprises with few resources of their own may improve their access to resources and markets. In developing rural regions with unstable markets, the recurrent cash-flow problems caused by seasonal and climatic cycles in agriculture may be partly overcome, but at the cost of a new instability caused by a lack of control of markets, prices and technological change. Collective efficiency in such a cluster is not based primarily on collaboration between the small enterprises in the cluster, but on reduced transaction costs with the large enterprises, which may also appropriate most of the benefit. On the other hand, through collaboration, the small sub-contractors may be able to improve their competitive power both vis-à-vis alternative suppliers and in bargaining for better conditions with the larger enterprise.

3   Finally, in the third scenario, the small town develops into a petty commodity cluster which diversifies vertically from trade into services and production based on small micro-enterprises with very few resources. The cluster may or may not be specialized in a specific sector. The new small enterprises will both compete with and complement local retailers, but will hardly be able to expand into non-local markets. Some collaboration between small enterprises may take place, but the collective efficiencies achieved through clustering in the small town will be primarily due to reduced transaction and search costs for the customers. The small enterprises in the petty commodity cluster operate with very little capital in a very unstable environment. They therefore tend to be closely linked to the household economy of the entrepreneur and highly dependent on his wider family/social networks and patron-client relations. Thus the petty commodity cluster is unlikely to transform the structure by itself.

The actual outcome of the development process and its ability to transform the rural economy depends on both local and non-local forces, and on small and large enterprises and the diverse set of resources they can mobilize. Therefore, the three scenarios may not really be alternatives, but would rather have to complement each other if successful development is to be achieved.

Small enterprises cannot develop where large enterprises have obtained monopoly status. But where there are no large enterprises or they are very inefficient, it may also be difficult for small enterprises to expand outside the local market. This is either because small enterprises often obtain access to non-local resources and markets via large enterprises and their national and international networks, or because large enterprises may be instrumental in the initial expansion of a monetized rural economy.

In addition, small and large enterprises tend to supply partly different markets and use different resources, thus often benefiting from one another. Where the large enterprise operates in a quasi-monopoly, it may be forced to carry out peripheral tasks which a large centralized organization cannot do efficiently, or it may leave them undone. On the other hand, where the large-scale sector collapses, small enterprises may operate in large markets which may well be profitable for them but where they do not run efficiently, and where competition is limited so that prices rise and markets decline.

Policies to develop clusters of enterprises and collective efficiencies in small rural towns should therefore seek to develop a balance between small and large enterprises by demonopolizing the large enterprises and developing markets for small enterprises. Corresponding to the three sources of small-town growth presented at the beginning of this section, such policies should attempt to:

– increase money incomes in the rural areas by increasing agricultural productivity and prices;

– demonopolize the commercial, industrial and financial sectors and support the development of small and medium-size enterprises. The primary goal of such a policy should be not to increase employment and incomes in the small enterprise sector, but to increase the overall efficiency of the production and distribution system, in order to lower prices and increase the buying power of the rural population. Policies which go directly for increased employment and income in the small towns are less likely to increase the efficiency of the agricultural sector and thus improve living conditions in rural areas;

– expand small-town production and distribution to the large towns and export markets through the liberalization of both foreign trade and trade in the national market. Although few small-town enterprises can enter

202

the export market, they may benefit from export-orientation policies if these encourage large urban enterprises to reorient their production towards the export market and thus open up the national market to smaller enterprises. However, export-orientation policies tend to conflict with policies to raise low incomes, partly because they attempt to reduce wages and partly because they tend to shift the focus of agricultural policies from food crops to export crops. They also tend to favour large enterprises and thus may be in conflict with policies to demonopolize. At the same time, import liberalization leads to increased competition, which may hurt small-scale producers badly unless they are able to increase their efficiency; on the other hand, competition can lead to a reduction in prices and thus increase the total buying power of low income and rural consumers and therefore of the market.

The policy elements proposed here are very much the same as those proposed by the current wave of structural-adjustment programmes. However, in structural-adjustment programmes the order of implementation has usually been the opposite, and policy conflicts have tended to be resolved in favour of export expansion at the expense of income expansion and the diversification of products and services for the home market.

A policy to develop the small towns and their rural hinterlands should first aim at a better utilization of local resources and market potentials by developing a more diversified economic structure which allows for both small and large enterprises and for different organizational forms (private, cooperative, public). This requires change in the institutional and administrative practices of the public sector at both national and local levels, and decentralization of competence in order to reduce the use of standardized national-development programmes and make it possible for local governments to interact with other local actors. This change should lead to a public sector which is not only geared towards a monopolistic large-scale sector, but which is also prepared to accept both large and small, formal and informal enterprises, as well as civil organizations, as legitimate partners in the development process. Such acceptance of both small enterprises and civil organizations and of their potential contribution to development is a prerequisite for the establishment of reasonable conditions for their operation, rather than the blind harassment and even eradication with which they are often met today.

The second aim should be to reduce the negative impact of the great instability of the rural economy. This will require the intensification and diversification of the links between the rural and urban economies in order to gain access to urban markets and resources. The rural-urban link today is greatly dominated on the one hand, by internal contacts within large monopolistic public and private enterprises, and on the other, by personal relations within family networks. This limits access to urban resources. A more diversified enterprise and organizational structure in the small towns and rural areas could be instrumental in strengthening rural-urban relations, just as public policies to redistribute state resources between rural and urban areas are important in securing more resources for the rural areas and reducing the impact of economic instability.

References

Aboagye, A.A. (1986), *Informal sector employment in Kenya: A survey of informal sector activities in Nairobi, Kisumu and Mombasa*, ILO, Jobs and Skills Programme for Africa: Addis Ababa.

Amin, N. (1989), 'Market reform in Zimbabwe: Peasantry, maize marketing and food security', paper presented at an UNRISD seminar on Food Pricing and Marketing Reforms, November, Geneva.

Arrighi, G. (1973a), 'Labour supplies in historical perspective: A study of the proletarization of the African peasantry in Rhodesia', in G. Arrighi and J.S. Saul (eds.), *Essays on the political economy of Africa*, New York Monthly Review Press.

Arrighi, G. (1973b), 'The political economy of Rhodesia', in G. Arrighi and J.S. Saul (eds.), *Essays on the political economy of Africa*, New York Monthly Review Press.

Aschwanda, H. (1987), *Symbols of death*, Mambo Press: Gweru, Zimbabwe.

Ærøe, A. (1992), 'The role of small towns in regional development in south-east Africa', in J. Baker and P.O. Pedersen (eds.), *The rural-urban interface in Africa: Expansion and adaptation*, Scandinavian Institute of African Studies: Uppsala.

Baker, J. (1990), 'The growth and functions of small urban centres in Ethiopia', in J. Baker (ed.), *Small town Africa: Studies in rural- urban interaction*, Scandinavian Institute of African Studies: Uppsala.

Baker, J. and Pedersen, P.O. (1992), 'Introduction', in J. Baker and P.O. Pedersen (eds.), *The rural-urban interface in Africa: Expansion and adaptation*, Scandinavian Institute of African Studies: Uppsala.

Basera, B. (1994), 'Changing population structure and characteristics of a small urban centre since independence: The case of Gutu-Mupandawana', unpublished BA thesis, Department of Geography, University of Zimbabwe: Harare.

Becattini, G. (1990), 'The Marshallian industrial district as a socio-economic notion', in F. Pyke, G. Becattini and W. Sengenberger (eds.), *Industrial districts and interfirm cooperation in Italy*, International Institute for Labour Studies: Geneva.

Belsky, E.S. and Karaska, G.J. (1990), 'Approaches to locating urban functions in developing rural areas', *International Regional Science Review* 13: pp. 225–40.

Berg, L. van den (1981), *Central place theory and planning of rural service centres in Africa*, Zambia Geographical Association Occasional Study, No. 11, Lusaka.

Berry, B.J.L. (1967), *Geography of market centres and retail distribution*, Prentice-Hall: Englewood Cliffs, NJ.

Bessant, L. and Muringai, E. (1993), 'Peasant, businessmen and moral economy in the Chiweshe Reserve, colonial Zimbabwe 1930–68', *Journal of Southern African Studies* 19, 4: pp. 551–92.

Billetoft, J. (1989), *Rural non-farm enterprises in Western Kenya: Spatial structure and development*, CDR Project Paper 89.3, Centre for Development Research: Copenhagen.

Billetoft, J. (1995), *Between industrialization and income generation: The dilemma of support for micro activities. A policy study of Kenya and Bangladesh*, Centre for Development Research: Copenhagen.

Blunt, P. (1983), *Organizational theory and behaviour: An African perspective*, Longman: London.

Bonnevie, H. (1987), *Migration and malformation: Case studies from Zimbabwe*, CDR Project Paper A.87.1, Centre for Development Research: Copenhagen.

Bourdillon, M. (1987 [1976]), *The Shona peoples*, Mambo Press: Gweru, Zimbawe.

Brand, V. (1986), 'One dollar work places: A study of informal sector activities in Bagaba, Harare', *Journal of Social Development in Africa* 1, 2: pp. 53–74.

Brand, V., Mupedziswa, R. and Gumbo, P. (1995), 'Structural adjustment, women and informal trade in Harare', in P. Gibbon (ed.), *Structural adjustment and the working poor in Zimbabwe*, Scandinavian Institute of African Studies: Uppsala.

Bromley, R. (1984), 'The urban road to rural development: Reflections on USAID's "urban functions" approach', in H.D. Kammeier and P.J. Swan (eds.), *Equity with growth planning perspectives for small towns in developing countries*, Asian Institute of Technology: Bangkok.

Bryceson, D. (1990), *Food security and the social division of labour in Tanzania 1919–85*, MacMillan Press: London.

Burrows, S. (1992), 'The role of indigenous NGOs in the development of small town enterprises in Ghana', in J. Baker and P.O. Pedersen (eds.),

The rural-urban interface in African expansion and adaptation, The Scandinavian Institute for African Studies: Uppsala.

Business Extension and Advisory Services (BESA) (1992), IBDC: Membership profile and business extension and advisory services, Annex 13 to *Technical Report: Survey of small scale industries and indigenous ownership in Zimbabwe*, DP/ZIM/90/005 (20 May 1993), UNDP: Vienna.

Castells, M. and Portes, A. (1989), 'The world underneath: The origins, dynamics and effects of the informal sector', in A. Portes, M. Castells and L. Benten (eds.), *The informal economy: studies in advanced and less developed countries*, Johns Hopkins University Press: Baltimore.

Central Statistical Office (1988/89), *The census of production 1988/89*, Harare.

Central Statistical Office (1989), *Statistical Yearbook of Zimbabwe*, Harare.

Central Statistical Office (1991), *Quarterly digest of statistics, December 1991*, Harare.

Central Statistical Office (1994), *Quarterly digest of statistics, October 1994*, Harare.

Chipika, S. (1993a), 'ESAP and the small scale foodstuffs sector in Zimbabwe', unpublished ms, Intermediate Technology Development Group: Harare.

Chipika, S. (ed.) (1993b), *Report on decentralized agro-industry seminar, 30 March 1993*, Intermediate Technology Development Group: Harare.

Christaller, W. (1933), *Die zentralen Orte in Süddeutschland: Eine ökonomisch- geographische Untersuchung über die Gesetzmässigkeit der Verbreitung und Entwicklung der Siedlungen mit städtlichen Funktionen*, Gustav Fischer Verlag: Jena.

Cousins, B. (1993), 'Debating communal tenure in Zimbabwe', *Journal of Contemporary African Studies* 12, 1: pp. 29–39.

Cousins, B., Weiner, D. and Amin, N. (1992), 'Social differentiation in the communal lands of Zimbabwe', *Review of African Political Economy* 53: pp. 5–24.

Daniels, L. (1994), *Changes in the small-scale enterprise sector from 1991 to 1993: Results of a second nationwide survey in Zimbabwe*, Gemini Technical Report no. 71, Gemini: Bethesda, Maryland.

Dicken, P. (1994), 'The Roepke lecture in economic geography. Global-local tensions: Firms and states in the global space-economy', *Economic Geography* 70, 2: pp. 101–28.

Drakakis-Smith, D.W. (1994), 'Food systems and the poor in Harare under conditions of structural adjustment', *Geografiska Annaler* 76B, 1: pp. 3–20.

Evans, H.E. and Ngau, P. (1991), 'Rural-urban relations, household income diversification and agricultural productivity', *Development and Change* 22: pp. 519–45.

Evers, H.-D. and Schrader, H. (eds.) (1994), *The moral economy of trade, ethnicity and developing markets*, Routledge: London and New York.

Fafchamps, Marcel (1992), 'Solidarity networks in preindustrial societies: Rational peasants with a moral economy', *Economic Development and Cultural Change* 41, 1: pp. 147–74.

Fallon, P.R., and Lucas, R.E.B. (1991), 'The impact of changes in job security regulations in India and Zimbabwe', *The World Bank Economic Review* 5, 3: pp. 395–413.

Freeman, D.B. and Norcliffe, G.B. (1985), *Rural enterprise in Kenya: Development and spatial organization of the non-farm sector*, Research Paper no. 214, University of Chicago, Department of Geography: Chicago.

Friedmann, J. (1988), *Life space and economic space*, Transaction Books: New Brunswick.

Friedmann, J. and Douglass, M. (1978), 'Agropolitan development: Towards a new strategy for regional planning in Asia', in F. Lo and K. Salih (eds.), *Growth pole strategy and regional development policy*, Pergamon: Oxford.

Friedmann, J. and Weaver, C. (1979), *Territory and function: The evolution of regional planning*, Edward Arnold: London.

Funnell, D.C. (1976), 'The role of small service centres in regional and rural development: With special reference to Eastern Africa', in A. Gilbert (ed.), *Development Planning and Spatial Structure*, John Wiley & Sons: London.

Funnell, D.C. (1988), 'Urban-rural linkages: Research themes and directions', *Geografiska Annaler* 70B, 2: pp. 267–74.

Gaile, G. (1988), 'Choosing locations for small town development to enable market and employment expansion: The case of Kenya', *Economic Geography* 64, 3: pp. 242–54.

Gasper, D. (1988), 'Rural growth points and rural industries in Zimbabwe: Ideologies and policies', *Development and Change* 19: pp. 425–66.

Gebre, S. (1991), 'The interaction between small towns and their hinterlands: Implications for rural development in Ethiopia', *African Urban Quarterly* 6, 3–: pp. 229–34.

Giaoutzi, M. (1990), 'Multinational corporations versus SME's: A dilemma for local development', paper presented at the 30th Congress of Regional Science Association, August 1990, Istanbul.

Gibbon, P. (ed.) (1995a), *Structural adjustment and the working poor in Zimbabwe*, Scandinavian Institute for African Studies: Uppsala.

Gibbon, P. (1995b), *Structural adjustment in Zimbabwe 1991–94*, Centre for Development Research: Copenhagen.

Göttlisher, M. (1986), *Zentrale Orten im Koncept der ländlischen Regionalentwicklung*, Remag: Bonn.

Government of the Republic of Zimbabwe (1989), *The promotion of investments: Policy and regulations*, Harare.

Government of the Republic of Zimbabwe (1993), *Poverty alleviation action plan*, Ministry of Public Service, Labour and Welfare: Harare.

Grierson, J. and Moyo, S. (1993), *Advocacy, enterprise extension and indigenous enterprise institution development: A programme of support for the small and medium enterprise sector in Zimbabwe*, Report to the Norwegian Agency for Development Cooperation (NORAD): Harare.

Gugler, J. (1988), 'Over urbanization reconsidered', in J. Gugler (ed.), *The urbanization of the third world*, Oxford University Press: Oxford.

Hägg, I. and Johanson, J. (eds.) (1982), *Företag i nätverk*, SNS: Stockholm.

Haggblade, S., Hazell, P. and Browne, J. (1987), *Farm/non-farm linkages in rural sub-Saharan Africa: Empirical evidence and policy implications*, Report no. ARU 67, World Bank: Washington DC.

Hardoy, J.E. and Satterthwaite, D. (1986), *Small and intermediate urban centres: Their role in national and regional development in the third world*, Hodder and Stoughton, in association with the International Institute for Economic Development: London.

Harris, J. and Moore, M. (eds.) (1984), 'Development and the rural urban divide', *The Journal of Development Studies* special issue 20, 3.

Heath, R.A. (1978), 'Rhodesian service centres and service regions', MPhil thesis, University of Rhodesia.

Helmsing, A.H.J. (1987), *Non-agricultural enterprises in the communal lands of Zimbabwe*, RUP occasional paper no. 10, Dept. of Rural and Urban Planning, University of Zimbabwe. (Also chapter 9 in Mutizwa-Mangiza, N.D. and Helmsing, A.H.J. (eds.) (1991), *Rural development and planning in Zimbabwe*, Avebury: Aldershot, UK.)

Helmsing, A.H.J. (1991), 'Rural industries and growth points: Issues in an ongoing debate', in N.D. Mutizwa-Mangiza and A.H.J. Helmsing (eds.), *Rural Development and Planning in Zimbabwe*, Avebury: Aldershot, UK.

Hesselberg, J. (1986), 'Tre myter om Afrika', *Nordisk Samhällsgeografisk Tidskrift* 40: pp. 3–7.

Hinkerdink, J. and Titus, M.J. (1988), 'Paradigms and regional development and the role of small centres', *Development and Change* 19: pp. 401–23.

Holm, M. (1994), 'Rural-urban migration and urban living conditions. The experiences in a case study of Tanzanian intermediate towns', unpublished PhD dissertation, Department of Geography, Royal Holloway, University of London and Centre for Development Research: Copenhagen.

Hosier, R.H. (1987), 'The informal sector in Kenya: Spatial variation and development alternatives', *The Journal of Developing Areas* 22: pp. 383–402.

Hydén, G. (1983), *No shortcuts to progress: African development management in perspective*, Heineman: London.

Hydén, G. (1985), 'Urban growth and rural development', in G.M. Carter and P. O'Meara (eds.), *African independence: The first twenty-five years*, Hutchinson: London.

Hydén, G. (1986), 'African social structure and economic development', in R.J. Berg and J.S. Whitaker (eds.), *Strategies for African development*, The University of California Press: Berkeley.

International Foundation for Education with Production (1990), *Education and employment in Southern Africa: Defusing the time-bomb?* Report on a seminar on education and training for employment and employment creation in the SADCC countries held in Zimbabwe, April 20–28, 1989, Harare.

ILO (1985), *Informal sector in Africa*, ILO, Jobs and Skills Programme: Addis Ababa.

ILO (1972), *Employment, incomes and equality: A strategy for increasing pro duction employment in Kenya*, ILO: Geneva.

ILO/Southern African Team for Employment Promotion (1991), *The employment and training programme of the Social Development Fund*: Harare.

Isard, Walter *et al.* (1960), *Methods of regional analysis: An introduction to regional science*, John Wiley & Sons: New York and London.

Jackson, J.C. and Collier, P. (1988), *Incomes, poverty and food security in the communal lands of Zimbabwe*, RUP Occasional Paper no. 11, Dept. of Rural and Urban Planning, University of Zimbabwe. (Also chapter 2 in Mutizwa-Mangiza, N.D. and Helmsing, A.J. (eds.) (1991), *Rural development and planning in Zimbabwe*, Avebury: Aldershot, UK.)

Jamal, V. and Weeks, J. (1988), 'The vanishing rural-urban gap in sub-Saharan Africa', *International Labour Review* 127, 3: pp. 305–29.

Jamal, V. and Weeks, J. (1993), *Africa misunderstood or whatever happened to the rural-urban gap?*, MacMillan Press: London.

Jansen A. and Olthof, W. (1993), *Small centres and enterprise characteristics in Makoni District, Zimbabwe*, RUP Occasional Paper no. 26, Department of Rural and Urban Planning, University of Zimbabwe: Harare.

Jayne, T. S. and Chisvo, M. (1991), 'Unravelling Zimbabwe's food insecurity paradox: Implications for grain market reform in Southern Africa', *Food Policy* 16, 4: pp. 319–29.

Jayne, T. S. and Rubey, L. (1993), 'Maize milling, market reform and urban food security: The case of Zimbabwe', *World Development* 21, 6: pp. 975–88.

Johanson, J. and Mattson, L.-G. (1986), 'Interorganizational relations in industrial systems: A network approach compared with the transaction cost approach', *International Studies of Management and Organization* 40, 3: pp. 307–24.

Johnson, E.A.J. (1970), *The organization of space in developing countries*, Harvard University Press: Cambridge, Mass.

Kammeier, Detlef, H. and Swan, P.J. (1984), *Equity with growth? Planning perspectives for small towns in developing countries*, Asian Institute of Technology: Bangkok.

Kanji, N. (1995), 'Gender, poverty and economic adjustment in Harare, Zimbabwe', *Environment and Urbanization* 7, 1: pp. 37–55.

King, K.J. (1987), 'Training for the urban informal sector in developing countries: issues for practitioners', paper presented at Workshop for Experts on Training in the Urban Informal Sector of Developing Countries: Turin.

King, K. (1989), *In-service training in Zimbabwe: An analysis of the relations amongst education and training, industry and the state*, Occasional Paper no. 3, Human Resources Research Centre: Harare.

Knorringa, P. (1995), *Economics of collaboration in producer-trader relations. Transaction regimes between market and hierarchy in the Agra footwear cluster, India*, Free University: Amsterdam.

Kongstad, Per, and Mette Mønsted (1980), *Family, labour and trade in Western Kenya*, Centre for Development Research Publication no. 3, Scandinavian Institute of African Studies: Uppsala.

Kongstad, P. (1985), *Lønarbejdet som reproduktionsform i den tredje verden*, (Wage labour as a form of reproduction in the third world), Research Report no. 45, Institute of Geography, Socio-Economic Analysis and Computer Science, Roskilde University Centre: Roskilde.

Kongstad, P. (1986), *Work and reproduction: How to survive in third world countries*, Working Paper no. 50, Institute of Geography, Socio-Economic Analysis and Computer Science, Roskilde University Centre: Roskilde.

Lerise, F.S. (1991), 'Development of urban functions in villages of Tanzania', *African Urban Quarterly* 6, 3–4: pp. 258–65.

Liedholm, C. and Mead, D. (1987), *Small scale industries in developing countries: Empirical evidence and policy implications*, MSU International Development Paper no. 9, Michigan State University: East Lansing.

Lipietz, A. (1985), *Mirages et miracles. Problèmes de l'industrialisation dans le tiers monde*, Edition de la Découverte: Paris.

Lipton, M. (1976), *Why poor people stay poor: Urban bias in world development*, Avebury: Aldershot, UK.

Little, I.M.D. (1987), 'Small manufacturing enterprises in developing countries', *The World Bank Economic Review* 1, 2: pp. 203–35.

Long, N. and Long, A. (eds.) (1992), *The battlefields of knowledge: The interlocking of theory and practice in social research and development*, Routledge: London and New York.

Lösch, A. (1954), *The economics of location*, Yale University Press: New Haven.

Makombe, G., Bernsten, R.H. and Rohrbach, D.D. (1987), 'The economics of groundnut production by communal farmers in Zimbabwe', in M. Rukuni and C.K. Eicher (eds.), *Food security for Southern Africa*, UZ/MSU Food Security Project, Department of Agricultural Economics and Extension, University of Zimbabwe: Harare.

Malecki, E.J. 1990, 'New firm formation in the USA: Corporate structure, venture capital and local environment', *Entrepreneurship and Regional Development* 2, 3: pp. 247–65.

Masinde, C. (1996), 'Small enterprise development through vertically-integrated production and distribution systems in Kenya's motor industry', in D. McGormick and P.O. Pedersen (eds.), *Small enterprises: Flexibility and networking in an African context*, Longhorn Publishers: Nairobi.

Maskell, P. (1984), 'Industriens omlokalisering 1972–1982: Dens omfang, årsager og erhvervsstrukturelle konsekvenser' (Relocation of manufacturing 1972–1982: Its extent, reasons and structural consequences), in S. Illeris and P.O. Pedersen (eds.), *Industrien – koncentration eller spredning*, Amtskommunernes og Kommunernes Forskningsinstitut: Copenhagen.

Massey, D. (1984), *Spatial divisions of labour, social structures and the geography of production*, MacMillan Press: London.

Massey, D. and Meegan, R.A. (1979), 'The geography of industrial reorganization', *Progress in Planning* 10: pp. 155–237.

Mbonile, M.J. (1994), 'Trading centres and development in a remote district in Tanzania', *Review of African Political Economy* 50: pp. 7–20.

McCormick, D. (1994), 'Industrial district or garment ghetto: The case of Nairobi's mini-manufacturers', paper presented at EADI workshop on Industrialization, Organization, Innovation and Institutions in the South, Vienna, November 17–18, 1994.

McCormick, D. and Pedersen, P.O. (1996), *Small enterprises: Flexibility and networking in an African context*, Longhorn Publishers: Nairobi.

McGrath, S. (1993), *Changing the subject: Curriculum change and Zimbabwean education since independence*, Occasional Paper no. 44, Centre for African Studies, Edinburgh University: Edinburgh.

McPherson, M.A. (1991), *Micro and small-scale enterprises in Zimbabwe: The results of a country-wide survey*, Gemini Technical Report 25, Gemini: Bethesda, Maryland.

Mead, D.C. and Kunjeku, P. (1993), 'Business linkages and enterprise development in Zimbabwe', unpublished ms, Harare.

Mellor, J.W. (1986), 'Agriculture on the road to industrialization', in J.P. Lewis and V. Kallob (eds.), *Development Reconsidered*, Transaction Books: New Brunswick, USA and Oxford, UK.

Mellor, J.W., Delgado, C.L. and Blackie, M.J. (eds.) (1987), *Accelerating food production in sub-Saharan Africa*, John Hopkins University Press: Baltimore and London.

Mkandawire, T. (1986), 'The informal sector in the labour reserve economics of Southern Africa with special reference to Zimbabwe', *African Development* 11, 1: pp. 61–86.

Mlalazi, A. (1993), 'Small urban centres' development in Zimbabwe', paper presented at a technical meeting on the role of small urban centres in economic recovery and regional development in Africa, organized by UNCRD in Nyeri, Kenya, Dec. 1993.

Moore, M. and Hamalai, L. (1993), *Economic stabilization, political pluralism and business associations in developing countries*, IDS Discussion Paper no. 318, IDS: Brighton.

Moser, C. (1984), *The role of the informal sector in small and intermediate-sized cities*, UN Centre for Regional Development: Nagoya.

Moyo, N.P. *et al.* (1984), *The informal sector in Zimbabwe: Its potentials for employment creation*, Report for the Ministry of Labour, Manpower Planning and Social Welfare, Department of Economics, University of Zimbabwe: Harare.

Moyo, S. (1995), 'Background paper on growth points development', unpublished ms: Harare.

Mudimu, G.D. (1987), 'The oil seeds sub-sector and household food security in the communal farming areas of Zimbabwe: A preliminary research proposal', in M. Rukuni and C.K. Eicher (eds.), *Food security for Southern Africa,* UZ/MSU Food Security Project, Department of Agricultural Economics and Extension, University of Zimbabwe: Harare.

Mugabi, E.A. (1993), 'The role of small urban and trading centres in regional economic development: A case study from Uganda', paper presented at a technical meeting on the role of small urban centres in economic recovery and regional development in Africa, organized by UNCRD in Nyeri, Kenya, Dec. 1993.

Mugambiwa, T. (1989), 'Action to assist rural women in Zimbabwe', Ministry of Community and Cooperative Development: Harare.

Mulenga, M.C. (1993), 'A country profile: Zambia', paper presented at a technical meeting on the role of small urban centres in economic recovery and regional development in Africa, organized by UNCRD in Nyeri, Kenya, December 1993.

Müller, J. (1980), *Liquidation or consolation of indigenous technology,* Development Series no. 1, Aalborg University Press: Aalborg.

Mulligan, G.F. (1984), 'Agglomeration and central place theory: A review of the literature', *International Regional Science Review* 9, 1: pp. 1–42.

Mushauri, J. and assoc. (1994), 'Identification of vocational training and business development opportunities at Bhasera rural service centre: Gutu East constituency', unpublished ms, Harare.

Musyoki, A.K. (1987), 'The hierarchy of centres and the urban balance strategy in Kenya: The case of Machakos District', *Journal of Eastern African Research and Development* 17: pp. 74–87.

National Economic Planning Commission (1993), 'Policy on measures to support small-to-medium scale indigenous enterprises', unpublished letter, Harare.

Närman, A. (1991), *Education, training and agricultural development in Zimbabwe*, International Institute for Educational Planning: Paris.

Nattras, N. (1987), 'Street trading in Transkei: A struggle against poverty, persecution and prosecution', *World Development* 15, 7: pp. 861–75.

Ndlela, D.B. (1993), Subcontracting for SSE's in Zimbabwe, Annex 11 to *Technological report: Survey of small scale industries and indigenous ownership in Zimbabwe*, DP/ZIM/90/005 (20 May 1993), UNDP: Vienna.

Ngethe, N. and Ngunyi, M. (1991), 'The role of small urban centres in Kenya's national development', *African Urban Quarterly* 6, 3–4, pp. 236–50.

NORAD (1989), *Dairy sector evaluation*, ZIB402, Hifab International, Oslo, Zimconsult: Harare.

NordREFO (1988), 'Om regionalpolitikken som politikområde (Regional Policy as a policy area)', Helsinki.

NordREFO (1987), 'Regionalpolitik i en nätværksekonomi: En seminarierapport' (Regional policy in a network economy: A seminar Report), *NordREFO*, 4.

Obudho, R.A. (1993), 'The role of small and intermediate urban centres in economic recovery and regional development in Kenya', paper presented at a technical meeting on the role of small urban centres in economic recovery and regional development in Africa, organized by UNCRD in Nyeri, Kenya, Dec. 1993.

Østergaard, T. (1994), 'The role of the national bourgeoisie in national development: The case of the textile and clothing industries in Zimbabwe', in B.J. Berman and C. Leys (eds.), *African capitalists in African development*, Lynne Rienne Publishers: Boulder and London.

Peattie, L. (1987), 'An idea in good currency and how it grew: The informal sector', *World Development* 15, 7: pp. 851–60.

Pedersen, P.O. (1978), 'The interaction between short- and long-run development in regions: The case of Denmark', *Regional Studies* 12: pp. 683–700.

Pedersen, P.O. (1986a), *Business service strategies: The case of the provincial centre of Esbjerg*, Report EUR 10611, FAST Series no. 19, Brussels: Directorate-General: Science, Research and Development, EEC.

Pedersen, P.O. (1986b), 'The role of business services in regional development: A new growth centre strategy?', *Scandinavian Housing and Planning Research* 3, 3: pp. 167–82.

Pedersen, P.O. (1987a), 'Impact of advanced technology in the production sector on freight transport and communications', in P. Nijkamp and S. Reichman (eds.), *Transportation planning in a changing world*, Gower: Aldershot.

Pedersen, P.O. (1987b), 'Netværk i den regionale erhvervsudvikling' (Network in regional industrial development), *NordREFO* 4: pp. 70–81.

Pedersen, P.O. (1990), 'The role of small towns in development', in J. Baker (ed.), *Small town Africa: Studies in rural-urban interaction*, Scandinavian Institute of African Studies: Uppsala.

Pedersen, P.O. (1991a), 'The restructuring of wholesale and retail trade in Zimbabwe's new district service centres', *African Urban Quarterly* 6, 3–4: pp. 292–303.

Pedersen, P.O. (1991b), 'A network approach to the small enterprise', in E. Bergman, G. Maier and F. Tödtling (eds.), *Regions reconsidered*, Mansell Publishing: London and New York.

Pedersen, P.O. (1992a), 'The structure of small service centres under conditions of uncertain supplies', *International Regional Science Review* 14, 3: pp. 307–16.

Pedersen, P.O. (1992b), 'Entrepreneurs and managers in Zimbabwe's district service centres', *Entrepreneurship and Regional Development* 4, 1: pp. 57–72.

Pedersen, P.O. (1994a), *De-agrarianization in Zimbabwe: A process of diversified development*, CDR Working Paper 94.8, Centre for Development Research: Copenhagen.

Pedersen, P.O. (1994b), 'Structural adjustment and the economy of small towns in Zimbabwe', in P.O. Pedersen, A. Sverrisson and M.P. van Dijk (eds.), *Flexible specialization: The dynamics of small-scale industries in the south*, Intermediate Technology Publications: London.

Pedersen, P.O. (1994c), *Clusters of enterprises within systems of production and distribution*, CDR Working Paper 94.14, Centre for Development Research: Copenhagen.

Pedersen, P.O. (1996), 'Flexibility and networking in a European and an African context', in D. McCormick and P.O. Pedersen (eds.), *Small enterprises: Flexibility and networking in an African context*, Longhorn Publishers: Nairobi.

Pedersen, P.O., Sverrisson, A. and van Dijk, M.P. (eds.) (1994), *Flexible specialization: The dynamics of small-scale industries in the South*, Intermediate Technology Publications: London.

Perroux, F. (1955), 'Note sur la notion de pole de croissance', *Economie Appliquée* 8: pp. 307–20.

Piore, M.J. and Sabel, C.F. (1984), *The second industrial divide*, Basic Books: New York.

Rasmussen, J. and Aeroe, A. (1987), 'Byen med de mange ansigter: En analyse af udviklingen i større og mindre byer i et af Afrikas mindst udviklede lande – Malawi' (The town with many faces: An analysis of the development of large and small towns in one of Africa's least developed countries – Malawi), unpublished MA thesis, Roskilde University Centre: Roskilde, Denmark.

Rasmussen, J. (1992), *The local entrepreneurial milieu: Enterprise networks in small Zimbabwean towns*, Research Report no. 79, Dept. of Geography, Roskilde University: Roskilde, with Centre for Development Research: Copenhagen.

Rasmussen, J., Schmitz, H. and van Dijk, M.P. (1992), 'Introduction: Exploring a new approach to small-scale industry', *IDS Bulletin. Flexible Specialization. A new view of small industry?* 23, 3: pp. 2–7.

Redclift, N. and Mingione, E. (eds.) (1985), *Beyond employment: Household, gender and subsistence*, Basil Blackwell: Oxford.

Republic of Zimbabwe (1988), *First five-year national development plan 1986–1990, Volume II*, Government Printer: Harare.

Republic of Zimbabwe (1990), *Economic policy statement: Macro-economic adjustment and trade liberalization including the budget statement, 1990, presented to the Parliament of Zimbabwe on Thursday, July 26, 1990, by the Senior Minister of Finance, Economic Planning and Development, The Hon. Dr. B.T.G. Chidzero*, Government Printer: Harare.

Republic of Zimbabwe (1991a), *Second five-year national development plan 1991–1995*, Government Printer: Harare.

Republic of Zimbabwe (1991b), *Zimbabwe: A framework for economic reform 1991–95*, Government Printer: Harare.

Riddell, Roger C. (1988), *Industrialisation in sub-Saharan Africa: Country case study: Zimbabwe*, Working Paper no. 25, ODI: London.

Riddell, R.C. (1990a), *Manufacturing Africa: Performance and prospects of seven countries in sub-Saharan Africa*, Heineman: London.

Riddell, R.C. (1990b), *ACP export diversification: The case of Zimbabwe*, ODI Working Paper 38, Overseas Development Institute: London.

Roe, E.M. (1995), 'More than the politics of decentralization: Local government reform, district development and public administration in Zimbabwe', *World Development* 23, 5: pp. 833–43.

Rondinelli, D.A. and Ruddle, K. (1978), *Urbanization and rural development*, Praeger: New York.

Rondinelli, D.A. (1982), 'The potential of secondary cities in facilitating deconcentrated urbanization in Africa', *African Urban Studies* 13: pp. 9–29.

Rondinelli, D.A. (1983a), 'Dynamics of growth of secondary cities in developing countries', *Geographical Review*, 73, 1: pp. 42–57.

Rondinelli, D.A. (1983b), 'Towns and small cities in developing countries', *Geographical Review* 73, 4: pp. 379–95.

Rondinelli, D.A. (1983c), *Secondary cities in developing countries*, Sage: Beverly Hills.

Rondinelli, D.A. (1984), 'Cities, market towns and agricultural development: A regional perspective', *Regional Development Dialogue* 5, 1.

Rondinelli, D.A. (1985), *Applied methods of regional analysis: the spatial dimension of development theory*, Westview Press: Boulder.

Rondinelli, D.A. (1986), 'The urban transition and agricultural development: implications for international assistance policy', *Development and Change* 17: pp. 231–63.

Rondinelli, D.A. (1987), 'Roles of towns and cities in the development of rural regions', in R. Bar-El, A. Bendavid-Val, and G.J. Karaska, (eds.), *Patterns of change in developing rural regions*, Westview Press: Boulder.

Rondinelli, D.A. (1988), 'Market towns and agriculture in Africa: The role of small urban centres in economic development', *African Urban Quarterly* 3, pp. 1–2.

Rondinelli, D.A., McCullough, J.S. and Johnson, R.W. (1989), 'Analysing decentralization policies in developing countries: A political economy framework', *Development and Change* 20, 1: pp. 57–87.

Rondinelli, D.A. (1990), 'Locational planning and regional economic development: Appropriate methods in developing countries', *International Regional Science Review* 13: pp. 241–48.

Sabel, C.F. (1982), *Work and politics: The division of labour in industry*, Cambridge University Press: Cambridge.

Salais, R. and Storper, M. (1992), 'The four 'worlds' of contemporary industry', *Cambridge Journal of Economics* 16: pp. 169–93.

Sanyal, B. (1991), 'Organising the self-employed: The politics of the urban informal sector', *International Labour Review* 130, 1.

Schatzberg, M.G. (1979), 'Islands of privilege: Small cities in Africa and the dynamics of class formation', *Urban Anthropology* 8, 2: pp. 173–90.

Schatzberg, M.G. (1980), *Politics and class in Zaire: Bureaucracy, business and beer in Lisala*, Africana Publishing Company: New York and London.

Schmith, G. (1979), *Maize and beans in Kenya: The interaction and effectiveness of the informal and formal marketing systems*, Occasional Paper no. 31, University of Nairobi, Institute for Development Studies: Nairobi.

Schmitz, H. (1990), 'Small firms and flexible specialization in developing countries', *Labour and Society* 5, 3: pp. 257–85.

Schmitz, H. (1995a), 'Shoemakers and Fordist Giants: Tale of a supercluster', *World Development* 23, 1: pp. 9–28.

Schmitz, H. (1995b), 'Collective efficiency: Growth path for small-scale industry', *The Journal of Development Studies* 31, 4: pp. 529–66.

Scoones, I. *et al.* (1994), 'A hazardous existence: Farming livelihoods in dryland Zimbabwe, Part 1', in *Coping with uncertainty in African drylands*, final technical report of a collaborative research program submitted to the Science and Technology for Development Programme, International Institute for Environment and Development: London.

Scott, A.J. (1988), 'Flexible production systems and regional development: The rise of new industry spaces in North America and Western Europe', *Inter national Journal of Urban and Regional Research* 12, 2: pp. 171–86.

Scott, A.J. and Storper, M. (1988), 'The geographical foundations and social regulations of flexible production complexes', in M. Dear and J. Wolch (eds.), *The power of geography*, Routledge: London.

Scott, E.P. (1995), 'Home-based industries: An alternative strategy for household security in rural Zimbabwe', *The Journal of Developing Areas* 29: pp. 183–212.

Secretary for Higher Education (1991), *Annual report for the year ended 31 December 1989*, Government Printer: Harare.

Seierup, S. (1995), 'Conceptualizing small town business activities in Kenya: On socio-economic differentiation, symbolic distinctions and entrepreneurship', unpublished ms, Centre for Development Research: Copenhagen.

Sengenberger, W. and Pyke, F. (1992), 'Industrial districts and local economic regeneration: Research and policy issues', in F. Pyke and W. Sengenberger (eds.), *Industrial districts and local economic regeneration*, International Institute for Labour Studies: Geneva.

Silitshena, R. (1990), 'The Tswana agro-town and rural economy in Botswana', in J. Baker (ed.), *Small town Africa: Studies in rural- urban interaction*, Scandinavian Institute of African Studies: Uppsala.

Simon, D. (1992), 'Conceptualizing small towns in African development', in J. Baker and P.O. Pedersen (eds.), *The rural-urban interface in Africa: Expansion and adaptation*, Scandinavian Institute of African Studies: Uppsala.

Slater, D. (1989), 'Territorial power and the peripheral state: The issue of decentralization', *Development and Change* 20: pp. 501–31.

Smith, C. (1976), 'Causes and consequences of central place types in western Guatemala', in C. Smith (ed.), *Regional analyses, Vol. 1: Economic systems*, Academic Press: New York.

Southall, A. (ed.) (1979), 'Small towns in African development', *Africa*, special issue 49, 3.

Southall, A. (ed.) (1988), 'Small towns in Africa revisited', *African Studies Review*, special issue 31, 3.

Soya, E.W. (1968), *The geography of modernization in Kenya*, Syracuse University Press: New York.

Stewart, F., Klugman, J. and Helmsing, A.H. (1994?), *Decentralization in Zimbabwe*, Occasional Papers no. 15, Human Development Report Office, UNDP: Vienna.

Stoneman, C. (1978), 'Skilled labour and future needs', *From Rhodesia to Zimbabwe* no. 4, Mambo Press: Gweru.

Stoneman, C. (1981), 'The economy: An overview', in C. Stoneman (ed.), *Zimbabwe's inheritance*, Macmillan: London.

Storper, M. (1991), *Industrialization, economic development and the regional question in the third world*, Pion: London.

Stöhr, W. and Fraser Taylor, D.F. (1981), *Development from above or below? The dialectics of regional planning in developing countries*, John Wiley and Sons: Chichester, UK.

Sunga, E., Chabayanzara, E., Moyo, S., Mpande, R., Mutana, P. and Page, H. (1990), 'Farm extension base-line survey results', unpublished ms, Department of Agriculture and Rural Development, Zimbabwe Institute of Development Studies: Harare.

Sverrisson, A. (1990), *Entrepreneurship and industrialization: A case study of carpenters in Mutare, Zimbabwe*, Discussion Paper no. 186, Research Policy Institute, University of Lund: Lund.

Sverrisson, A. (1993), *Evolutionary technical change and flexible mechanization: Entrepreneurship and industrialization in Kenya and Zimbabwe*, Lund University Press: Lund.

Sweeney, G.P. (1987), *Innovation entrepreneurs and regional development*, St Martins Press: New York.

Therkildsen, O. (1991), 'Public sector driven urbanization in Tanzania', *African Urban Quarterly* 6, 3–4, pp. 252–56.

Thwaites, A.T. (1978), 'Technological change, mobile plants and regional development', *Regional Studies* 12: pp. 445–61.

Tirfie, A. (1993), 'A country profile – Ethiopia', paper presented at a technical meeting on the role of small urban centres in economic recovery and regional development in Africa, organized by UNCRD in Nyeri, Kenya, December 1993.

UNIDO (1988), *Feasibility study for increasing the oil production capacity from cotton seed in Zimbabwe, Multipurpose Factory*, Volume I, final report, UNIDO Contract No. 88/19.

van Dijk, M.P. (1995), 'Structural adjustment and the role of different actors in Zimbabwe', *Nord-Südaktuelt* 9, 1: pp. 103–08.

Varshney, A. (1993), 'Beyond urban bias', Special issue of *The Journal of Development Studies* 29, 4.

Wanmali, S. (1991), 'Market towns and service linkages in sub-Saharan Africa: A case study of Chipata, Zambia; Salima, Malawi; and Chipinge, Zimbabwe', *African Urban Quarterly* 6, 3 and 4: pp. 267–77.

Wanmali, S. and Zamchiya, J.M. (1992), *Service provision and its impact on agricultural and rural development in Zimbabwe: A case study of Gazaland District*, International Food Policy Research Institute: Washington, and Department of Physical Planning, Ministry of Local Government, Rural and Urban Development, Government of Zimbabwe: Harare.

Watts, H.D. (1981), *The branch plant economy*, Longmans: London.

Watts, H.D. and Stafford, H.A. (1986), 'Plant closure and the multiplant firm: Some conceptual issues', *Progress in Geography* 10, 2: pp. 206–27.

Weber, A. (1929), *Theory of the location of industries*, The University of Chicago Press: Chicago.

Wekwete, K. (1987), *Growth centre policy in Zimbabwe: A focus on district centres*, RUP Occasional Paper no. 7, Department of Rural and Urban Planning, University of Zimbabwe: Harare.

Wekwete, K. (1990), 'Rural urbanization in Zimbabwe: Prospects for the future', in J. Baker (ed.), *Small town Africa: Studies in rural-urban interaction*, Seminar Proceedings no. 23, Scandinavian Institute of African Studies: Uppsala.

Wekwete, K. (1991), 'Growth centre policy in Zimbabwe, with special reference to district service centres', in N.D. Mutizwa-Mangiza and B. Helmsing (eds.), *Rural development and planning in Zimbabwe*, Avebury: Aldershot, UK.

Wield, D. (1981), 'Manufacturing industry', in C. Stoneman (ed.), *Zimbabwe's inheritance*, Macmillan: London.

Williamson, O.E. (1981), 'The economics of organization: The transaction cost approach', *American Journal of Sociology* 87, 3: pp. 548–77.

World Bank (1982), *Zimbabwe agricultural sector study*, Mimeo: Harare.

World Bank (1992), *Zimbabwe: A review of primary and secondary education from successful expansion to equity of learning achievements*, Report no. 8976 – ZIM, Population and Human Resources Division, Southern Africa Department: Washington DC.

Zimbabwe Press Mirror (1992), Bonn.

Zinyama, L.M. (1990), 'Retail sector responses to changing markets in Zimbabwe: Some geographic perspectives', *Geographical Journal of Zimbabwe* 21: pp.32–49.

Zvogbo, R.J. (1986), *Transforming education: The Zimbabwean experience*, College Press: Harare.